WORKING ACROSS THE GAP

WORKING ACROSS THE GAP
The Practice of Social Science in Organizations

Lisl Klein

KARNAC
LONDON   NEW YORK

First published in 2005 by
H. Karnac (Books) Ltd.
6 Pembroke Buildings, London NW10 6RE

British Library Cataloguing in Publication Data

A C.I.P. for this book is available from the British Library

 ISBN: 1-85575-382-0

10 9 8 7 6 5 4 3 2 1

Edited, designed, and produced by Communication Crafts

Printed in Great Britain

www.karnacbooks.com

CONTENTS

ACKNOWLEDGEMENTS

Many individuals and organizations have contributed to the work that is reported in this book; without them neither the work nor the book would exist. They are, first and foremost, the organizations and the many people in them that have either been clients or have been willing to take part in research. And second, they are the professional colleagues with whom I have worked over the years. Where possible, I have acknowledged their contributions in the text.

There are some names that occur in the text, of colleagues and teachers to whom I owe a special debt of learning:

Joan Woodward was the industrial sociologist whose groundbreaking research led to her pioneering the teaching of industrial sociology to engineers at the Imperial College of Science and Technology (as it then was) in London. It was she who supervised my first research activity when there was no other professional supervision and then engaged me for her project on management control systems. Harold Bridger was one of the pioneering founders of the Tavistock Institute. He was a psychoanalyst who turned to consulting with organizations and developed a model of group relations training. How we met is described in the last of these papers (chapter 16); working with him and learning from him over the course of forty years has been one of the richest experiences of my life. Marie Jahoda became a friend when she came to England in 1958. She became a founding trustee and then President of the Bayswater Institute and remained a friend and teacher until her death in 2001. I have been very lucky in my teachers.

In saying something about these three, I am conscious of many others to whom I also owe a debt of learning, influence, and support, which is perhaps less clearly articulated: in particular, Sylvia Shimmin and Brian Shackel have been fellow travellers as well as friends over the years, working across the same gap in their own fields. So has Ken Eason—he is not only joint author of two of the chapters, but has been enormously helpful and supportive in the work of putting the book together. As the new director of the Bayswater Institute he has protected me from the intrusion of other work, has read and commented—with great tact—on early drafts, and has firmly (and frequently) reassured me that it was worth doing. I hope he was right.

* * *

Acknowledgements are due to the following:

To the current management of Freightliner, the company (now privatized) that features in chapter 6, for permission to reproduce the consultancy report that forms that chapter.

To Blackwell Publishing Ltd for permission to reproduce, in chapter 2, my article "Rationality in Management Control", published in the *Journal of Management Studies*, vol. 2, no. 3 (October 1965), and to change the title to "Prescription and Rationality in Management Control"; and for permission to reproduce, in chapter 3, parts of my article on "The Role of the Anaesthetist", published by the Association of Anaesthetists as an occasional paper in *Anaesthesia; Journal of the Association of Anaesthetists of Great Britain and Ireland* (1980).

To Cambridge University Press for permission to reproduce, in chapter 3, a modified version of my chapter "A Framework for Diagnosis" and, in chapters 12 and 13, the joint chapter with Ken Eason "Elements of Practice", both from Lisl Klein and Ken Eason, *Putting Social Science to Work: The Ground between Theory and Use Explored through Case Studies in Organisations* (1991).

To the Economic and Social Research Council, which commissioned the study forming chapter 10, for permission to publish it. The views expressed in that chapter are not necessarily those of the ESRC.

To Karnac Books for permission to reproduce, in chapter 14, an edited version of my chapter "Three Cases of Transitional Interventions", which appeared in Anthony Ambrose and Gilles Amado (Eds.), *Transitional Thinking* (2001).

To John Benjamins Publishing Company, Amsterdam/Philadelphia and the editors of *Concepts and Transformation, International Journal of Action Research*, for permission to reprint, in chapter 15, my article "On the Use of Psychoanalytic Concepts in Organizational Social Science", published in vol. 6, no. 1 (2001).

Chapter 8 is taken, courtesy of the New Statesman, from an article that first appeared in *New Society*.

FIGURES

PREFACE

This book brings together papers on the relevance and use of social science for organizations: the gap referred to in the title is that between the world of the social sciences and the world of organization. The traffic across this gap, as some of the papers show, is by no means all in one direction.

It is hard to believe that I have now been working on this topic, one way or another, for nearly five decades. The impetus has been the same, whether the work was done from a university base, from inside an industrial organization, from the Tavistock Institute, or now from the Bayswater Institute. The organizations involved were at first mainly in industry and later in other spheres, such as banking and hospitals.

The practice of social science in organizations is one of two topics that have preoccupied me. The other one is work organization and the meaning of work, and there will be another volume about that. The two books are independent of each other, although there has sometimes not been a clear-cut way of allocating material between them. Chronologically, the preoccupation with meaningful work came first, arising out of my own early work experience. But it became clear very quickly that work organization could not be separated out from broader questions of organization, and this brought with it an interest in organization in its own right. In turn, an interest in questions of organization came to be linked to, and sometimes overtaken by, the question of how to apply and make use of the social sciences—again in its own right.

In terms of my own work and career, this apparently logical progression has of course not been quite as logical as, with hindsight, it now sounds. There is much chance in the opportunities that do or do not present themselves, as well as in what one does with them. The introductory historical chapter includes a little of my own history; I have written a personal memoir elsewhere and here, too, there has sometimes not been a clear-cut way of allocating material.

In selecting the papers, which were written over a period of some forty years, I have tried to give them some coherence around a thread rather than bringing together a random collection. The practice of social science requires two frames of reference to be held in mind simultaneously: one that regards it as a question of getting knowledge—that is, concepts, methods, and research findings—into use; and one that is concerned with the dynamics of action. The papers are grouped in a way that reflects my developing thinking and learning in relation to these two frameworks. Although there is some overlap, I have tried as far as possible to avoid repetition.

The trustees of the Bayswater Institute first suggested in 1998 that I should put together a collection of papers. It was an intriguing idea, but there was never time to carry it out. As director of a small institute there were always more urgent things to deal with: clients, colleagues, work—getting it, doing it, writing it up—landlords, stationery, budgets, auditors. I have often remembered a conversation with Federico Butera, the Italian industrial sociologist who founded the Institute for Action Research on Organization Systems in Italy. I had said, "Oh, I would so like to start a new institute"; it was during one of the periods of upheaval that regularly beset the Tavistock Institute where I was then working. Federico replied, "Problem is, now you think about ideas and work. If you start new institute, you will think about furniture and tax." He was right! When the Bayswater Institute first started in 1991, with a sponsor, an office, a planning group, and a part-time secretary, I remember a serious discussion with the secretary about whether it would be irresponsible to buy more than one wastepaper basket.

For about five years the idea of a collection of papers kept sliding to the bottom of my inexhaustible list of things to do. Then, at the beginning of 2003, three things happened which, between them, propelled it to the top. The first was that the Institute found a new director in Ken Eason. So now he is the one who never has any time. The second thing was a bout of illness which served to remind me that, if I am going to do this, I had better get on with it. And the third was a publishing contract. These three things exemplify one thread in my work—the way in which factors inside and outside the individual combine and interact.

I think of this collection as work in progress. I have a strong sense of it being incomplete, first in the sense that it is hard to know when to stop editing and tweaking a text. Second, and more importantly, it is work in progress in the sense that one's work is always incomplete.

My friend and colleague Albert Cherns, who was the first Secretary of the Social Science Research Council in the United Kingdom and who founded a Centre for the Utilisation of Social Science Research in Loughborough University, once said: "Lisl, I do admire the way you keep on saying the same things." Yes, well . . .

WORKING ACROSS THE GAP

CHAPTER 1

Introduction—the context

No scientific work is truly context-free, and in the social sciences this is more so than in most others. This first chapter is therefore concerned with context, both in terms of what has been happening in relevant parts of the social science scene, mainly in Britain, and about how the personal context—my own history and values—interacted with it.

The social science background

There is a pattern in the way in which some sciences have developed: from intuitive application, through systematic investigation (science), to more knowledgeable application (technology). People were using levers long before they investigated the principles on which levers work. Having established the principles, they can now use levers more effectively. The development is similar in the matter of human relationships and behaviour: for a long time, people have been relating to others and co-operating in work; societies have evolved rules and customs and ways of having them kept; children have learned from the responses of their parents what pays and what does not; armies have been inspired to commit suicide. Moreover—and this is a further stage in sophistication—people have thought about these processes and in-

stitutions. Much has been written, on the basis of intuition and experience and sometimes with great wisdom, on law, government, education, the division of labour, and more recently management and
organization.

What is recent is the systematic, and therefore scientific, study of
these things. It may not always yield better answers than the intuitive
wisdom of the specially gifted—but then, achievement in any applied
science is to raise average standards of performance, not necessarily
the standards of the outstanding individual. It also provides an essential means of testing the intuitive answers—too often for comfort, these
turn out to be wrong.

I have not set out to write a history of the subject—that would need
to be much richer, and there are other histories and surveys (see, for
instance, Brown, 1954, chap. 1; Cherns, 1979; Pugh, Mansfield, &
Warner, 1975; Shimmin & Wallis, 1994). I want only to explain those
parts of the relevant background and context against which the work
in these papers was carried out, interspersing this with some anecdotes
and experiences. The early parts of the story are therefore given only in
very brief summary form.

1915–1945: the first thirty years[1]

Industrial psychology began in Britain during the First World War.
The urgent need for munitions and the fear of industrial unrest gave
the government a keen and unprecedented interest in industrial efficiency as well as industrial peace. In 1915, a Health of Munition Workers Committee was set up to investigate the influence of hours and
conditions of work on the output and health of workers—a virtually
uncontroversial topic. The model was that knowledge about these
topics could be discovered and would then be put to use.

The first studies were set up to test the assumption that women
could fill twice as many shells if they did twice as many hours of work.
Few people will be surprised that the assumption was found to be
wrong. Equally naïve was the belief that absenteeism among shipyard
workers working a seventy-hour week was due solely to incorrigible
drunkenness. However, the fact that research is relevant does not
necessarily mean it gets used. Those early findings led to changes in
practice at the time, but they did not enter into the general stock of
knowledge, and in the Second World War similar mistakes were made
about the connection between hours of work and output.

Here is another, less clear-cut and more debatable, but also perhaps more far-reaching example of the consequences of failing to recognize the significance of an empirical finding: empirical research in the late 1920s showed that, given the opportunity, people varied their working pace in the course of the day, without loss of output. This knowledge never found its way into the design strategies of production engineering. Production engineers continued to work on the assumption that controllability and predictability required evenly spaced—that is, mechanical—pacing. Then, in the 1950s, when basic standards of living were recovering from the Second World War, the motor industry began to suffer from waves of strikes, most of which were unofficial and short. No one recognized that an important function of a short strike is simply to create a break, an interruption from work, and that such strikes were happening in situations where work was machine-paced. The pattern of unofficial strikes became a culture known as "the British disease", and this in turn had major political and economic consequences.

While the First World War provided the stimulus for psychological research in British industry, it faced the American army with the problems of classifying and training vast numbers of men from widely varied backgrounds, many of them illiterate. The response was the use of psychological testing, on a mass scale, to classify men for immediate vocational training.

After the war, industrial psychology in Britain moved along both these paths. To continue sponsoring studies, the Health of Munition Workers Committee was re-structured, first into the Industrial Fatigue Research Board, and then into the Industrial Health Research Board— the remit broadening with each step. And in 1920 the National Institute of Industrial Psychology (NIIP) was founded, developing methods of selection, training, and vocational testing and guidance. It was independent both of government and of the universities, with the advantages and disadvantages of having to earn most of its bread and butter by solving problems put to it by industry and providing services for which businessmen were prepared to pay. It therefore also had the function of getting industry used to collaboration with psychologists.

From the early 1930s, work was much influenced by the famous Hawthorne Investigations in the United States (Roethlisberger & Dickson, 1939). These began as what were, at the time, conventional studies of the effect on output of changes in lighting, rest pauses, and other factors in the environment. They were very comprehensive and were carried out under the most careful experimental conditions. It was found that output went up with every change that was made in environmental conditions, no matter of what kind or in what direction, and that it went up both in the experimental group and in the control group. The researchers concluded that the operators were responding to the experiment itself, and that what stimulated them was the fact that they were the centre of interest and attention. A second series of experiments drew attention to the work group and the way in which it controlled and regulated the behaviour of its members.

I once referred to this study in a talk to the Fabian Society in Birmingham. During the discussion period, an elderly gentleman in the audience stood up and said, "My name is Sargent Florence. I was around at the time you are talking about. What people don't realize, and what did not find its way into the reports, is that these girls were having a lot of attention paid to them by two very good-looking young Englishmen. That was part of it, you know." Context, context, context.

These experiments drew attention to "human relations" in industry. Emphasis on permissive methods of supervision and on the training of managers and supervisors in human relations techniques, and the further study of industrial sociology, all arose from the impact of the Hawthorne experiments. Later, some of the teachings and practice of the human relations school came to be severely criticized. There is often an assumption that work satisfaction, "high morale", and high output must go together; that conflict is always avoidable by better management and always bad in its effects; and that, in the last analysis, the interests of workers and management are identical. For the first— but by no means the last—time, scientific findings and the moralistic and political conclusions drawn from them got mixed up. In both, the discovery of human relations as a factor in the work situation tended to make people forget or ignore the existence of other factors. This confusion persists.

The dilemma came to light rather early. The Harwood Manufacturing Co., headed by Alfred Marrow, who had graduated in social psychology, opened a new factory in West Virginia and had to train and get the co-operation of girls who had never been in a factory before. Marrow brought in Alex Bavelas, a psychologist, and later Lester Coch and John French , whose work in this factory became a classic (Coch & French, 1948). They set up teams that set their own targets and made group decisions on methods of work, on the distribution of work, and on changes in the work place. In fact, all important matters were decided by the teams of girls themselves.

Output was good, the girls were happy, and the psychologists published their studies of group decision-making under different forms of leadership. They did not, of course, mention the name of the plant, but Marrow himself published an article in *Fortune* magazine about it, mentioning the name of the firm and saying, incidentally, that everyone was so well satisfied that the firm had escaped unionization. Whereupon the International Ladies' Garment Workers Union sent a representative to the factory who stood at the gates handing out leaflets with Marrow's article, across which was written "To the workers of Harwood Manufacturing: Do you know that you are being used as guinea pigs?" The plant became unionized.

It is a sad reflection that both world wars provided a context of urgent problems which stimulated developments in social science as an aid to problem-solving, and for which there has not been the same focus in peacetime. What links the examples that follow is that they arose in response to specific problems. An important aspect is that the professionals involved later took their experience out into civilian posts and institutions.

The work that had to be done in the Second World War in relation to aircraft cockpits, radar screens, and operations control-rooms presented unprecedented problems in selection and training, as well as creating some tasks that were simply not suited to human abilities. One characteristic of the new highly skilled complex tasks was the emphasis on their perceptual rather than motor aspects. The actions required were simple; the skill lay in interpreting information and deciding on the right action. The science of ergonomics emerged in part from the problem of arranging and presenting information in such a way as to enable the operator to perform a task with least error and strain.

Another wartime problem was in the supply of officers for the services. When officers had been drawn from a fairly narrow sector of society, it had not been too difficult for those interviewing and selecting to make reliable judgements about their qualities. It is relatively easy to interpret correctly small differences in such things as dress, speech, or behaviour, in someone who comes from the same social background as oneself. But when there was suddenly a need for a very much larger number of officers, who had to be drawn from a much wider range of social backgrounds, selection became more difficult and less reliable, and psychologists were called in to help. They developed the system of group leadership testing that, in the shape of the War Office Selection Boards, later became the model for the postwar "house party" method used by leading industrial firms, the civil service, and some of the nationalized industries.

Lastly, the war brought problems of morale. At the psychological level, these were studied far more in the American than in the British services where the tradition was strong that morale is a matter of leadership and where, therefore, permitting an outside expert to study and to offer advice can look like an admission of failure. It was, then, the American studies that provided the methods of investigation of group functioning and of the interactions of the individual's motivation with the values and goals of the group and with the aims of the organization as a whole. But there was also some British work done on morale. In a different approach, a study of low morale in an RAF fighter station involved the whole station and its activities as the system, approached the process in a grounded way, and proceeded along lines that would nowadays be regarded as action research (Paterson, 1955).

After the Second World War

From this point on, I want to expand the scale a little.

A good way to understand what is happening in the social sciences is to look at the sources of funding: who is prepared to pay for what at any particular time. It is not simply that he who pays the piper calls the tune—sometimes a piper can negotiate, or can appear to be playing one tune while really developing another. It is also that he who pays the piper creates pipers. Some of the confusion and conflict we and our users and clients experience can be understood when one recognizes that the direction set by the priorities of funding at any one time affects the training and development of the next generation, and therefore exerts an influence beyond the time-scale of the funding strategy.

After the Second World War, there was in Britain a high regard for science and its potential contribution to industrial development, based mainly on the contribution to the war effort that had been made by operational research (see Stansfield, 1981). This had meant first-hand observation, generally from the perspectives of several disciplines, of what was actually going on, not primarily laboratory experiments or applied mathematics. The aim had not been to develop the various sciences involved, but to solve problems. Paradoxically, in the process there was much scientific development. In addition, the practical applications of experimental, occupational, and social psychology to the wartime problems of the services had done much to make the image of the subject respectable and help the postwar expansion of teaching and research.

Under the postwar Attlee government, the same optimism and idealism that led to social security legislation and the creation of the National Health Service lay behind the wish to use science in the service of problem-solving. A Scientific Civil Service was created, and an Advisory Council for Scientific Policy was set up. One of the first tasks of the Advisory Council was "to advise the appropriate form of research effort to assist the maximum increase in national productivity during the coming decade". The Advisory Council recommended setting up a new type of body, representative of "Government, employers and workers in industry, and of the natural and social sciences". So already in 1947 the reference was to the "natural and social sciences" and the importance of understanding the "human factor"; this was at the request not of social scientists but of other scientists who saw, and recommended, that this contribution was needed.

A Committee on Industrial Productivity (CIP) was set up and, in turn, set up four panels to deal with specific aspects of its remit. One of them was called the Panel on Human Factors, chaired by Sir George Schuster. The "Schuster Panel" sponsored a number of psychological and sociological investigations into industrial problems. Under its auspices the NIIP carried out research into methods of foremanship (National Institute of Industrial Psychology, 1951). Joint consultation was the subject of two projects, one conducted by the NIIP (National Institute of Industrial Psychology, 1952) and the other from a sociological standpoint by Liverpool University (Scott, 1952). The Tavistock Institute of Human Relations, itself a postwar development, made a major study of the human effects of technological change in the coal mines (Trist, Higgin, Murray & Pollock, 1963). This study gave rise to the concept of the work system as a "sociotechnical system", which was to become very influential.

The Tavistock Institute also launched pioneering studies in the Glacier Metal Company (Jaques, 1951). This became the first instance of a full-time social science consultant working with a firm. The fact that the consultant was a psychoanalyst brought new types of insight and knowledge and new techniques to bear on the human problems of industry. Not least among them was the realization that the mere uncovering of a problem and making it explicit can in itself be part of the solution. The Glacier study was also breaking new ground in that it was looking at problems of organization and the proper definition of roles and relationships within a company. Altogether there was a shift after the war, from looking at the worker to looking at management problems or whole organizations—for instance, at the ways in which organizations adapt to change.

In 1950, at the time the CIP decided to dissolve itself, the Department of Scientific and Industrial Research (DSIR) and the Medical Research Council (MRC) were working out a joint scheme to cover the national needs for research in this field. They divided it into three areas—industrial health, individual efficiency, and human relations in industry—and they set up committees to look after each. The members were academics, top-level industrialists and top-level trade unionists.

The 1950s were the time of the Marshall Plan, the programme of support for economic recovery in Europe voted under the United States Economic Co-operation Act of 1948 and Mutual Security Acts of 1951 and 1952. Politically there was ambivalence about this American support in Europe, because it clearly had some political aims. However, as part of the Marshall Plan, under the so-called Conditional Aid scheme, funds were made available for industrial social research. With the coming of the Conditional Aid funds, the joint DSIR/MRC committees now had bigger resources to spend, and there began the first broad-based programme of industrial social science in this country.

The essential feature of the scheme was that the problems being tackled should have some bearing on productivity, and that the research carried out should produce practical results within three years. The Individual Efficiency Committee supported research on the influence of equipment design and working conditions on operator efficiency, as well as research on the acquisition of skill. The projects supported by the Human Relations Committee were mainly in the fields of technological change, management organization, incentives, training and promotion, and the problems of special groups in industry, such as married women. Project steering committees included industrialists and trade unionists, and they interpreted their briefs with flexibility. Paradoxically, therefore, although the expressed aim of the programme was to produce practical results, some of these studies brought with them major theoretical and methodological advances.

The programme was administered by the DSIR. Until then, the DSIR had been responsible for research in the physical and engineering sciences only. Their remit covered "pure" research such as that carried out at the National Physical Laboratory, and "applied" research like the work of the Road Research Laboratory. They also made some contribution to industry-based research associations such as the British Iron and Steel Research Association, the Cutlery and Allied

Trades Research Association, and the British Boot, Shoe and Allied Trades Association. Some of these now also became involved in human sciences research.

Administering social science research was new to the DSIR, and they had decided to locate one of the Conditional Aid projects in their own headquarters, in order to understand better the issues involved in social research. It was a project on the Human Implications of Work Study.

The personal background—moving into research

I became a junior research assistant in the Human Implications of Work Study project, so my own involvement began at this point. I will need to include something about it in the account from here on: I had left university in 1949 with a degree in modern languages, not knowing what kind of work I wanted to do. I had tried work in a library organization and in a specialist library and had been very bored and unhappy. Still not knowing what to do, I took what was meant to be a temporary job as a general factory hand in a pharmaceutical company, packing pills and stuffing envelopes with advertising material. Factory life, it turned out, was interesting, lively, and stimulating.

For instance: once a month there was a one-day induction course for all those who had joined the company during the previous month, from the chief accountant down to the lowliest factory hand. We were told about the company and its products, heads of departments explained what their departments did, and there was a tour of the plant. It was totally fascinating: wheat was purchased from Rank Hovis and brought to the factory in barges. The first production process was to extract the wheat-germ from the whole grain. What was left after that was pressed to extract an oil that was rich in vitamin E. And what was left after that was sold—for more than had been paid for the original wheat—to Heinz for thickening soups. Marvellous! No such explanations of the bigger picture had been made available in the library.

Instead of leaving after a few weeks as I had intended, I stayed for a year. But I certainly did not regard it as an "experiment", as people since then have sometimes tried to suggest. It was real, and I was a real part of it, not an observer.

Two things remained with me from that experience: the first is a life-long love affair with industry, which later came to include other kinds of organization. It may be kinky, but I am never as happy as when I am puzzling out how it all works and fits together—the materi-

als, the customers, the suppliers, the machinery, the people, the relationships, the dynamics, the economics—the sheer life of it. The second
is a life-long fascination, not to say obsession, with the question of
work satisfaction. Why was working in a factory so pleasant and
interesting and alive, when working in a library—*prima facie* a much
more suitable job for an educated young woman—had been so miser-
able?

Now I knew what I wanted to do. I took a year's training in personnel management, and then worked as a factory personnel officer for
the Metal Box Company in Bermondsey. When Metal Box decided to
close that factory, in 1955, I went to see my former tutor, Nancy Seear,
to ask about the job situation in personnel management. She asked
whether I had ever thought of doing research. Up to then I hadn't.

Nancy Seear had become a member of the DSIR's Human Relations
Committee. The secretary of the committee was Ronald Stansfield, a
physicist and senior civil servant within the DSIR, and Nancy suggested that I should go and see him. It happened that a young research
assistant on the DSIR's Work Study project had given her notice on the
day I met him, and, to cut the story short, I was offered that job.

The Work Study project involved case studies in two firms and
lasted five years. Fuller details of the project itself, with its findings
about work organization, belong to the other topic of the meaning of
work (as does the answer to my earlier question about why factory
work had been so much more enjoyable for me than work in a library)
and can be found in Klein (forthcoming). What belongs here is what
we learned from the project about the process of doing empirical social
research in the real world.

There were three of us in the research team, and none of us had any
formal qualifications in social science. It made us read a lot and be very
careful and rigorous about methods. One of my colleagues was undergoing psychoanalysis and, apart from the fact that it made him stare
out of the window a lot of the time, he alerted us to the fact that the
people and situations we encountered would be having some effect on
us and that we needed to deal with that.

I discovered early that conventional academic ideas of "rigour"
could turn out to be superficial. When we were preparing for the
second case study, in an engineering company, I was sent to consult a
very eminent professor of occupational psychology about research
methods. "Work Study" included incentive payment schemes, and to
study the effect of these he proposed that we should set up a group of
operators who would be on piecework and another group, doing the

same work, who would be on flat rates of pay. Having come to this research from industry, I found it inconceivable that one would go into a company and play with people's wages in this way. Besides, we knew from the Hawthorne experiments that this method would not tell us anything reliable.

The fact that we came from the world of practice also made us very rigorous about not publishing a text without working it through with the people in the field site. This sense of responsibility towards the field site must also (although I have no conscious memory of it) have been influenced by the nature of the project's steering committee, with its management and trade union representation. In the first case study, getting agreement to publish took four years (Dalziel & Klein, 1960).

The company, which we called "Pakitt Ltd", had a lively and forceful woman managing director, and in the course of these four years she and I had long, tough sessions about the text of the report. During one of these, her phone rang. She tore a strip off whoever it was on the other end of the line and then said impatiently to me, "Why will they come to me like children, with every little detail?" I said, "But look: you expect them to come to you with this; and with this; and with this. How can you be surprised if they also come to you with something small when it happens to be inconvenient for you?" She was a person of integrity and intelligence, and there was a long silence while she thought about this. It was my first experience of consultancy, and my first experience of that buzz that tells you that a nail has been hit on the head. Getting the text cleared for publication became much easier after that.

It was apparent that research involving people brought with it ethical obligations that were different from those of other scientific research. They involved explaining the nature of the research to those who were being asked to take part and making the participation of any individual voluntary; guaranteeing the anonymity of individuals or, if that was impossible, getting their agreement to what was to be quoted; giving people the opportunity to see reports; and not publishing reports without having cleared the text. This did not mean necessarily agreeing to changes, but it did mean serious efforts at "working through"—which, in turn, usually yielded more information. All of these were, in some sense, interventions in the field, however much one tried to minimize intervention. So when debates arose later within the social sciences about the scientific validity of action research, it seemed to me that ethically conducted empirical research already blurred the boundary between research and intervention; the rest was merely a matter of degree. Rigour then meant being aware of what one was doing and its consequences, and choosing strategies in the light of this knowledge. That, in fact, is a very demanding kind of rigour; the blurring of the boundary did not mean that action research could serve as a front for "letting it all hang out".

I also had a first experience of social science making it possible to predict things. There was a good deal of research on accidents going on at the time. Industrial accidents were classed under two headings— severity and frequency—and the severity rate and frequency rate were thought to have different meanings. At the same time, it had been postulated that every accident is the result of a false hypothesis (e.g., "There is no one around that corner", "I can reach that kettle", etc.). Putting these two ideas together made me think that in a paternalistic firm, with policies that took good care of workers, there would be a prevailing hypothesis that "they will take care of me", and that there would therefore be a high rate of minor accidents such as falling or dropping things on one's foot.

"Pakitt Ltd" was very paternalistic. There were welfare arrangements far beyond what was required by law, leave for educational activities—provided that management approved of the kind of activity—and so on. Accidents were not the reason why we were there, but I ventured a prediction that they would have a high rate of minor accidents. And lo, they did. Their rate was relatively much higher than the national average, which puzzled them greatly. It was exciting to find that one can predict such things, because it also suggested that one might be able to choose policies in knowledge of their outcomes.

So this first case study in my first experience of empirical research sowed the seeds of the two frames of reference of my later work. First, there was a possibility of making use of knowledge—that is, of empirical findings, of approaches engendered by those findings, as well as of methods and concepts. Second, engagement with the field was a process that brought with it dynamics that needed to be understood and managed in their own right. The relative salience of these two frames of reference, and the relationship between them, were to become a dominant theme.

A programme-wide perspective

Being located in the DSIR itself, from where the Conditional Aid programme was being administered, meant that one saw much more than one's own work. I developed a feel for the whole programme and got to know many of the researchers, who came in to discuss their projects. I also saw the administrative end of it, with civil servants agonizing about how to handle the applications of researchers from the Tavistock Institute, who required large salaries because they had to pay for psychoanalysis. By chance, I had landed right in the centre of this ground-breaking programme, and the perspective that this gave me has influenced everything that came later. Only the reflection of hindsight has made clear to me how I came to value the range of perspectives that can be brought to bear on situations and problems. From my junior position in the DSIR, I saw the contributions of ergonomists as well as those of sociologists and psychoanalysts; I have been uncomfortable ever since with academic requirements to be wholly focused on one discipline. When I later became social sciences adviser in Esso Petroleum Company, it seemed obvious that one would draw in contributions from a range of disciplines to address different kinds of issue.

So, for instance, it was from within the DSIR that I first heard about group dynamics. The Tavistock Institute had been asked to develop a design for group relations training of the kind that was being carried out in the National Training Laboratories in the United States, but suitable for British conditions (Bridger, 1990). In 1957 the Institute announced its own first group relations conference at Leicester University, and out of curiosity I attended it. I went there 95% sceptical, and came away 90% sceptical. Every few years I tried again, and by now I run Harold Bridger's model of group relations training (see chapter 16).

A large part of the research in the Conditional Aid programme turned out to be about the interplay between structure and behaviour. The Tavistock Institute carried out the second study in its coal-mining project, which was looking at the effects of a new technology on the social system at the level of the primary work group or shop floor, and at the interaction between the two systems (Trist et al., 1963). Other researchers in the same programme were also looking at such interactions, but from a sociological point of view at the level of the organization rather than the shop floor: between organization and the technology of production in the case of Joan Woodward (1965), and between organization and the technology of products, and therefore their markets, in the case of Tom Burns and George Stalker (1961). Although the term "contingency theory" only came into use later (Lawrence & Lorsch, 1967; Perrow, 1986), these studies constituted the major foundation stones of the contingency approach, which holds that the right way to organize depends on the circumstances and the contingencies affecting the organization.

With the passing of time and the coming of information technology, which pervades management systems, operations planning, design, and other organizational functions, the boundary between the shop-floor interdependencies and the organizational ones is now somewhat blurred. But in any case, at both levels—the sociotechnical and the organizational—these emerging concepts about the interdependencies between structure and behaviour were potentially eminently usable and applicable, both for prediction and for design. There simply seemed to be no conflict between usefulness and theoretical development; in Kurt Lewin's words, there is nothing so practical as a good theory.

In the course of the work study project, my two colleagues moved on, and I was left to write it up. I had been "spotted" by Joan Woodward, who offered to supervise the analysis and write-up, and she invited me to join her at Imperial College, where she was pioneering the teaching of industrial sociology to engineering students. When the book was finished (Klein, 1964), I took a sabbatical year out, reading in sociology, psychology, and methods of research at the London School of Economics and taking degree exams, since I could not go on for ever without formal qualifications. Then I rejoined Joan Woodward at Imperial College, where she was beginning the sequel to the work on technology and organization, a research project on the behavioural consequences of management control systems (chapter 2).

The use of research—
moving into practice[2]

To the postwar optimism that I have mentioned must be added the optimism generated by this body of promising research, which not only produced substantial conceptual and theoretical development, but which could be used. In a review of the outcome of the Conditional Aid projects, evidence was given by industry which ranged from putting into effect drastic reductions in the length of training courses to the seeking of advice on far-reaching problems of organization by many large and medium-sized firms (Department of Scientific and Industrial Research/Medical Research Council, 1958). Because the social sciences had produced creative and valued results, industry was becoming interested: there were many meetings between industrialists and researchers, and the DSIR commissioned journalists to write short, simple accounts of research reports (Department of Scientific and Industrial Research/Ministry of Technology, 1957–67).

Partly in view of the likely growing demand, the government also set up a committee chaired by Lord Heyworth, the chairman of Unilever, to look into the organization of social research and the supply of researchers. As a result of the Heyworth Committee's work (Department of Education and Science, 1965), a Social Science Research Council (SSRC) was set up, on a par with other government research councils (though, of course, with nothing like their budgets).

The Heyworth Report is suffused with the belief that research in the social sciences is important and valuable and should be used. It therefore also discusses the issues involved in use:

> In expressing their research needs and in constructing research divisions or units, user organisations must bring social scientists into a close working relationship with administrators. In all kinds of social science research the application of results is not likely to be simple and straightforward: it is often a matter for sophisticated judgement. In the physical sciences the translation of research findings into practical applications is the function of the specially trained development scientist or engineer, who understands both the relevant scientific discipline and the technology of the establishment in which he is employed. In the social sciences, even when allowance is made for the difference in the nature of applied research, there are very few people whose functions correspond to the engineering or development function in the physical sciences, and nowhere are such people trained. If anything approaching the full potential value is to be obtained from research in the social sciences, an attempt must be made to define and analyse this function. [p. 39]

Two further concrete expressions of the optimism about the value of social science research were aimed at addressing the issues referred to in the Heyworth Report: first, a Centre for the Utilisation of Social Science Research was set up in Loughborough University. Its head was Albert Cherns, who had been secretary of the Heyworth Committee and then scientific secretary of the SSRC when that was set up. And second, Esso Petroleum Company decided in 1964 to experiment with appointing an industrial sociologist in-house, to "help in the analysis of the social pressures in a large industrial organisation [and] . . . advise on all aspects of human science research . . .").

The company's employee relations adviser had been one of the people giving evidence to the Heyworth Committee. He was interested in the subject, and he was a friend of A. T. M. Wilson, a former chairman of the Tavistock Institute, who had become social sciences adviser to the Board of Unilever. He had gone on to persuade the Board of Esso Petroleum to create the post of social sciences adviser there as well. In the first of two major efforts at exploring the practice of social science, I took that job.

Inevitably, addressing "the engineering or development function" meant that one needed to take an interest in the methodological examination of advisory and consultancy roles. There had been one earlier attempt to describe and codify the role of a consultant in a continuing relationship with an organization, in Elliott Jaques's book about his work in the Glacier Metal Company (Jaques, 1951). Using the term "consultant" in the sense of a clinical or medical consultant, not a management consultant, Jaques established some principles that were very quickly accepted: that a consultant is independent and cannot be captured by one side in a dispute, does not make private reports about people to others, and does not reveal what people say without their consent.

Jaques himself was a psychoanalyst. On the one hand, it was widely accepted, even by those who were not in the world of psychoanalysis, that people who move into consulting and advisory roles needed to have an analysis: it was felt that such people needed to make sure that they were not using their clients to work out their own problems and therefore needed some other locus where this could be done. On the other hand, for a professional psychoanalyst to be in this role seemed to me to create too "special" a situation for wider diffusion. If the use of the social sciences was to become widespread, there would have to be a more "ordinary", less esoteric way of doing it. This was what I joined Esso to explore.

While being very much influenced by the Glacier work, I had also, rather early on, developed considerable scepticism about the way so-called landmark studies become idealized. In the second case study in our work study research, my colleague John Snelling and I conducted unstructured interviews, asking almost no questions and encouraging people to talk freely about whatever was important to them in their work situation. If we were forced to ask a question, it would take its cues from something the person had said rather than what we were pursuing. For consistency, we sat in on a sample of each other's interviews.

That was how I came to be sitting in on one of John's interviews when it turned out that the lathe operator he was interviewing had recently joined the firm from Glacier Metal. The company was very famous at the time, in the social science world and beyond it, especially for the joint consultation system that had been established there. I could see John tense up with excitement, but his professionalism held:

"What was it like there?" he asked, in best non-directive style.

"Oh, it was all right", said the man. "In the shop I was working in the floor was wet. You used to get your feet wet, and I didn't like that. But apart from that it was okay."

"Anything else?" asked John.

"Not really", said the man. "They didn't have piecework. Here they have piecework, so if I'm late in the morning it's my own money I'm losing. It's better than having a supervisor breathing down your neck."

"Anything else?"

"No, not really. It was all right."

John cracked. He could bear it no longer. Breaking his own very strict rule, he asked: "Don't they have some kind of . . . ah . . . joint consultation system there?"

"What's that, then?" asked the man.

Reality, reality, reality.

The context changes

I held the Esso post from 1965 to 1970 (see chapter 4). During those five years the context underwent major change.

First, there was in this country a massive expansion in the number of universities, with many new social science departments and senior posts. These were now mainly occupied by people who did not share the history I have described, and who had other areas of interest. Research moved away from application: in psychology, much of the emphasis shifted to methodology, and in sociology it shifted to macro-societal and gender issues. On both counts, applied work was considered suspect. From a methodological perspective, the methods involved in application and utilization were not considered to be scientifically "pure". From a societal, neo-Marxist, perspective, helping organizations to function better—especially industrial organizations—meant colluding with capitalism.

Where application and intervention were still debated within the academic community, it was now not in terms of the design and development of organizations and institutions, the area that had held so much promise. Rather, it was in terms of policy-making, of "scientific answers to major national social issues". The distinction between these levels has never been clearly articulated, and this continues to cloud the debate. With it, the two frames of reference became separated. At the institutional and organizational level, there has been much learning about implementation, such as the need for and necessary characteristics of processes of transition (see chapter 14). Learning about these processes has not carried over into the use of research for policy. This is why policy initiatives that may in substance be quite soundly based fail again and again.

In the debate about research for policy guidance, it was assumed that such research would need to be in a "scientific" tradition, mainly of survey research, that would give "reliable" answers. It was therefore felt to be very limiting to the development of the discipline itself, or else applicants for research funds would be forced to make their plans appear more positivistic than they were—or could be—in reality (Williams, 1980). The irony was that a funding body set up as the direct result of creative and useful research at the level of institution-building was now unable to support the very research that had given rise to it.

A gap had opened up between social science and industry. Since industry was now more open to collaboration with social science than it had been in the past, the need came to be filled in other ways. There was therefore, second, an increasing number of consultants, many of them American, carrying out "applied behavioural science" projects in UK organizations. Many of these assignments did not come from a research base at all; some of them were standardized forms of intervention designed to be applicable in all situations, and which came to be known as "packages". And third, the content of these projects was often not concerned with appropriate structure or the fit between structure and behaviour, but with influencing people's behaviour.

This kind of work was well established in the United States. At a conference on Operational Research and the Social Sciences in 1964, Warren Bennis gave a paper entitled "Theory and Method in applying Behavioural Science to Planned Organizational Change" with 117 references, most of them American (Bennis, 1966).

In Esso we experienced this trend when, after three years of a developing social science activity, the parent company brought in a team from the Institute of Social Research, Michigan, whose aim was to change the behavioural style of managers. To help work on the turbulence this created (chapter 7), I turned to a consultant from the Tavistock Institute, Harold Bridger. However, the social science operation in Esso did not recover. When it wound down, I joined the Tavistock Institute; I was there for nineteen years.

The context diversifies

By the end of the 19970s, the context of the work was too diffuse and complex to be easily summarized. I can only pick out a few of the relevant threads:

- At the time I joined the Tavistock Institute, the climate in the funding environment was still favourable to a concern for applied work, and I had obtained a grant from the SSRC to write up the Esso experience (Klein, 1976). But by the time I wanted to take the topic further, a few years later, antipathy among the new social science establishment to application and utilization—which had in fact been the original remit of the SSRC—was probably at its fiercest (see chapter 9).

- The gap between research and problem-solving had widened; its boundaries had hardened and were for a long time impermeable. When problems were publicly recognized, institutions that appeared designed to deal with them were set up, but could only respond with more research. A Technical *Change* Centre was set up, to carry out *research* studies, and was then closed. The research councils formed a joint committee between the Social Science and the Science and Engineering Research Councils to fund linked studies: funding a Work Organisation Research Centre, which did research, and again was closed; funding a Programme for Information and Communication Technologies, which in turn created a number of centres researching the impact of these technologies on society. In all of these, researchers were being funded to do more research. The only exception was a small unit originally set up within the Department of Employment and called, for the sake of respectability, the Work Research Unit, which was actively concerned with dissemination and application.

- In this climate I lost contact with the Social Science Research Council. So I don't know exactly how it came to be nearly abolished. It was investigated by Lord Rothschild (Rothschild, 1982) and survived, eventually re-emerging as the Economic and Social Research Council (ESRC).

- The National Institute of Industrial Psychology lost its core funding from government and closed down.

- On the other hand, universities came under pressure to earn income and undertook consulting activities.

- There were also many new consultancies with some behavioural science component.

- In some circles, novelty began to acquire a value of its own, transcending the content of what was being attempted. In the London Underground one day, I met a young colleague going in the other direction. In the thirty seconds it took us to pass, he said: "Well, last year was job-design year. What's next?"

- Some parts of national research budgets went into the research programmes of the European Commission, with the result that national governments set themselves targets about what their own nationals should be able to claw back. Getting involved in European Commission-funded projects was hard to avoid and at the same time was complex, time-consuming, and frustrating. The rules and customs created a world of their own. They seemed to be designed to foster European collaboration more than to foster research and development—in the welter of acronyms, bullet points, PowerPoint presentations and executive summaries it was hard to hang on to substance.

- In some ways, policy and research came to be brought together through evaluation research, with associated methodologies and institutions.

The recent past

I left the Tavistock Institute in 1989. Since then I have been pursuing the same objectives as always—working with the problems of organizations, working on questions of work organization and job satisfaction, and continuing to explore the use of the social sciences for these purposes, through the work programmes of the Bayswater Institute, which I founded in 1990.

In 1994 I saw an article by Professor Howard Newby, the then chairman of the ESRC, which sounded as if the policy climate might be changing in favour of the use and application of research. I wrote to him. With my customary bad timing, this was two weeks before he was due to leave the ESRC, but he sent copies of the letter to colleagues, and it led to my being invited to do a seminar for ESRC staff, because "we are very exercised—in the wake of the White Paper—about the relationship between research and practice which you have addressed over many years and in many different contexts . . .".

Having lost contact with public funding policy, I now discovered that in 1992 the government had set in train a number of substantial changes in the U.K.'s science and technology infrastructure. In 1993, a White Paper, *Realising Our Potential* (Cabinet Office, 1993) set out a strategy that led to a major reorganization of the research councils, with each of them being required to produce a mission statement making explicit commitment to their contribution to wealth creation. The government reaffirmed its commitment to the "customer–contractor principle" of research, set out in another, earlier, report of Lord Rothschild.

The broad strategy led specifically to a new mission for the ESRC:

> To promote and support high quality basic, strategic and applied social science research and related postgraduate training to increase understanding of social and economic change, placing special emphasis on meeting the needs of the users and beneficiaries for research and training, thereby enhancing the United Kingdom's economic competitiveness, the effectiveness of public services and public policy, and the quality of life.

The first step in this approach to meeting the needs of users was "relevance", much of the ESRC's available research resource now going into programmes developed and selected "for their relevance to policy and business needs alongside their academic quality and promise".

The next step, they felt, was to see whether and how this clear aim of relevance related to engagement with users or potential users of research. To explore this, the ESRC commissioned me in 1996 to look at one of their programmes from the point of view of relations between researchers and users (chapter 10). Although I saw serious problems with the structure and direction being taken, it seemed churlish, after all these years, to quibble. In a short piece in the ESRC's newsletter I wrote of "coming in from the cold".

About this book

The grouping of the papers is not chronological. Nevertheless, they show an overall shift, from emphasis on research in the early phases to greater emphasis on the dynamics in the later ones:

> Section 1 contains a paper reporting on research that turned out later to be very useful for practice, plus one that presents and illustrates a framework for organizational diagnosis.
>
> Section 2 brings together some experiences from practice.
>
> Section 3 looks at practice taking place within a changing context and describes some of the issues involved in relating to the context.
>
> Section 4 contains reflective papers that attempt to generalize from the experience of practice.
>
> Section 5 contains two papers that are more personal and concern my own continuing efforts to learn and to integrate learning.

* * *

The brief history that I have given here shows that the "knowledge-into-use" framework has had some forms of institutional support for nearly a hundred years. The "dynamics-of-action" framework came into play alongside it rather later and is less institutionalized, less regulated, and even more open to the vagaries of fashion, ideology, and personal idiosyncrasy. It is, however, vital: one needs to be both researcher and consultant—each one by itself will not do. Throughout my professional life I have struggled with the difficult, infuriating, and fascinating task of trying to hang on to both frameworks and the dynamic interaction between them, at the same time as their meaning has evolved and changed. The occasions on which I have had a sense of having successfully resolved this task are fairly rare. I hope that this collection of papers can make the task a little easier for others who want to see the social sciences put to use.

Notes

1. This part of the story draws on a paper that was first written in 1965 to introduce industrial managers to the social sciences. The paper incorporated a contribution from Albert Cherns.

2. In this part of the story, I have drawn on the first chapter of Klein (1976).

ORGANIZATION RESEARCH AND DIAGNOSIS

This section represents the beginning of the journey from research into use. The first paper reports on a piece of research on systems of management control, which was funded as research and not intended to lead to action in the firm in question. Nevertheless, I have found the idea derived from it—that behaviour in organizations is influenced by the control systems that are in place—probably more useful than any other in understanding organizations and in contributing to their design. The second paper brings together a broader range of areas of research and theory into a model for organizational diagnosis and design.

CHAPTER 2

Prescription and rationality in management control

This is an example of research that can be used, not in the sense of applying findings directly to other situations, but of highlighting mechanisms (in this case, control systems) that will be at work in other situations. It also generated a method—the tracer study—that has turned out to be useful in practice.

In the 1950s, the industrial sociologist Joan Woodward had conducted research in a hundred firms in Essex to see whether those that followed the precepts of current management teaching were more successful than those that did not. Instead of finding that successful firms had features of organization in common, however, the research found a relationship between technology, organization, and success: if one ranged the firms on a scale of production technology—from unit production through small-batch, large-batch, and mass production, to process production at the complex end of the scale—there were forms of organization common to these production processes. Successful firms tended to adhere to these forms of organization, unsuccessful ones to deviate from them. The research also found that at the two ends of the scale, in unit production and process production, it was possible to make predictions from the technology about behaviour in the firm, whereas in the middle of the scale it was not (Woodward, 1965).

Joan Woodward then formulated a second project, on the hypothesis that in batch production the control system would be the intervening variable making prediction possible. At the time she was in the Mechanical Engineering Department of Imperial College, University of London, and I joined her there for that project: in its first phase, three of us each took a product and followed it through—from the marketing decision to make it, through everything that happened to it until it left the factory gates—in order to elicit the control systems that impinged on it. We called this method a "tracer study", and I have used it many times since then. My "tracer" was a brand of soap and is described in this paper.

Two versions of the paper were originally published; this is the shorter one (Klein, 1965), slightly amended. The fuller version appears in Woodward (1970). Although this project is not as well-known as the first one, I have in fact found it more useful in application: production technologies are ephemeral, whereas control systems exist in all situations.

To make the complexities of industrial behaviour more readily amenable to investigation, one can isolate some of the more important variables that appear to be at work in any organizational context. We know that behaviour, and observed situations, are the result of the interaction of these variables and not of their separate impact; we also know that things are not so arranged that one can play around experimentally with one variable while keeping the others constant. However, while one has constantly to remind oneself of this, it is still possible to increase understanding of how the major variables operate, and various pieces of research have concentrated on one or other of them.

The study on which this chapter is based formed part of a research project on the impact of different types of control system. The assumption behind the research was that there will always be a control system of some sort—that is, that every activity, one way or another, goes through a cycle: objectives are decided, plans are made for realizing them, the plans are carried out, information is generated about how successful they have been, and in the light of this information the objectives are modified or some corrective action is taken. The process may be explicit or implicit; how plans are made and control information obtained may be closely limited by the technology or by the market, or may be very much a matter of choice; the choices may be deliberate or by default. But the nature of these choices, and the way in which control is exercised, will be one of the main components of the total situation.

In the effort as far as possible to capture whole situations in this project, the "tracer" method turned out to be very useful. Case studies were carried out in which a product was isolated and then tracked through all the processes and decisions that impinged on it. All the planning, decision-making, and control procedures of the firm concerned were analysed as they affected the particular tracer. The usefulness of this device, both in making the research manageable for the research worker and in making it real and meaningful for the people in the firm, is hard to exaggerate.

The "tracer" in this case, called here "Product Four", was a batch of a brand of household soap tablets representing one month's production of a small department. The factory as a whole employed about 600 people, roughly one-fifth of whom were managerial and clerical staff. The chief executive on the site was the works manager, to whom were responsible a general production manager with five group managers under him, as well as the heads of four functional departments—the chief chemist, responsible for quality, the personnel manager, the chief engineer, and the industrial engineer.

The basic liquid from which "Product Four" was manufactured was common to some other products; "Four" began to have its own identity in the "Four" department, into which it was pumped from a storage tank. In the department, it went through a number of physical and chemical processes, at the end of which it was extruded in solid form as a bar. It was then cut into tablets, stored on racks, dried, stamped, packed, and despatched to a warehouse. All of this took place in one room, and involved about fifteen operators and one manager, who was in turn responsible to one of the group managers referred to above. At the same time, all the policies of a very large international company impinged on this small department. Scheduling and production control, budgeting and cost control, the determining and implementing of working methods, all took place with regard to "Four" as much as to any of the company's products and activities, and caused the occasional flurry, but on a small enough scale for one research worker to be able to see them in operation and talk to the people involved. The department also formed a unit for most of the firm's accounting procedures. In the words of the works manager, "It's a microcosm". However, in some ways "Four" was also not typical of the firm's products. To a greater degree than with some of the other products, its market was well-established, steady, and predictable, and methods of production for it were also long-established and seldom changing.

Methods of research

The fieldwork was carried out in two phases: interviewing and observation. During the first phase, interviews were held with everyone who was involved with the making and packing of "Four" (omitting the processing of the basic liquid). This included:

1. *Line management*: the works manager, the group manager, and two "Four" department managers, as the post changed hands during the course of the research.

2. *The operators in the department*: five men and eleven women.

3. *Service personnel*:
   — the industrial engineer and, in his department, the chief job study engineer, the job study engineer, and the bonus checker attached to the "Four" department; also the control engineers responsible for fuel, water and power costs; losses and depreciations; repairs and expenses; wage control and methods;
   — the chief chemist, the laboratory manager, and four inspectors;
   — the chief engineer, the section engineer, and two mechanics;
   — the accountant;
   — the personnel manager;
   — the manager of manufacturing at the company's head office, as well as the head of the management systems department and one member of his staff.

The interviews were focused but unstructured. They always started off by asking the people concerned what they actually did in relation to "Four", and this always produced responses on which further questions could then be based. It also provided information on how people perceived and structured their jobs.

The second phase of fieldwork consisted of four weeks spent in the "Four" department. Production was scheduled in four-week periods. One whole schedule was traced: from the decision to make it, at head office, through the various incidents that happened during its production, to the collection and assessment of all the control information relating to it. During the four weeks, the same people (operators, mechanics, department manager, group manager, works manager, inspectors) were visited each day and asked what had happened since the previous visit. For the department manager, there was a questionnaire that was filled in with him every day. For the process operator, there was also a questionnaire. The other operators were asked what had been happening in relation to (a) the product, (b) the equipment, (c) people. The group manager and works manager were asked whether "Four" had come to their attention since the previous visit, again under the headings of product, equipment, and people. Where incidents cropped up involving people not on the regular "visiting list", these were followed up as well. All the relevant management meetings during the month were also attended.

In addition, activity in the department was observed in detail for two hours at a time, covering the whole working day once—that is, observing everything that happened from 6 to 8 a.m. one day, from 8 to 10 a.m. another day, and so on.

This extensive fieldwork yielded a mass of information. Within the scope of this chapter the control system that emerged cannot be described in detail, but only discussed; its effects will be discussed only in relation to management.

The systems of control

It turns out that one has been looking at a firm where rationality of operation had been taken about as far as it can go. It was a firm that, consciously and deliberately, based its management practices on the concept of control systems. There was a management systems department that expressly[1] saw its function as:

1. designing, installing, improving, and maintaining control systems for business activities, resources, or objectives;

2. developing and improving organizations;

3. developing and improving the work place;

4. developing and installing improved working methods and procedures;

5. developing and promoting the widest possible use of tools and techniques, the application of which helps to maximize performance and effectiveness;

6. developing and maintaining the means for measuring the effectiveness of the use of resources and for appraising performance.

The thinking and the procedures did not all originate from the management systems department. Somewhere in the company there seemed to be a central intelligence, a mind, that had taken the trouble to think through the questions, "What do we want?" "How are we going to get it?" "How are we going to know whether we have got it?" "When we know, what are we going to do about it?"

In some instances, this "mind" appeared to be located at the international headquarters of the company, in some instances at the British head office, and sometimes one could not give it a location. In a sense, this impression corresponds with reality, in that the power of decision lay at different levels of the organization, according to the size and importance of the issue involved. But the mode of approaching a decision or a problem was consistent, irrespective of its size and importance and of the level at which it was being made, and it is this consistency of approach that was so striking and gave the impression of some kind of invisible central direction.

As regards the actual control of operations, the explicitness of the systems approach meant that, for all the parameters of quantity, quality, and the different types of cost, targets were set; methods for arriving at targets were laid down; and ways of auditing the methods for arriving at targets were laid down.

Similarly: actual performance was measured; methods for measuring the actuals were laid down; and ways of auditing the methods for measuring the actuals were laid down. The comparison between the targets and actuals, for each item in each department, yielded a performance factor, or PF, which was the main control tool.

And, again, systems were laid down for proposing and investigating amendments to any of these.

As an example: cost control was the responsibility of the industrial engineer, and it was his department that operated the company's Cost Control Plan. For control purposes, costs were divided into wages costs, repairs and maintenance, losses and depreciation (in respect of materials used in making and packing the products), and fuel, water, and power costs. The methods used for setting the standards under these various headings were perhaps the most complex, analysing every possible source of costs into the degree to which it was knowable and controllable; for each source of costs, at each degree of controllability, there was then a number of ways of computing targets, in order of preference. In every facet of costs, the department manager was thus presented with a target in the same way that he was given targets for quantity and quality.[2] Similarly, there were mechanisms for measuring or calculating the actual as opposed to the target costs under each heading.

All the PFs were weighted at the end of each month according to their relative importance for the particular product and to ensure that they were reconcilable with each other. They were then brought together in a matrix-type cost-control summary. Read horizontally, the summary gave the overall performance of each production department. Read vertically, it showed the results obtained throughout the factory in respect of quantity, quality, and each type of cost. Thus the PFs were the measure of the effectiveness of line and service managers and influenced their bonuses.

Of course, in detail the system was sometimes difficult and often complex in operation, and not all the procedures were completely foolproof. But even those parts of the company's operations that had not yet been brought under detailed control were known, and hence circumscribed and limited, and therefore in a sense controlled after all. In three months of fieldwork one cannot possibly have discovered and recorded everything, but the general impression was that this was a company in which the last "i" had been dotted and the last "t" crossed. This is a state of affairs that yields both a certain aesthetic satisfaction and a certain frustration, not only for the observer but also for the managers operating the system.

One effect within the company could be that the rationality behind the aim to know what is happening, in order to control it, could on occasion yield to an irrational and obsessive desire for detailed knowledge for its own sake. One system that may have begun to cross this borderline was "work assignment". Under this a manager was supposed to plan and assign in detail the work of every operator under him at the beginning of every day. In some departments this may have been useful, but in the "Four" department, where the operators knew the work, which was more or less the same each day, and where the small variations due to machine stoppages could in any case not be predicted, there seemed little point in this, except perhaps as an exercise for a trainee manager.

The expressed objective, "that any senior manager walking through the department at a quarter to eleven should know exactly which bit of the floor the clean-up man is supposed to be cleaning", seems to show anxiety rather than rationality.

Irrationality, however, was rare. On the whole, the systems were to a high degree rational, and they were effective. Moreover—and this is an important factor in the situation—they were explicit and documented. Every manager and senior manager had a bookshelf full of manuals, describing and prescribing the different aspects of his job. One of them, the "Job Control Book", he would have compiled himself while he was learning the job. Between them, these various manuals provided instructions or guidance for how to proceed in every imaginable circumstance, sometimes down to the most minute detail. For instance, the "Manager's Manual" included instruction to managers on what to say to an employee who asked whether he should join the trade union. The answer he was to be given was a sensible one and would ensure that an inexperienced manager could not harm the industrial relations of the company. On the other hand, only an inexperienced manager was likely to welcome, or indeed tolerate, being told exactly what to say.

We begin to see, therefore, some of the consequences of managing in this particular way. One consequence was that the company could have surprisingly young and inexperienced men as managers, since the accumulated experience of the company existed on paper in the form of detailed explanations and instructions for everything, and very few contingencies could arise that had not been foreseen and allowed for. A second consequence was that for the same reasons it did not take very long to learn to run a department, and a third consequence was that managers could therefore also be moved quite easily from job to job.

Managerial job rotation

The company's practice was to recruit good-quality graduates straight from university, in fairly large numbers. A young man recruited in this way was placed with an existing manager—line or service—for about six months, to learn the job. He then took over that particular department, or service job, and ran it for perhaps eighteen months. By then he would in turn be teaching the job to his successor and would then himself be moved on to another management post. Moving around could also include moving between the company's factories, but this was more usual for senior managers. It was reckoned that by the time a man was twenty-six or twenty-seven years old he would have held two or three management posts, probably one in a line department, one service post such as job study, and probably one in personnel, such as safety or training manager.

At about that stage the young manager would be considered for promotion to the senior grade of group manager. If such promotion was not forthcoming and the young man was ambitious, the chances were that he would leave the company, and many managers did in fact leave at this stage. They were then in a very good position in the labour market, since they had had an undoubtedly excellent training, and it was known that some firms would automatically short-list a man if he came from this one.

This frequent moving of managers from job to job was perhaps a unique feature of this company. I believe that it explains to a large extent the remarkable consistency of approach noted earlier. It led the manager to identify himself with a way of tackling a new task, a way of approaching a problem, rather than with the problems of a particular department or function.

This was also suggested by a comment made by several managers, that the main disadvantage of this system lay in relation to projects. During his tenure of a post, a manager might initiate one or more projects to tackle the problems of that department. He might then be moved from the department before such a project was completed, and it was unlikely that his successor would identify himself with the project to the same extent. Projects, especially difficult ones, were therefore sometimes left incomplete. The operators in the "Four" department, for instance, complained that a difficult cleaning job had no time set for it, since over the years successive job-study engineers had begun to study it but had never actually settled a time.

Although this loss of interest in particular projects could in practical terms have some disadvantage, it emphasizes the way in which managers acquired a company-wide perspective, thus avoiding the problems of limited perspective that are associated with long tenure of a particular post. The disadvantage was to some extent mitigated by the Methods Programme, under which every manager was allocated into one of a number of methods teams. The teams worked to financial targets on cost-reduction projects, their success in reaching the targets influencing the PFs of the members. A methods team cut across departments and thus provided a little more continuity in the pursuing of projects (although the criteria for deciding on projects were different ones, and therefore the type of project tackled may have been different). Again, however, being involved in an inter-departmental methods team was at least as likely to impress on the young manager the methods approach as to impress on him the details of any particular project he worked on.

In the main, continuity, and any undocumented know-how there might be in a department, were provided by the operators, and not by the manager. Operators saw managers come and go, and they appeared not to mind this. An operator on "Four" explained that "a manager in this firm is a chap who asks you how to do the job", but he said it in a tolerant and good-humoured way. This acceptance was helped by the fact that the managers were generally very young and, provided that their behaviour was not clumsy or arrogant, the operators could feel protective towards them. It was, however, a slightly uneasy relationship.

The control of managers

The fact that managers were moved around had important implications for control. A fairly short tenure of a job meant that one did not have time to learn to deviate from the job as it was laid down. There was a lot to learn, the procedures were often complicated, and one cannot normally develop short-cuts or by-pass procedures until one is very familiar with them. In this way, therefore, the moving of people from job to job acted as a second-order control—it controlled the controllers. There is no way of telling whether this was the purpose of the mechanism; one can only observe that this was its effect.

There was another, perhaps more deliberate, way of controlling the behaviour of managers. When a trainee had been with a manager for about six months and they both felt that he was ready, he had to "qualify". That is, he was tested on his knowledge of the different aspects of the job and on his ideas for running it. This testing was carried out by various functional staff and the works manager. The manager from whom the trainee had learnt the job took no part in it. Before this, the trainee would also have had a full discussion about his findings and views on the department with the group manager, again without the presence of the manager, "in case the manager isn't operating according to the group manager's policy".

There can hardly be a more effective way of keeping control of what a manager is doing than by finding out what a trainee has learnt from him. If he is not "operating according to policy", but the results he produces are satisfactory, one may well allow him to continue operating in this way. However, at least his successor will not operate in this way and will revert to the proper way, so that the deviation will not be continued. And at least one knows the extent of the deviation. And the manager knows that one knows.

The "Four" department highlighted some of these points. Its manager and section engineer were the only two exceptions in the factory to the pattern of management training and development described. Both were older men who had held their jobs for a considerable time. Both therefore had the job at their fingertips and planned their activities in their heads, with as little use of the formal systems as they were allowed to get away with. They were the only two people of manager grade who, when interviewed, described their jobs without reference to a manual. (It seems likely that the habit of training others, as well as moving around and being at the receiving end of training, helped to ensure conformity to procedures.)

The "Four" manager had been running the department, on and off, for about twenty years. Every now and again he would be moved out of the department to allow a new, young manager to run it for a time, and would then come back to pick up the threads again. During the periods that he was running the department, there were greater differences between the formal and the informal systems than at other times or than elsewhere in the factory. He flatly refused to do work assignment, and there were various other procedures that, through experience and familiarity with the job, he bypassed or used flexibly.

There had been rows about this with senior management, but his informal handling of his job was tolerated because he was an old servant of the company, for whom there was considerable affection, and because his PFs were good. The problem of what attitude to take towards him was mainly resolved by treating his behaviour as a joke – "Oh well, everybody knows Peter!"

There was, however, an interesting ambivalence in the attitude of senior management towards this deviant. Mostly the attitude was one of exasperation, tempered by affection and made bearable by amusement. This was reversed in a dramatic way during a meeting held in the firm to present the findings of this study. Peter, who had been rather a thorn in the flesh, suddenly became a hero, an example of individuality and initiative, of whom the whole body of management was proud.

There is a well-known difficulty in presenting a descriptive account without having feelings of praise or blame projected on to it by the audience or reader. When presented to an audience of this company's managers, the present account evoked the reaction, "You think we are all 'organization men'[3]—you think this is bad" (and then, by implication, "we would think it is bad too, if it were true. But then it is not true—look at Peter!"). In a different context, the reaction is, "You are holding this up as a perfect system. You think this is good." In fact, the situation includes something of both these elements. It comprises both excellence in the system and conformity in the people who operate it, and to say this is neither praise nor blame (cf. Fred Emery's comment that "love and hate . . . are a basic defence against informational complexity"!).

"Perfection" is, of course, too absolute and philosophical a term, but it must be true that the nearer a system gets to meeting the requirements it is set up to serve, and the less a reasonable person can find in it to criticize and improve, the more it must call forth acceptance and therefore the "organization man" type of behaviour. This fact in itself then becomes a source of criticism to those who, like Whyte and possibly many people in this country, are still rooted in the protestant ethic, with its emphasis on the virtues of individualism and independence. But Whyte only concerned himself with the last part of the equation, the behaviour of the organization man. He avoided either accepting or rejecting the need for the organization itself, and therein lies the rub. One must quarrel with the objectives or raison d'être of the organization; or one must quarrel with the systems set up to achieve these objectives; or one must accept. If none of these postures is tolerable, then one is in an insoluble dilemma.

Initiative

There remains the question of where and how initiative occurs within the organization. On this subject, the control system described presents some apparent contradictions.

The managers in this firm genuinely did not know whether their jobs were challenging and exciting, or merely routine. At different times they claimed both, and the movement from job to job helped to confuse the issue and prevent them from finding out. As one senior manager put it: "It takes six months to learn the job, it's exciting then. Then for about three months you develop it and have ideas. Then it would begin to get boring, but if you are moved around you don't get bored and you don't discover that it's essentially routine."

But even without the moving around, the contradiction exists. Two examples will serve to illustrate it. In line management, it is a valid question to ask in what sense the "Four" department manager was "managing" at all. If he had suddenly disappeared, the department would have continued to function. The operators knew what to do, the product would continue to be produced and packed, and it might be two or three months before anything started going seriously wrong. On the other hand, after a time the PFs would begin to deteriorate, costs would go up, quality problems would become more frequent, and the co-ordination with other departments would begin to creak. Senior management would eventually have to intervene, or the operators be given some additional training.

An example from a service management post is that of the engineer responsible for losses-and-depreciations cost control. This meant losses in material being processed, through inefficient processing, leaks, evaporation, and so forth. The post was held by a young philosophy graduate, in his first job, with no vocational training except a two-week course in statistics organized within the company. Loss of material was the biggest potential cost item in the factory, 1% loss involving a cost of £6,000 per month. On the one hand, it was tremendously exciting and challenging to think that only his own intelligence stood between him and savings of this order to the factory. On the other hand, if he merely read the meters, filled in the forms, applied the formulae, and did the routine calculations, he would still be fulfilling his job adequately, and the result at the end of the month might be no different.

In these conditions it becomes very much a matter of the perceptions of the individual how he interprets the job. There were some who felt constrained by the comprehensiveness of the systems. The majority appeared to feel that this very comprehensiveness set them free to think creatively about the job. Constraint was, in any case, not direct: managers frequently set their own targets. It was the methods of arriving at targets which were laid down, and these, too, were subject to systematic review and modification. Whether the resulting feelings of freedom were real or illusory would depend on how much objective possibility there was of making improvements.

We are brought a little further, therefore, in the elucidation of the ever-vexing question: "What is management?" Industrial management involves three distinct types of activity:

(a) the setting up of a workable system for production or service;
(b) the maintaining of the system by planning the work, co-ordinating the materials and services needed, keeping quality and costs within acceptable limits, and so on;
(c) improving the performance of the system and improving the system itself.

Activities (a) and (b) are essential in every industrial situation; (c) may be essential if competition is intense, although sometimes it would be nice to have but not essential—the icing on the cake of profitability.

Firms in different technical or economic conditions use the energies and skills of their managers to different degrees in different parts of this schema. In the situation of small-batch production engineering in the firm of "Multiproducts Ltd" (Klein, 1964), the problems of (a) and (b), and especially of (b), were so great that they took up all the energy and initiative of the managers who were on the spot. For "Product Four," and for the service systems surrounding it, the problems of (a) had been largely resolved. The challenge to management ability no longer lay in working out how to make it. Activity (b) still required attention and ability, and a little initiative in spotting problems, but the solving of problems could be handled in a routine manner since the problems that arose were hardly ever new ones. The real challenge lay in (c), in improving performance—perhaps in devising a better way of keeping product meters consistent, or a way of setting a more specific target for the department's "ideal" use of electric power.

The important difference between (a) and (c) on the one hand, and (b) on the other, is that (a) and (c) are never as urgent as (b); or rather, even if economic circumstances make them urgent, their urgency is not as immediately apparent as that of (b). If one does not feel like working on the new formula for inventory control today, one can work on it tomorrow, without any apparent harm coming to the company. Indeed, if one does nothing at all to improve the system, it may be a long time before anything very terrible happens.

This is without doubt one reason for the atmosphere of calm that was a marked feature in the factory. The observer—especially an observer with experience of batch production engineering—is very impressed by a general atmosphere of security and confidence, an absence of panic and pressure (always remembering that this was only in relation to the tracer product; there were other parts of the company where things were less calm). It is an interesting exercise to assess how much of this is "luck" and how much is "judgement". There is no space here to go into details of the market and the technology, but it is certain that economic and technical circumstances helped to minimize problems—there was quite a lot of luck. On the other hand, the company had itself taken an active part in developing the technology and the market.

It is also certain that the intelligence and sophistication that had gone into devising the control system meant that it was not difficult to keep it running. Attention therefore became focused on the actual performance of the system. The importance attached to "performance factors" supports this, as does the fact that the flurries of activity that took up a large part of the day-to-day happenings around the tracer during the observation period were nearly all concerned with changes in performance.

* * *

This study was part of a programme concerned with "generating a body of knowledge and methodology that can be communicated and used" (Woodward, 1970, p. 235). It had no local action agenda, but there is an action element in the process of feedback to the firm, and in the firm's response. Once the study was over, I was asked to come back to the firm as a consultant. That episode is reported in chapter 5.

Notes

1. The list that follows is taken from an internal report dated June 1962.
2. The masculine pronouns in this chapter will sound strange in this day and age. However, all the managers in the company at that time were in fact men.
3. See Whyte (1956).

CHAPTER 3

Theories of organization— a framework for diagnosis

A first formulation of the framework presented here was included in *Putting Social Science to Work* (Klein & Eason, 1991). In the form of talks it has continued to evolve over time. One version of it is used during the Bayswater Institute's regular Working Conferences, to help participants make sense of their experience. The version below is an amalgamation of the various threads: it is still in the form of a talk, in which the listener or reader is invited to join in the learning process. It has not been published in this form.

I find myself constantly using this framework as an aid to diagnosis. I don't explicitly set out to do that—it just keeps happening. The paper includes two examples of using it.

Theory is about explanation. We all have a powerful need to make sense of our environment. The environment consists of an infinite number of bits of information, and unless we arrange these for ourselves in some meaningful way, we cannot function. We all need to have some basis for believing that the floor will not melt when we put a foot on it. Whether it is a theory about the properties of wood and stone, or a statistical theory that since the ground did not melt the last six thousand times it is unlikely to melt the next time, or a theory that the angels will look after us—without some theoretical basis for putting one foot in front of the other, we are paralysed.

Insofar as we spend our life in organizations, we are all organization theorists. We go through the day, the week, the month, with a kind of running commentary going through our heads: if we do this, that is likely to happen; if we hadn't done X, then Y would not have happened. These are statements of theory and prediction. The only difference between that and what researchers do is that they do it more systematically and perhaps comparatively.

Organizational diagnosis serves both the frameworks that are necessary for the practice of social science: knowledge-into-use and the dynamics of action. In the framework of knowledge-into-use, a diagnostic study produces a picture or information that may then be used. To form the picture, those carrying out diagnosis need to have a background of knowledge to which to relate what they find, and a capacity for rigour in the way they set about finding it. In the framework of dynamics of action and change, a diagnostic study provides a "transitional system", entered into jointly by the practitioner and client systems, enabling them to explore each other to develop confidence, to enter into each other's frames of reference, and to test out working together. It is a vehicle for "getting to know you". Information will become explicit that may not have been so in the past, or may be interpreted in ways that are new. If any of that is disputed, there is an opportunity for working through, on both sides. Learning, and with it change, will take place on both sides.

Ordering theories of organization — a framework for diagnosis

I came to organization consultancy from research in the area of contingency theory. So there was one part of the field which I knew fairly well. But the first time I had to give a lecture on organization in the broader sense, I felt I should read around more systematically, and I found the literature very confusing. There would be a study by Dr X, which was quite interesting, and a book by Professor Y, which was also quite interesting, but apparently no kind of connection between them. And the quantity of material was enormous. The environment of which I had to make sense was the literature and, again, without a way of making sense of it I couldn't function. A situation or problem

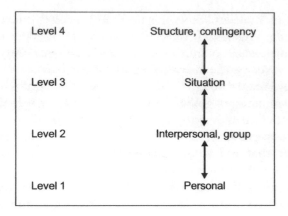

FIGURE 1.   A model for diagnosis.

may be studied from many disciplines or points of view, and each of them may shed some light on it. But it will be a partial light, like the light that has been separated out from a prism; it will not by itself serve for resolution or development. The mass of ideas and theories appear to be unrelated to each other and merely competing for attention; it is indeed paralysing.

It is important not to avoid or try to cut short the confusion, painful and difficult though it is—in other words, to "stay with the madness". It is also important not to stay there for ever. Eventually, I worked my way through to a framework or model for ordering this confusing literature. Once the various ideas are seen as having a place in a broader framework, it should be easier to select points of entry for diagnosis and to make judgements about diagnosis itself.

The model has four levels: the personal, the interpersonal or group, the situational, and the structural, as shown in Figure 1.

Level 1.   Individuals affect organization

The most direct and immediate explanation of the experience of or-ganizational life is in terms of the people in it. If one's superiors were less autocratic or more far-sighted, if one's peers were not so competi-tive, if one's subordinates were more able or more committed, one's experience of the organization would be different. And, indeed, it would be. There is some truth in explanations at all of these levels.

At this first level, there exists a great deal of research and theory about personality and personal development. It is, in the main, the psychology literature that features here, and some of it has been used to devise methods of selection and training. Those who favour this level of explanation are likely to look to selection and training for solutions to organizational problems.

However, people don't always make the right connection between problem diagnosis and solution. When I joined Esso in 1965, I started my tenure with a round of interviews with senior managers. This was partly to learn about the company and partly to let people know about the new function of in-house social sciences adviser. Esso managers were very good at explaining the problems the company was experiencing. For instance, Esso Petroleum UK was not responsible for buying crude oil in the world market; its function was to process the crude oil allocated to it by the parent company, Standard Oil New Jersey (now Exxon). Now, if one of the main parameters—raw material purchase—is not under your control, it is very difficult to know what is meant by success and to devise appropriate control systems, and it is therefore also very difficult for managers as individuals to know when they are doing well.

Or again: a few years previously the company had built a new refinery at Fawley, near Southampton. This meant that a large number of young graduates had been recruited, and these were beginning to move upwards in the hierarchy, as well as outwards to other functions and departments. The result was a diamond-shaped age structure: a large number of middle-level people aged around 30 were competing for a very small number of senior posts, with uncomfortable and sometimes distressing results. Or again: competition had recently sharpened, with a number of new, small oil companies appearing in the market, and this too, of course, had consequences.

Yet, having described and explained a situation of this kind, managers would quite often sit back, reflect for a moment, and conclude: what we need is bright people with ideas. It was a solution at the personal level to problems that were not at this level.

Level 2. Relationships affect individuals

The influence of individuals is important, but individuals are not limited to one way of behaving. They have a repertoire of behaviours available to them, and which one they select will depend on a number of things, including how they themselves are treated. Thus interpersonal relations—the effect of the group on the individual, and the behaviour of groups as such—represent the next level of explanation.

These, too, have been the focus of much research, as well as experimentation.

The body of literature here is enormous. From the Hawthorne experiments of the late 1920s (Roethlisberger & Dickson, 1939), through the study of the morale of an Air Force unit in the Second World War (Paterson, 1955), to studies of supervisory style in industry in the 1950s (Likert, 1961), the impact of the social context on individual attitudes and behaviour has been documented again and again. Those who are drawn to this level of explanation will look to behaviour modification for solutions, and there are many forms of training and of giving feedback about behaviour that attempt to achieve this. Often they are aimed at shifting behaviour towards some culturally acceptable norm, perhaps that of being more "democratic" or "participative" in relation to others. More rarely they are aimed at helping people to understand better the roots and dynamics of their own behaviour and become, as it were, more truly themselves. In any case, social process is here seen as a causal factor, sometimes as the principal or only causal factor, explaining the problem or situation being considered.

At this level, confusion often creeps in between "behavioural science" and ideology, and there is some tendency for the work to become normative: not so much trying to convey understanding as trying to turn bad guys into good guys.

Level 3. Situations affect relationships and roles

However, it is coming to be recognized that social processes, too, are subject to external influence. There is no single style of behaviour that is appropriate to all situations. A managerial style that is appropriate when a new field of endeavour is being explored may not be appropriate when a fire breaks out. Batch production manufacture requires many managerial decisions per day; process production requires few, as many decisions have already been built into the design of the plant. The implications for managerial style, and the personal qualities needed to survive and be successful in these situations, are different. It is also clear that people who have been influenced by programmes that attempt to modify behaviour may only be able to manage it until they come under pressure—say, time pressure or money pressure. An autocratic manager is easier to relate to than an inconsistent one.

Time presents a good illustration of a situational constraint that affects relationships. For instance, in the organization of newspaper production, the time when the paper has to be "put to bed" has a pervasive impact on most aspects of the organization, its activities and relationships, from the bottom to the top. Or again, when a research department working to a six-monthly or annual time-cycle has to relate to a production department working to a weekly cycle, the people involved are likely to find each other insensitive to need and difficult to relate to, and they may well attribute these difficulties to personality factors.

Such situational factors may, in turn, be influenced by what I am calling structure. The time boundaries, for instance, may be due to the technology of the product or of distribution. There is not much research literature isolating these situational factors as such, and this level is not always distinct. But there is a body of research and writing at the next level, which considers what gives rise to such situations—that is, structure.

Level 4.   Structure and contingencies affect situations

Structure is defined differently in different disciplines. I am using the term here to indicate those things that, although they may be influenced in the long term, cannot be influenced in the short term and therefore at any particular point in time are given and create the environment within which organizations and their members have to function.

As regards society as a whole, for example, people may influence the size of the population to some extent with their decisions about family size or emigration. In the short term, however, a country's demographic structure, including its age distribution, with the profound effects that has on resources and the provision of services, and consequently also on politics, is part of the environment within which families have to function.

As regards organizations, factors that have such pervasive effects include: ownership (whether an organization is public or private, family-owned, a subsidiary, part of a chain); the legal system within which the organization operates; the characteristics of the markets within which it operates; the level of scientific and technical development and therefore product technology and production technology; geographic location; size. Control systems have a similarly powerful effect but, of course, mainly arise within the organization.

In many of these areas, research has shown the consequences of different kinds of structure for attitudes, behaviour, and experience. For instance, there are built-in structural differences between the marketing function and the production function in manufacturing. It is predictable that marketing managers and production managers will have difficulties with each other, and it helps to point out that this always happens and is no one's personal fault. Geographical location is another such situational factor. When people from different functions or departments are geographically separate, there is more chance of incomplete information—leading to fantasy in their perception of each other—than when they are together in the same location.

The discussion has thus moved from a psychological level of explanation to a contingency level. This means that there is not a single right way to be, but that whatever way one chooses will have consequences, and these can often be predicted and therefore selected: "if this . . . then that".

* * *

There is little doubt that, currently, the most popular levels of diagnosis and consequent action in the behavioural sciences are the first two. It may be that this is because selection and skills training on the one hand, and human-relations-type training activities on the other, actually seem to offer some hope of change. Managers feel able to do something in these areas, whereas, on the other hand, gaining an understanding of structural influences may leave them intellectually convinced but feeling either helpless or required to take on something more fundamental than they feel able to handle. As some of these connections become better understood, however, there may be a willingness to move into areas of influence that were previously thought to be inaccessible. Certainly it is coming to be recognized that technology is a matter of choices and that technology design itself can be influenced (Rosenbrock, 1979, 1983).

As I said earlier, a situation may be studied from many points of view. If one is in the business of research, research questions can be formulated at any of these levels. But if one is in the business of diagnosis, the real skill (and the real fun) lies in moving between these levels—as it were, playing the piano up and down this scale—asking oneself: with regard to this problem that I am observing, or experiencing:

- What component of it lies at the personal level?
- What component lies at the interpersonal or group level?
- What component lies at the situational level?
- What component lies at the structural level?
- And how do these interact?

Doing this, I have repeatedly found that the model is robust. It works.

Of course, it would be nice to think that one had managed to encapsulate all the complexities of organizational theory into a four- or five-line model! Much as I am drawn to the simplicity of it, it has to be acknowledged that it is not comprehensive, and I can refer to at least one theoretical approach that does not fit in.

During the 1970s a view of organizations became prevalent that perceives the "skin" around the organization as being rather thin, and the organization itself as a temporary container for members of other institutions with which they are more strongly identified than with the organization itself. These might be, for example, the trade union movement, or the function of management, or the profession of marketing or IT. The roots of this approach are perhaps political, but its validity goes beyond the political. I once worked on a project in a medium-sized company that was a subsidiary of a large conglomerate. About two years after the work was finished, I wrote it up for possible publication. When I went back to the company with a draft, to get clearance for publication, I found that not one of the managers with whom I had worked was still there. Every one of them had moved on to another part of the parent company, as part of the parent company's management development scheme. So this aspect, too, needs to feature in the mind of the diagnostician.

Two examples of diagnosis

Example 1.   The role of the anaesthetist

An example may serve to illustrate the interplay of factors at different levels of the model in the search to understand organizations. It concerns the roles of hospital anaesthetists.[1] The professional association of anaesthetists had some concerns about its membership. They thought—though they did not have definite data—that anaesthetists were difficult to recruit, were tending to retire early, and generally showed signs of low morale. The association's research and education committee sponsored four small studies, three of them focusing on fatigue aspects of the job; but one study was commissioned to explore role and organizational aspects. This turned out to illustrate the interplay between the different levels of structure, situation, and social and personal dynamics.

It was decided to carry out an exploratory case study of the Division of Anaesthesia in a district general hospital, with 850 beds. (Incidentally, the process of obtaining their agreement to the study also showed something of the value of this framework at work. The anaesthetists were in the habit of meeting over sandwiches and coffee once a week for professional discussions. I was invited to one of these meetings to put the case for the study. I did so, and then they explained a little about how they worked. They serviced the hospital's general operating lists, as well as providing a service for dentistry, obstetrics, and psychiatry. But the general operating lists had priority. However short-staffed they might be, "if you are scheduled to have an operation, you will have your operation". I asked whether this meant that I might come across an obstetrician in the hospital grumbling that "you can never get hold of an anaesthetist when you need one!" One of the consultants frowned into his coffee for some lengthy moments and then said, in a surprised and thoughtful voice, "Yes. I suppose you might." The trouble is, one gets so used to thinking in this detective-story way that my prediction just seemed like common sense. But to them it was not "mere" common sense, but served to show that there was some scientific underpinning to a social scientist's approach. They agreed to the study.)

In the Division of Anaesthesia there were fourteen anaesthetists, seven men and seven women. Unstructured interviews, averaging about two-and-half hours, were conducted with all the anaesthetists, with two consultant surgeons, and with a senior nursing officer. In addition, about fifteen hours, spread over a week's operating lists, were spent in theatre, observing the work there.

Unstructured diagnostic research of this kind yields very rich data. But the richer the material, the less easy it is to analyse. I spent a long time soaking up, assimilating, and trying to understand the material, with its many apparent contradictions and inconsistencies. It was the frequently experienced painful process of feeling confused and over-whelmed by the richness and forcing myself to stay with it. Eventually I had to say to myself, "you have a framework—use it!"

So I searched through the material for facts of structure (Level 4), and found three:

- the fact that an anaesthetic is a relatively bounded, short-cycle event;
- the fact that a patient comes into hospital for surgery and not for an anaesthetic;
- the scientific and technical content of anaesthetics.

These three—there were undoubtedly others—all had the quality of being given, at least in the short term. It then turned out that much of the material fell into place behind these structural facts (again, not all of it—life is not so tidy!), as outlined below.

Consequences of the bounded, short-cycle nature of the event

An anaesthetic is not only a relatively short event, it is one with relatively clear-cut, unambiguous boundaries. This has implications for Level 1 phenomena, because it helps to select the kind of medical practitioner who enters the role. For example, the bounded nature of the work makes it possible not only for married women, but for anyone who wants to pursue outside interests, to work part-time.

The short cycle of the anaesthetic means that one can experience a successfully completed service for patients quite often—things very rarely go wrong—and it also provides fairly quick feedback about how well one has performed—"It's nice to put a patient to sleep and then he wakes up and he's talking to you and you've done something for him. One moment they're asleep and then they are talking to you." "It's extraordinarily satisfying to have taken the patient through one of the most difficult times of his life safely and properly, and then they wake up and they don't even remember going to the theatre. That's one of the best things about it." It was pointed out that an anaesthetist may give between 30,000 and 40,000 anaesthetics in the course of a career.

By unambiguous is meant the fact that, once the patient is awake and breathing safely, the anaesthetic has been completed, whatever other problems the patient still has. Some people did not want the long-term care of the patient or the ambiguities of ill-health—"It's very much an open-and-shut sort of job. You meet the patient, you assess him, you put him to sleep, you go and see him once afterwards, hopefully, or twice. It's a unit, a complete entity." "I like finishing with them and then getting new faces." "In the house job, there is a ward full of problems, and the next day they're all there again, whereas in anaesthetics I come on in the morning, the patients . . . they've got me, they've got my undivided attention for an hour or two, and then they go back to the ward. It's not the same with a stroke or with some problem that I've made ten phone calls about."

On the other hand, there was some room for interpretation, depending on individual personality. What has been described was a rather bounded, closed system. If these aspects were not what appealed, the boundaries could to some extent be extended, and people then spoke of research, or pain clinics and intensive care, and of places where "they already look after them for twenty-four hours, fluid regulation for instance, and only then the surgical team takes over". Also the broader management of the patient—"some places have a preoperative clinic where you chat with the patient, see if they are allergic to anything, and so on. I hope this will spread. It would need more posts, but you would learn more by managing the patient." Taking the whole history was then perceived as an opportunity to learn rather than the chore of clerking, and the patient's long-term progress as necessary feedback.

An anaesthetic has a high proportion of technical and a low proportion of interpersonal content, at least as far as interaction with the patient is concerned, and this, too, helps to select the kind of medical practitioner who enters the role. In the vexed question of "patient contact", there was some room for individual differences to express themselves. This even influenced technique—for instance, whether the anaesthetist considered it kinder to give heavy premedication or to deal with patients' fears by talking to them.

Consequences of the fact that the earliest decisions concern surgery

That patients come into hospital for surgery and not for an anaesthetic is indisputable. This structural fact could be traced as having major implications at Level 2 for one of the most important role relationships in the operating theatre: that between the surgeon and the anaesthetist. Surgeons derived their authority from the fact that it was they who decided on the operation and performed it, and it was they who carried the overall responsibility for the patient. In the last resort, as one surgeon put it, "You don't say, 'I'm going to do an anaesthetic list next Tuesday, find me a surgeon.'" In addition, some had authority stemming from personal eminence. This authority then carried over onto a whole range of matters, in some of which its appropriateness was less obvious and where others could experience difficulty and resentment:

- Surgeons not only devised timetables and operating lists, they modified them at short notice and sometimes failed to make them known. They scheduled work to suit their own requirements and did so without consultation—"surgeons can really be outrageous.

They can be so demanding and rude and thoughtless . . . this business of putting patients on the list without the courtesy of saying, 'Can you manage?' They put eight hours' work on and don't dream of saying, 'Have you got a long list?' They assume that you are there as a service." "It's supposed to be ready at 5.00, but . . . I ring up at 8.00 or 10.00 and there's no list yet." In private practice, surgeons had the power of patronage, so one was dependent on them to get work. (However, one instance was quoted where a syndicate of anaesthetists had been set up to control their own access to work.)

- There was a general assumption that the surgeon's time was more valuable than the anaesthetist's. It was the surgeon who must not be kept waiting—"You've got ten minutes, then they start looking through the porthole."

- It was the surgeon who determined the general atmosphere in the operating theatre. Surgeons obviously needed to work in the way that suited them best, and they varied greatly. The atmosphere in theatre ranged from formality and silence to the surgeon beating a tattoo on an old lady's bottom as a signal for starting. In any case, the anaesthetists were constrained to take their cue from the surgeon and not the other way about.

- With their limited knowledge of anaesthetics, surgeons could have unreasonable expectations: "One surgeon actually said, 'You should be able to anaesthetize any patient if the heart is beating and the patient is breathing'". They could make unreasonable demands: "If everybody's in a hurry and you say you have to wait four hours because he's had a meal, they say, 'What does it matter if it's only two hours?'" They could fail to realize what was being achieved: "If things go well, you are hardly there. If they go badly, you are not doing your job well." They could make inappropriate requests: "Some surgeons believe in blood, that blood is good, and they give too much." They could seem indifferent to problems outside their own sphere: regarding a patient with heart trouble, "It's not his problem patient, it's my problem patient."

Consequences of the scientific and technical content
of anaesthetics

As regards scientific and technical developments, enormous strides had been made in recent years in the development of new drugs, new methods, and new equipment. Anaesthetics had expanded in scale and complexity and had become "a real science, as well as an art". Examinations were becoming more difficult. There was even a possibility that the qualities of modern anaesthetics could be exaggerated or too much taken for granted "They [surgeons] get a bit blasé. They think that anaesthetics 've got to such a pitch they can go on for ever."

Developments in anaesthetics had had a number of consequences:

- *Greater separation from surgery.* In the "old days", surgeons had known about anaesthetics and sometimes administered anaesthetics themselves. Exceptionally it could still happen that "some old-timer might tell the anaesthetist what anaesthetic to give, and it might be out of the ark". But the knowledge and methods, at the same time as growing, had established themselves as clearly different in kind from those of the surgeon. An operation used to be a single undertaking; it was now two distinct undertakings. Surgeons tended to opt out of knowing about anaesthetics. They were interested in the result—a safe and stable patient—but not in the choices and strategies involved in getting there, and this could be a cause for regret—"There was a partnership between the surgeon and the anaesthetist. You were looking after that patient together, you would exchange ideas about the patient. Now it's different; you are looking after different ends of the patient. The surgeon doesn't know about the anaesthetic side of it, there is more of a conflict therefore." A surgeon said, "Anaesthetic technique has left me behind. I don't really understand now, if he tells me what he's doing . . . and I'm not really interested."

- *Greater professional standing for anaesthetists.* At the same time as leading to greater separation from surgery, the distinctive nature of the scientific and technical content of anaesthetics had brought a sense of independent professionalism for anaesthetists, as well as high status, expressed in consultant posts. This had led to a more complex relationship with surgeons, both at the level of the specialty in general, and at working level. When GPs had done anaesthetic sessions in local hospitals, the question of competition for leadership would not have arisen, nor would the surgeon's right to dominate the scene and make the rules have been questioned.

- *Changes in surgery.*   Developments in anaesthetics had meant that more complex and difficult surgery could be carried out: "We can keep the patient alive while they do those fantastic things." It also meant that routine surgery had become easier: "They don't need such dexterity any more, because with improvements in anaesthetics we can keep the patient under for six to eight hours while the surgeon fumbles about." "I've anaesthetized for simple hernia, which should take forty-five minutes, and I've sat for three or four hours because the surgeon's not very good."

- *More patients could be anaesthetized.* Developments in anaesthetics had meant that not only could more types of operation be performed, but they could be performed on more types of patient. Patients with various kinds of ill-health, either associated with or independent of the reason for operation, could be successfully anaesthetized: "You very rarely turn a patient down, however ill he is." However, there was a cost in worry for the anaesthetist. One of the people interviewed admitted to being worried the whole time. A second was in two minds whether to give up the job for this reason. A third, fairly recently qualified, said that although with time the anxiety was getting less, "I still wake up in the night imagining procedures. I wake up and think the oxygen's run out or something." A fourth said, "sometimes I see a patient who's going to be operated on Monday morning, and I can worry all weekend about that patient."

It was an important aspect of medical policy that the pre-operative examination of patients should be carried out by those anaesthetists who were going to treat them, so that they could prepare their strategy and know what to expect. In the hospital under discussion this policy was carried out, but many of the anaesthetists referred to other hospitals where it was not. It seems at least possible that, where anaesthetists do not make a practice of doing the pre-operative assessment, this may be a defence against anxiety: "[Where I come from] the consultants don't go to the pre-med, because if there's a problem they wouldn't sleep."

So why was the policy sustained in this particular hospital? The operating-theatre complex, although old, was well designed. With the exception of an accident-and-emergency (A&E) theatre and the obstetric theatre, all the theatres were centrally located in one place, opening

FIGURE 2.   Radial layout of operating-theatre complex.

onto a common concourse, from which also opened the recovery-room, and coffee and changing-rooms (see Figure 2).

The advantages of this arrangement were frequently stressed: "It's not so at the Y where I do some sessions. I feel very cut off there, and isolated." It had a number of consequences, the first of which was that it facilitated the teaching of junior staff, since it was easy for senior staff to be present when needed and then to slip out and leave juniors on their own when things were routine.

Second, one could very easily ask a colleague to stand by for a while if something was complicated. The anaesthetists recalled an earlier time, when one theatre had been located in another block and a registrar would be alone there, no matter what happened. Moreover, doctors had almost certainly also gone home—again, no matter what had happened—directly from that building. For, a third consequence of this layout was that it provided the opportunity to discuss technical issues with colleagues both before and after operations, and therefore also to work through some of the anxiety. On a day when a difficult case was expected in the afternoon, the consultant concerned spent the whole morning in the coffee-room, discussing the case with the colleagues who came and went there.

This analysis suggests that an additional structural factor—the lay-out of the building—had consequences for Level 2, the impact of social processes on individuals. The shape of the building where the operating theatres were located was facilitating a form of social support among the anaesthetists that was important in helping them manage some of the most difficult personal aspects of their role. It seems very likely that this was the institution, or the means, that made it possible to sustain the policy of examining patients pre-operatively. (It was very unlikely that suggesting they purposely set up support groups would have cut much ice with these professionals.)

When a draft report on this study was sent to the association's research and education committee, one of its members, who was head of the division of anaesthesia in a large teaching hospital, telephoned me. In his hospital the operating theatres all opened onto a long corridor, as in Figure 3. He said, "You know, this is interesting. This morning I had a woman patient I was worried about. But I'm the boss, I'm not supposed to get worried. I have one woman colleague I don't mind admitting it to. But she was working at the other end of the corridor, and going all that way for help would have been a big deal. Anyway, I couldn't leave the patient that long."

To come back, therefore, to the framework for organizational diagnosis and the interplay between different levels: the structural factors of scientific and technical developments in anaesthetics (Level 4) had led to great advances, but had created situations and relationships that affected the roles involved. In particular, they had brought some psychodynamic consequences for anaesthetists in the form of anxiety (Level 1). The architecture of the building (Level 4) made it possible to work through this anxiety by means of social and professional support from colleagues (Level 2). This, in turn, made it possible to sustain medical policy.

From this diagnostic study, one may see that a single level of analysis would not have captured the range of factors and the interplay between them that produced critical effects for the anaesthetists.

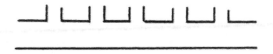

FIGURE 3.   Linear layout of operating-theatre complex.

Example 2.   The organization of hospital wards:
the clinical condition of the patient as determinant

In the case of the organization of hospital wards, as in the previous example the model was the key to making sense of overwhelmingly rich data.

During the 1990s, the Bayswater Institute was part of a multidisciplinary consortium doing evaluation research around electronic patient record (EPR) systems being implemented in NHS hospitals. Our part of the research was to answer the question: "What is the experience of living and working at the implementation sites?" This was explored in three hospitals: the Queen's Hospital, Burton-on-Trent; the Wirral Hospital; and St. Paul's Hospital, Winchester.[2]

For the purpose of this chapter, two of the hospitals, Burton and Winchester, are particularly relevant. At Burton, the initial EPR implementation was in orthopaedics and general medicine, and the locus of study was an orthopaedic ward and a general medical and coronary-care ward. At Winchester, also for reasons of the technology implementation, we studied two linked wards for the care of the elderly. The research in the two wards at Burton was repeated after eighteen months.

Activities during the fieldwork included: observation, planned interviews, interviews that developed spontaneously, accompanying or "shadowing" a person (e.g., a ward sister, a health care assistant, an outpatient), tracer studies of activities (e.g., an occupational therapist's home visit, a discharge as far as the patient's GP practice and district nurse), sitting in on ward meetings and outpatient consultations, observing activities (ward rounds, drug rounds, nursing shift handover), and getting people to talk us through what they were doing. As a result, we had an enormous amount of data.

At the beginning of the fieldwork at Burton, the ward manager of the orthopaedic ward explained the work of the ward and the characteristics of the patients. An important feature of the work in the ward was that much of it was predictable. The patients had been booked in in advance; when they came in they were already known, because of their history as outpatients and because they would have had a pre-operative assessment. Their recovery after their operation was monitored against well-established paths. When staff introduced a patient to colleagues, during ward rounds or nursing handover, it was in terms of "This is Mr X. He is total hip replacement plus three", meaning it was three days since his operation. Everyone then had a broad idea of what to expect in relation to him. Operations, too, were predictable, not only the operation itself but the habits of the surgeon: "The computer records and updates how long I take for a hip replacement or a knee." The general atmosphere was one of calm and order. The patients were lying quietly in their beds or being walked by physiotherapists, visitors were calm and quiet, there was little overt excitement or distress. Also, there were some empty beds as two consultants were on holiday.

Orthopaedics is a very optimistic specialty. Patients arrive in pain and in difficulty, have their operations, and can then be observed recovering and progressing. It is very satisfying to look after orthopaedic patients and to see them going out in a substantially better condition than when they came in: "Orthopaedic patients are lovely to nurse, you see them getting better. I couldn't work in a hospice. They come in in pain, you can see the pain in their face, the greyness, they're bent double, but after the operation you can see them improve."

Death is very rare on this ward. When there is a death, it is very traumatic for the staff. There had been a death some two-and-a-half months before this period of fieldwork, and staff were still dealing with it and talking about the unusual combination of circumstances that had led to it.

The ward manager's introduction had to be interrupted because there was a ward audit. The outcome was positive, there was very little to criticize. One of the few critical comments was about the crash trolley: it needed up-dating, some things about it were out of date. I reflected on this—"Hang on a minute! They don't use the crash trolley. They don't have that kind of emergency." The fact that a piece of equipment did not have equal relevance for all wards alerted me to the idea of the clinical condition of the patient being a major determinant of the organization and life of the ward.

In contrast to this, in the medical ward there were patients with many different conditions, non-planned admissions, and medical emergencies. And there were deaths—"We are level pegging with A&E in cardiac arrests", said a nurse. Diagnosis was sometimes a complex process happening over time. Many of the patients were immobilized, either because of their condition or because of monitors and IVs (intravenous drips). A few patients were confused. Although some of the conditions were chronic, most patients did not stay long. They moved in and out of the ward quite rapidly and were often moved from bed to bed within the ward, to free up for new patients the limited number of beds with monitors. It was challenging for staff to keep up with them.

The telephone at the nursing station rang constantly during the day—patients' relatives seeking news, social workers, other hospital departments and wards. During the first period of observation there was no ward clerk, and the phone was felt as a constant burden by nursing staff—"It never stops".

Visitors came and went throughout the day—not only patients' friends and relatives, but specialist staff (physiotherapists, social workers, occupational therapists, phlebotomists and others). Consultants arrived in a flurry of activity, requiring notes, X-rays, nurses. Junior doctors came and went; there was hustle and bustle, a constant coming and going.

In this context, the ward staff were able to maintain the appearance of calm, routine, and preparedness through apparently seamless teamwork. Staff noted the high level of qualified medical staff on the ward, and many spoke of the strong degree of teamwork achieved. Health care assistants and cleaners collaborated in this smoothness, referring to nurses things of which they should be aware (a patient is looking sick, needs a cuddle, is anxious). The only time the smooth routine was disrupted during fieldwork was when a patient died: the "crash" brought staff at a run, and it was clear that something untoward was happening. For the most part, staff were constantly working to create routine and calm in a situation that was often unpredictable and defied standardization: where patients' conditions were irregular, changing, serious.

In addition to experiencing this contrast between the medical and orthopaedic wards, we had by that time also experienced two wards for the care of the elderly, which were different again. Care of the elderly is difficult; so much so that we were told that nurses used to be put onto it for their first three months because if they could handle that they could handle anything. There were occasional triumphs—for instance, a patient who turned out to be only suffering from neglect: short-term memory loss made him forget to eat, and with warmth, rest, and three meals a day he flourished. There were also, of course, tragedies, not only when patients died but when they discovered that although they knew they were going to die, death was nearer than they expected. One patient died during the week we were there, and some staff were quite distressed; four had died during the previous six weeks.

But most of the experience is not at these levels of triumph or tragedy. It is caring for people whose progress is slow, who are there for a long time, who need help with ordinary things like washing, dressing, and toileting, who may be incontinent, or demented, or both, who forcibly remind one of what is going to happen to oneself and one's parents, and whose own frustration may make them just plain difficult. We asked a nurse, "Do you ever feel like hitting them?" "Oh yes!" she answered. "What do you do then?" "I just walk away till I've got hold of myself." We don't, of course, know how often it gets like that.

The process of care planning, and especially of collaborative discharge planning, is an opportunity for staff to make up for these negative feelings and experiences. An important function of collaborative discharge planning is that it helps to take care of the staff. All one's positive skills and intentions can come into play. The multidisciplinary ward round, and especially the multidisciplinary review meeting that takes place after it, seal the integration of the different professional contributions with doughnuts and chocolate biscuits, in a kind of celebration. This is very different from the mundane handover meeting, concerned with the tedious realities of levels of continence and who wandered during the night. However, multidisciplinary assessment and planning are not the same as multidisciplinary care, and there may be occasions when there is a difference between the quality of the strategic level of planning and the patient's immediate experience of care. (Also, at the boundary of the hospital, multidiscipline becomes multi-agency, and that is a very different matter.)

It began to look as if one—or perhaps the—major determinant of the life and work of the ward was the actual clinical condition of the patient. While this may seem stunningly obvious, much of professional practice seems to be predicated on general rather than condition-specific bases.

Both hypotheses—that the condition is a determinant of work organization and that this is not explicitly recognized in practice—were further fuelled in the course of the second visit to Burton Hospital. The patient population had changed in the intervening eighteen months, and this provided the opportunity to observe the organizational consequences, in a kind of "natural experiment".

The same four consultants still had their elective orthopaedic patients in the ward, but there was now, in addition, a rheumatology consultant with four rheumatology beds. All the beds were occupied, not only by the orthopaedic and rheumatology patients, but by some trauma patients, more than there had been before, and also by some "outlier" medical patients,[3] one of whom had cancer which was thought to be terminal.

Life was not only very much busier than before, but staff were encountering situations they were not used to and having to do things that were unfamiliar. For instance, a patient needed to be weighed every day but the nurses had not known this. The doctors responsible for these "outlier" patients were not generally on the ward to give these new and different instructions. There was therefore also not the same opportunity to develop collaborative relationships between doctors and nurses. Responses on the phone to the worried wife of the cancer patient needed to be different from the usual up-beat responses to relatives of orthopaedic patients. Caring for trauma patients was also different from elective orthopaedic surgery, because one was generally not sure what was happening with them and was waiting/looking for indications. For instance, a patient cannot pass urine—does that change the picture of what has happened, is it the effect of the accident she was in? Did she black out and then drive into something, or drive into something and then black out?

Again, the kind of demands that rheumatoid and osteoarthritis make on staff appear to be very different. The conditions subsumed under rheumatology brought with them a great deal of ambiguity. Patients were brought in for assessment; there was one patient whose diagnosis was uncertain during the whole week of fieldwork and was still uncertain at the end of the week. The patient needed to be able to tolerate ambiguity, and so did the staff. This was very different from the clarity and predictability associated with orthopaedic surgery. Rheumatology also had other kinds of impact on staff—"She's only just older than us!"

This framework of explanation—that a major determinant of organization is the clinical condition of the patient—seems to be fairly robust. It also brings coherence to other findings that might otherwise seem arbitrary. Some showed some interaction with the computer system:

- Care of the elderly requires the collaboration of physiotherapists and occupational therapists with doctors and nurses; multidisciplinary working is a matter of necessity, not of dogma or lip-service. The reality of this need may then influence systems design, and in Winchester there was congruency between systems design and the objectives of ward staff. Written records from the different professions were colour-coded, nursing staff writing in black, physiotherapists in blue, occupational therapists in green, social workers in red. Others (dietician, chiropodist, speech therapist) did not have a code and usually wrote in blue. The colour coding was copied on the system. Discharge planning came out multidisciplinary; for admissions, the physiotherapist and the occupational therapist had their own screens. But their notes could be transferred to the multidisciplinary screens and accessed there by others. The screen, with its colour-coded contributions, reinforced the culture of multidisciplinary working every time one looked at it. It could not by itself have created such a culture, but clearly was helping to sustain it.

- Consultants tend, on the whole, to be more sceptical about the hospital's computer system than are junior doctors, who have to use it in the nature of their work and who are saved a lot of running around by it. Often this is because consultants have developed their own departmental systems, evolved over time to meet their needs, and dislike having to give these up for a generic hospital-wide system. Yet in Wirral we encountered a consultant who both had his own system and was enthusiastic about the hospital's. It turned out that his specialty was diabetes. A high proportion of the work with diabetics is outpatient work; they are only rarely admitted for inpatient episodes. So it was perfectly possible for this consultant to have his own system, tweaked to his own needs, and still support the hospital's system. Patients only rarely needed to be transferred from one to the other.

Other findings were independent of the computer system:

- The clinical condition of the patient influenced the presence of doctors on the ward. In the medical ward at Burton, there was always at least one junior doctor present; in the orthopaedic ward, junior doctors mostly spent their time in theatre or clinics. There was therefore also a knock-on effect on relationships: "I'm going down to the main theatre to find a surgical doctor, and I'm not coming back till I find one. Seven bleeps annoys me; I've tried three different ones."

* * *

It will be clear that, when the material is rich and complex, and in the absence of strong indications otherwise, I tend to look for structural aspects to help understand what is happening at other levels. It does not matter where one begins, as long as all the levels in the model, as well as their interaction, eventually feature in the diagnosis.

Notes

1. A detailed account of this study was published as an occasional paper by the Association of Anaesthetists of Great Britain and Ireland (Klein, 1980).
2. This research was carried out jointly with Dr Lesley Mackay. A short version of our part of the report (Manchester Centre for Healthcare Management et al., 2001) is included in the volume on the meaning of work (Klein, forthcoming).
3. An "outlier" is a patient who is admitted to a ward that does not normally deal with that patient's condition, when the ward that does deal with that condition has no beds.

SOME ACTIVITIES
IN THE FIELD

In a sense, moving into the field is what it is all about. Sometimes this takes the form of "projects", and examples of the project format can be found in the volume on the meaning of work (Klein, forthcoming). The three papers in this section are different in kind. The first is an account of what was at the time considered, both in the company involved and in the academic social science community, not as a project but as an open-ended experiment to see how putting a social scientist inside a company would work out. The second paper gives four episodes from experiences in the field, in order to illustrate the relationship between knowledge-into-use and the dynamics of action, both when these are integrated and when they are not. Finally, the third paper is an example of a project report to a client, reproduced verbatim. In such a situation, where the client organization then takes on any further action, one does not necessarily know what happened next.

CHAPTER 4

The Esso story

In 1965 I joined Esso Petroleum UK as "social sciences adviser". This paper is based on a lecture given in 1971, summarizing that project and pulling out some of the issues it raised; the full story was written up as a book (Klein, 1976).

I am calling it a "project" now, though it was not intended to be a project but, rather, the beginning of a new function in the organization. Although I did not articulate until later the importance of infrastructure and institutionalization for the use of social science (see chapter 13), it was already very much in my mind. This is witnessed by the point made to the Esso Board about the need to make this a "routine, ordinary, even boring" part of what goes on.

Origins and beginning of the Esso experiment

For five years, from 1965 to 1970, I was in a role in Esso called "social sciences adviser". It was the time of the Heyworth Committee, which was looking at the organization of research and teaching in the social sciences, and which had led to the setting up of the Social Science Research Council (Department of Education and Science,

1965). The Secretary of the Heyworth Committee, Albert Cherns, started a unit in Loughborough University concerned with the utilization of social science research, and it was at about the same time that Esso decided to launch an experiment in making use of the social sciences inside a company. The impetus came from the company's employee relations (ER) adviser, a man who knew about the work of the Heyworth Committee and had given evidence to it. He also knew some of the social science community of that time. The people in the social sciences who were interested in utilizing them were a relatively small group, who knew each other and had rather similar kinds of approaches.

I was coming from a background of industrial experience and research in industrial sociology. I had been much influenced by the work of Elliott Jaques in the Glacier Metal Company (Jaques, 1951) but felt that this work could not easily serve as a model for wider use:

1.   Jaques was a psychoanalyst, and it was unlikely that psychoanalytic skills would become available to industrial organizations on a large scale.

2.   The managing director, Wilfred Brown (later Lord Brown), was exceptionally enthusiastic about the project, and it seemed equally unlikely that many managing directors would be as keen as that.

3.   The Glacier project focused on relations in groups in industrial settings. There were other frames of reference that were also relevant and applicable and should be used. The question was, how?

The appointment was made, I need to say, at the instigation of this rather powerful ER adviser and not at the instigation of the Board. The Board was permissive rather than positively enthusiastic, and this raises a first issue: is it essential to have the Board's enthusiasm and support, either for a project or an appointment, or is it possible to manage without it?

Every strategy has some benefits and some costs. The benefits of going in with the sanction of the Board—that is, with the positive enthusiasm of the people at the top—are obvious: you make greater initial impact, you have a power base, you have visibility. The costs are that you don't know whether people who do the kind of things you suggest will be doing them because of the pressure from above rather than because they really want to. If they do, that is something that will catch up with you eventually. If people at middle and junior levels accept an idea, agree to do a project, because they have been pressured into it, their real feelings are bound to emerge in the end. We were to see that later in the course of the project.

I accepted this position at middle-to-senior management level for a number of reasons: one was that I genuinely thought that there is a need to "earn the right". One needs to demonstrate value in a modest way before one can expect a broader and more strategic level of involvement and the support of the senior people. Another reason was that directors are not the only source of influence. There are other sources, other places where it was relevant to bring social science ideas to bear. A very important one was in the management service area, among the industrial engineers, the systems designers, the operational research people, who are in fact designing the working arrangements that other people live with. If you can influence *them*, if you can get the criteria and methods of the social sciences influencing the thinking of the management service people, that is a pretty valuable thing to be doing.

That raises another issue relevant for this part of the discussion: "social science" or "the human sciences" is much too vague, too global a phrase. There is a great range of methods, skills, and empirical research findings. No practitioner is in command of all of them, every practitioner has a different mix. It is therefore very hard for the customer to know what he is buying. If a company says to you, "We are using social science; we are doing something in the social sciences", there is no way of knowing what they are doing. If they say, "The consultant we are using is X or Y, Professor This or Doctor That", and you know those people, you begin to have some idea of what might be going on. Because every practitioner has a different mix of what is available, the field has unfortunately became very personalized.

We decided to regard the first twelve months as an experiment. By the end of that time, not very much had happened. I had conducted an interview survey of senior managers and written a report about the issues facing the company, but the ER adviser did not allow me to circulate it. There is a good case for saying that I should have resigned at that stage, but I was just too interested in what was going on. We decided that the verdict was "not proven" and to extend the experiment for another six months.

During those six months, work began to come in and then to come in more rapidly, to the extent that I was very quickly overloaded. I acquired two assistants, and for about two years a programme of work began to develop, and with it something like a professional practice; it was very like the building of an accountancy, or law, or medical practice. We got into a number of pieces of work, which encompassed a wide variety of frames of reference and approaches. That was what had originally appealed to me: the company's wish for an eclectic approach that was not tied to one particular school or set of methods. The pattern that developed was that we would help departments formulate what was needed, and then we would bring in a range of outside researchers and consultants to carry out the work. By that stage the departments would need to show their commitment by budgeting for the work themselves; there was no major central budget for social science.

However, real eclecticism may be very threatening to the people at the receiving end. If there were individuals who really mastered all the concepts, methods, and insights of the social sciences, they would be impossible to cope with!

Projects and some issues arising from projects

The following are some of the projects that were carried out in this way.

1. *Product distribution.*   Esso had distribution plants around the country, where fuel oil was stored in large tanks and from which it was taken to customers. The Purfleet terminal was located on the Thames estuary and received product by ship from the refineries. The function of the terminal was to receive and store products and to distribute them by road, rail, barge, and pipeline. These products were, in the main, "black oil" (or fuel oils), "white oils" (petrols, paraffin, diesel oil, etc.), and bitumen. There was a small plant where lubricating oils, greases, and some additives were blended, and also a small distillation plant.

The plant employed some 340 staff, who were concerned with the technology of storage and packaging. The number also included about 100 drivers (truck operators), who drove approximately 70 company trucks; in addition, up to 70 or 80 non-company trucks and drivers were hired in under contract.

The work we did here fell into three stages. The first of these was support to an operational research project manager who was working on a project to automate some of the activities, preparing data-transmission links to the computer at head office, and who found the human and organizational unknowns of his project daunting.

Arising out of this work, the manager of the terminal asked for a study of the distribution-planning function—that is, the collating of customers' orders into truckloads and routes for truck drivers. In the management of the terminal there were many difficulties arising from the relationship between sales and operations, or, in functional terms, between the objectives of high volume and low cost. These tensions between sales and operations went right to the top of the company. At the grass roots they meant, for instance, that to keep delivery costs low the deliveries had to be grouped, in terms both of the amounts that fitted together to make a load, and of geographical location. This, in turn, meant that customers could not always get a delivery exactly when they wanted it, especially at short notice. They might then get in touch with the sales branch office, or even head office, and it could happen that there the customer would be given an unconditional promise, which the terminal was then obliged to fulfil.

For the exploratory study of the planning office, I interviewed all the planners and all the supervisors and held discussions with some drivers. I attended meetings of the Joint Consultation Committee and a series of planners' meetings, and spent some time in the planning office. The findings were reported back in two meetings. During the two weeks before this, the terminal manager himself paid a good deal of attention to the planning office. Indeed, the planners said that one good effect of the study was that management took more notice of them and their problems than they had before. He made a number of changes, including the creation of a level of shift supervision. This helped to mitigate one severe complaint of the planners, which was that if any problem arose with a driver, they did not have the authority to deal with it. They had to refer him to a supervisor, and a supervisor could usually not be found.

The feedback meetings were regarded as very successful. The discussion was of the kind which makes effort seem worthwhile, and which is difficult to describe—where people see themselves and their situation in a new way and are prepared to continue learning together. A number of suggestions for further work and for changes in organization emerged. However, the terminal manager also said that he would need more quantitative information to support organizational changes. The third phase of the work was therefore a detailed observation study of the planning office, and this was carried out by a research team from the London School of Economics.

Then we encountered a practical difficulty: at the point where we were ready to move into a more radical action frame, the manager who had commissioned the study, and who had become very committed to it, left the company. I discovered later that he had taken the report with him to his new post as distribution manager of a large company and had made use of it there. But in Esso, his successor was not as interested as he had been. The career and management development system in a company is generally not in line with the project and programme development system. This is true not only where social science work is concerned, but in relation to any kind of project work. It is an important part of the reality, but you don't find it in the literature. People change jobs. The same thing happens with project or steering committees: when the membership changes the policy may change, because people don't want to copy what their predecessors did. On the whole, in our culture, people want to innovate—the process of innovation seems more exciting to them than the content of what happens.

However, this was an instance where the continuing presence of an in-house role showed its value. The familiarity that this study had provided, and the relationships with staff and management that had developed in the course of it, had a number of consequences. There cannot be many companies where the engineer responsible for construction will come to a social scientist and say, "Can you give me any sociological advice on where to put the new office? If we build it by the gate instead of extending the existing one, what shall we be doing to working relationships and working groups?" These consequences culminated in a request to look at a distribution terminal as a whole, with a view to redesigning the whole system including, inevitably, tackling the relationship in marketing between sales and operations.

2. *Marine department projects.*   We did a good deal of work with the marine department. There were two different projects on Esso's oil-tankers: one was an ergonomics programme, consisting of a linked series of projects that eventually led to the redesigning of the ship's bridge of a small coastal tanker. It was contracted out to an ergonomics team, and the researchers involved were, in the end, able to go to the launching of a ship that they had had a hand in designing. It is not often in the human sciences that one has feedback as tangible as that, and it was very rewarding for them.

The other project on board ship was contracted out to the Tavistock Institute and was a "softer", anthropological, investigation of work and life at sea. The researchers made trips on oil-tankers and studied things like the drinking patterns, roles and role relationships, the concept of "shipmates", and the function of the bar in safeguarding private space. In the twenty-four-hour, total institution of a ship, there is need for some private space: in those ships where there was no bar, drinking took place in the crew's cabins; where there was a bar this was not necessary, and private space could be preserved.

These projects were so different from each other that I did some work with the teams to explore the nature of the frames of reference (this is discussed in chapter 11).

I also did work with the marine management group, sitting in on their management meetings once a week for about eighteen months in a process-consulting role. Something we learned from this was how one may, with consensus, change the rules as one goes along and as the relationship develops. The way we were working when we were eight or nine months into the process was quite different from the way we had set it up in the beginning: we had, by mutual consent, changed the rules as we got to know and trust each other.

3. *Aircraft refuelling.*   There was a design project about the refuelling of planes at London Airport (described in chapter 14), which was largely contracted out to a team of ergonomists. The key feature of the project was the experimental testing of alternative solutions before deciding on the one to implement. An interesting issue was the different perceptual sets of different kinds of scientist. This showed up when an ergonomist and I first went together to the control-room at London Airport (from which Esso sent out trucks to refuel the planes) to do some exploratory observation. During the first half-day's observation, the ergonomist noted people making near-mistakes under stress. What I noticed was people making cups of tea to cope with stress. There was a kettle and a set of old mugs, and anybody—however senior—who happened to have some spare time made a cup of tea for the others. The function of this was to provide some relief and a change of activity. It also had a social function in the sense of team-building and cohesion. But what was interesting theoretically was the influence that training and perceptual set had on the data that one takes to be relevant. I later used this example when teaching a group of postgraduate systems engineers, and I got a fairly angry response. They pointed out that people had no business making cups of tea in working time—it was not part of "the system" at all!

Some strategic issues

There is a question about how much one should be concerned with fieldwork projects. Once during the Purfleet study, the ER adviser said to me, "You shouldn't be grubbing around in the field, you should be influencing the Board." Well, of course, one should be doing both, but which is more effective? What is effectiveness anyway in this field? General euphoria? That may simply be a sign of how good one is at making people dependent.

In a local sense, I know what feels effective. The work with marine management felt effective; also, there were people in the company who would come and say "We are thinking of reorganization in such and such a plant, can we try out some ideas on you?" and who would go away saying "Thank you, that's helped me sort myself out, I think I know what I want to do now"

In a presentation to the Board in 1969, I said:

> "In a general sense I shall not feel that this has been effective until the incorporation of social science knowledge and methods becomes an absolutely routine, ordinary, even boring part of what goes on. Every system or gadget that is introduced brings with it social and organizational consequences, whether you like it or not, and it should be completely axiomatic that people take steps to predict these and to cope with them. It is not difficult to persuade middle managers of the sense of this, because they know it. But they won't do it until you hold them accountable in this way. When some bright spark comes to you with his pet project, ending up with a flourish that it will save 30% of manpower and the discounted cash flow is so much, you should be asking him, 'What are the changes in skills, in demands, in roles and relationships, and in organization that the remaining 70% will be faced with, and what are you doing about that? And what mistakes will the remaining 70% make as a result of the changes, and how does that affect your discounted cash-flow calculation?' Do that a few times and this company will be utilizing social science very quickly."

There was also the question of scale. In that same Board presentation I said that, while there must always be room for spontaneity and enthusiasm,

> "We have to do the dreary systematic part as well. . . . Clearly the potential for social science application is unlimited. Since you are not going to put unlimited resources into it, there is a big question of matching supply and demand. How much in the way of resources should one be putting into social science? . . . What are the criteria for deploying the resources? Should one respond to needs because somebody in the field has a problem? Should one consider

the payoff in terms of cash returns? In terms of better relationships (they don't necessarily always go together)? The payoff for knowledge? In terms of sales value for future social science work? . . ."

Changes in the context

During the course of my time with Esso, the environment changed in a number of significant ways.

With regard to the social science context, there was during those years immense growth of social science activity, both in universities and in applied work in industry. Getting people interested—not just in Esso, but in industry generally—was not the problem. Indeed, the climate of opinion was such that it became rather difficult for someone who was not interested to say so. The problem, rather, was getting industry to relate to social science in a systematic way. Fads and fashions predominated. What counted was the one book, or person, or article that people happened to come across when they happened to be in a receptive frame of mind.

But there was also a growing divergence between what was going on in the universities and what was going on in industry. University research became less concerned with usefulness and application, while less and less of the applied activity was research-based. More and more of it was training-based, human-relations based, aiming first at action. There were many action-oriented interventions, basically about behaviour and interpersonal relations, aiming to modify behavioural styles. During the year in which I left Esso, I collected about three or four months' worth of the brochures and advertising literature that were beginning to come in to organizations from consultants, from behavioural scientists, and from a range of agencies that offered behavioural science interventions. The advertising brochures often contained the word "psycho"—psycho-dynamics, psycho-cybernetics. The word "behaviour" appeared frequently. This approach takes personal behaviour as the independent variable.

To illustrate the growth and differentiation in types of development in the social sciences: when I first joined Esso, I had invited to a seminar all the people I, and Albert Cherns, could think of who were involved in application and utilization. This became a little club, which continued to meet two or three times a year for several years. We called it the Seminar in Applied Social Science. At the beginning of this period, they were the people who were involved in applied social science. At the end of the period, they were more like a group of émigrés meeting to comfort each other in the face of immense amounts of consultancy activity, often by visiting Americans: "change programmes", "OD programmes", Blake Managerial Grids, etc. etc.

These developments also raised a complicated question about the ethics of selling and the problem of competition, which from my sheltered academic background I had not been expecting. In ethical terms, from the point of view of protecting the client, and in terms of relationships with colleagues: to what extent is it professionally acceptable to "sell", and how do you cope with competition between professional colleagues? The somewhat idealizing social science literature does not prepare one to deal with this.

The context within the company

With regard to the environment within Esso, the man who had recruited and sponsored me retired in 1968, and his deputy, who had been very involved in the process and supportive, also left the company. It turned out that the new ER manager (not now titled "adviser"), was not interested in the experiment in the same way that the original sponsors had been.

Less clear-cut was the fact that colleagues in the personnel department were also moving out, either promoted or leaving the company, and were being replaced. The whole issue of how social science activities relate to personnel management is complex. When we first started, social science colleagues had said that the function should not be located in the personnel department, because of the difficulty of advising about personnel policies while being a subordinate or a colleague. The answer to that had been, if not in personnel, then where? It would have meant setting up somewhere else in competition with the personnel department. The problem of how to relate social science activities to those that were a more traditional part of personnel management was going to exist, no matter where the function was located. Because I was very aware of this, I had taken a lot of trouble to relate to colleagues in the personnel department when I first joined; and it had worked quite well. But as they left and were replaced, I was not taking the same amount of trouble with their successors. Partly this was because they did not all come at once, it was a gradual change and, therefore, one could not make the same kind of concerted effort; partly it was because I was by then very busy; and partly, I think, I was not really aware of the need. If I had thought much about it, I would probably not have felt the need to sell myself in the same way as at the beginning—that I ought by now to be accepted. In fact, the need was rather greater, because new people in the personnel department had not been involved in the original decision to engage with social science.

A third contextual factor was that there were structural changes in the organization of Esso's parent company, Standard Oil New Jersey (now Exxon), and these changes had major consequences for our social science function. In the course of the third year of the post, Standard Oil decentralized its activities, setting up regional boards around the world, including one for Europe. The headquarters of Esso Europe were in London, and there appeared on the scene an ER manager for Europe. His general approach was that Europe needed to be brought out of the dark ages. Esso was about to have a new chairman, who spent the three months between being appointed and taking up his post in Esso Europe. The departing chairman had been involved in the decision to create our function and had been kept in touch with it. The new one did not know it existed. He discussed with the ER manager the organizational problems that were awaiting him, and the ER manager suggested getting some social science help. He arranged for the chairman to meet Rensis Likert, chairman of the Institute of Social Research (ISR), Michigan, and when the new chairman arrived to take up his post he brought with him a $300,000 project to be undertaken by the ISR. With considerable pride and excitement, he was about to introduce social science to Esso.

The proposed Michigan project was to be led by Likert's successor, Dr Stan Seashore, and was along classic American "organization development" lines. It was about trying to change people's behaviour and was therefore fundamentally different from what we had been doing. (These differences in approach are discussed in chapter 7.) In a selected part of the company they would first diagnose the prevalent behavioural styles of managers by means of a detailed questionnaire; they would then introduce a "change agent" who would set out to shift behaviour towards more "participative" or "democratic" styles by means of various interventions; and then behavioural styles would be measured again.

Our policy of starting quietly at middle levels of the company and working outward from there had proved politically disastrous. My original sponsor was on the point of retiring, and his successor aligned himself behind the Esso Europe ER manager.

The two years that followed were to a large extent taken up with this very painful battle, in which territorial conflict and conflict about theory and values could never be clearly disentangled. Our work towards redesigning the work systems in a major distribution terminal became part of the controversy. In the end, both sides in the battle foundered. The marketing department, where the Michigan project was intended to take place, rejected it. That was perhaps some vindication of our original policy of working from the ground upwards rather than in a way that is imposed from above. But the in-house social science activities also wound down. The battle had used up too much of the available energy, and there was now no support from the new ER manager.

Some years later, when the dust had settled, I met Stan Seashore at a conference in Toronto. Standing talking with a group of colleagues, I told them that we had spent two years fighting each other. "It would have been more fun if she hadn't been right", said Seashore. It was gracious, but it didn't undo the damage.

When I later wrote the book about the Esso work, staff and directors of the company were generous about clearing the text for publication, including the parts they did not like, and came to a very pleasant launch party. The Michigan people also cleared the text for publication. One publisher had turned the manuscript down on the grounds that it was not clear whether this was social science or autobiography, and Marie Jahoda (at that time Professor of Social Psychology at the University of Sussex) made a feature of this in her preface.

Some episodes from the field

This paper presents four episodes from action-research experience, illustrating the relationship between "knowledge-into-use" and "the dynamics of action". They represent a learning process: in the first two, research was still in some sense dominant in a way that did not sufficiently accommodate the dynamics of action, in the last two, the two frameworks have become much more integrated.

A researcher's first step into consultancy

One essential for consultancy is "starting from where the other is". The episode described here happened at a time when I had not yet taken this on board in all its implications. It took place at the end of the control systems research described in chapter 2. We had used the tracer study method, three researchers each tracking a product or batch of products through a company, from beginning to end. My "tracer" had been a batch of soap, tracked through all the processes that impinged on it in a manufacturing plant of a large multinational company. In the course of the study, good relationships had developed with the people in the plant, and at the end of it I was asked to come back as a consultant. I had never done consultancy before. Two meetings were held with the senior management group, which went very well. Then, during the second meeting, one of them asked, "If we reorganize the packing line in the way you suggest, to improve the nature of the jobs, shall we be tapping untapped motivation—shall we get more production as well?" I said "I don't know, let's try"—and the whole thing collapsed. Visibly. You could see it die, and it could not be revived.

The works manager, who had very much wanted the project, was very disappointed. Years later, when I was working in Esso, he occasionally came to see me when he was in London, and every time he came back to this topic. Eventually, one day he thumped my desk and shouted, "Your bloody integrity!"

Now, as a scientist, "I don't know" was the only thing I could honourably say. But, as a consultant, I had not taken care of the reality of their anxiety. What I might do now is to suggest formulating the project in phases so that the risk could be limited and the work could be reviewed, and if necessary stopped, at points along the way. I would still, however, say that one could not predict the outcome—not "Yes, of course—trust me and you will be alright." That still seems to me to be unprofessional and unacceptable. At the same time, taking care of my "bloody integrity" had been starting from where I was, not from where they were.

A "research loop" within a consultancy programme

This example concerns work carried out in a bank. While in the previous example not enough care was taken of the client's anxieties, in this one not enough attention was paid to the institutional framework.

In 1972 I was approached by one of the clearing banks in the United Kingdom, not with a specific problem but with the question, "What can the social sciences do for us?" My answer was—again—"I don't know. Can we have a look?" This time, the answer was appropriate. I had no knowledge of banking; all my previous experience had been in manufacturing. A small exploratory piece of work within the personnel department gave them the confidence for a first consulting contract.

Around that time the bank had been going through a series of mergers and a wave of large-scale computerization, and they felt that customer service had probably slipped in the process. The question that was now put to us was, "How can we improve customer service?" They set up a Customer Service Working Party, consisting of people from different divisions, and then commissioned from us a diagnostic study of branch banking.

I got together a team of four people plus myself, and we spent one week in each of four branches: one in central London, one in a London suburb, one in a small provincial town, and one in the country. We interviewed staff and customers, observed a range of activities in the branch, "shadowed" some key people, tracked enquiries, and so on. This yielded a large amount of data, and the analysis and report writing took about three months. As research studies go, that was not very long, and the resulting report really was quite good, containing rich material (which, I am told, is still relevant to present-day banking). But I had become so immersed in the fascination of the material and its analysis that I neglected to maintain the institutions for making use of the study.

When the report was ready, I discovered that the Customer Service Working Party had been disbanded. The study therefore had no direct client, and some opportunities for effective action and change were lost. Nevertheless, the study of branch banking served as a kind of passport, providing the bona fides for seven further years of consultancy with the bank.

The framework of dynamics comes into its own

This third example involves the use of "transference", a concept that is central to psychoanalysis: during an analysis the patient is likely to develop feelings and reactions about the analyst. Since the analyst has not been active in doing anything that might provoke such feelings, it is likely that they have been transferred from some other situation in the patient's life; this becomes material for analyst and patient to work on.

From the time I joined the Tavistock Institute, I often talked work through with my colleague Harold Bridger, who had moved to organizational consultancy from being a psychoanalyst. Sometimes he would say, "You must use the transference", but I was not sure what this meant. I knew what it meant in psychoanalysis but not how it applied to organizational consultancy.

Then one day I showed Harold the report of a project in which I seemed to be bouncing like a tennis-ball between a tough and intransigent management group and an equally tough and intransigent trade union group. He said, "Read this again, and ask yourself what they are doing to you that they can't do to each other." Aha, I thought, it's not just transferring feelings onto the consultant; it's actually doing something to the consultant. This was news.

Some time later, I was involved in a "seeding contract" with the National Economic Development Office (NEDO). It was a time of great interest in questions of job satisfaction and job design, and under this arrangement firms in a particular industrial sector wanting to explore questions of job design could have four days of my time funded by NEDO; if this led to further work, the firm would then have to take on the further costs. In one such firm, an initial meeting was held with a group consisting of the managing director, staff from the production engineering and personnel functions, line management supervisors, and two shop stewards. My presentation about job design was received courteously, but without particular enthusiasm. Then the managing director said, "You know, what I would really like to have an outsider do is find out why we were late on the market with [a particular product]. What is it about our organization that made us miss the Christmas market last season?"

On the principle of "starting from where they are", I agreed to look at this problem, provided that the NEDO-funded assignment could be carried out as well, and a small study was formulated. A time was arranged when a week would be spent interviewing people who had been involved in the development of "Product X"; the material would be analysed during the weekend, and a feedback meeting would be held on the following Monday morning. At the same time, it was arranged that a feedback-and-review meeting on the job-design work would be held on the Monday afternoon.

Interviews were held with about fifteen people involved in the marketing, design, technical development, production engineering, and manufacture of "Product X", and two group discussions were held with operators assembling the product. This yielded a considerable amount of material, and the weekend, which was spent trying to organize and understand the material and preparing to report on it, was filled with a growing sense of pressure and anxiety.

Eventually I stepped back from the situation to ask some questions: "What are they doing to you, that you are spending Sunday, your so-called free time, trying to deal with this impossible task? Knowing that you have taken on more than can possibly be handled in the time? Eating margarine sandwiches because you haven't allowed time to buy and cook food? Knowing that the report is likely to be poor in quality because there just isn't time to do it properly? Nobody has forced you to schedule it this way!" The answer came: "They have turned you into a mini-version of the company! This is what *they* do. This is what happened to Product X, and it is already beginning to happen to the next product. You have absorbed and internalized the culture to such an extent that you are not analysing what happened to Product X, you are living it!"

It was this experience and understanding that formed the basis of the report back to the company the next day, margarine sandwiches and all. It formed the context and framework within which the organization around Product X was then discussed. The meeting was completely successful and established a credibility that also carried over onto the job-design activity. Transference is not only transferring feelings onto the consultant; it is also affecting the consultant. Where it is possible to understand and make use of this phenomenon, the two frameworks—of knowledge-into-use and the dynamics of action—come very close together.

Appropriate dynamics can also happen by accident

This incident concerns an opportunity to make use of "transitional space" (Winnicott, 1971), which arose by accident.

For four years the Bayswater Institute was part of a consortium funded by the European Commission to develop and test enhanced IT systems in the construction industry. The industrial partners in the consortium were construction companies in Finland, the United Kingdom, and Germany and some of their suppliers, clients and consultants; the Institute's part was to work with the human and organizational aspects.

In this project, which was called ProCure, we had some opportunity to accompany the technical developments being undertaken by the industrial partners for some three years. In the design and implementation of technology, there is need for a long-term relationship between social scientists and the technologists. The reason is that, while one can to a large extent predict issues that are likely to arise, one cannot predict what will turn out to be important when. There are many different kinds of issues; they can arise at many different stages, and they arise within the system that is designing and developing the technology as much as in the system at the receiving end. If one is not present, one does not see it.

During the first year of the project, the industrial partners planned their individual projects while the social scientists familiarized themselves with the construction industry and the project partners and reported on the partners' business strategies. Then workshops were held in the different countries:

- for the social scientists to learn more about the project plans of the partners
- for the participants to learn more about relevant areas of social science
- to start to identify the human and organizational issues within the pilot projects
- to agree methods for monitoring and working with these.

These launch seminars had the function of allowing the members to relate their own experience to the examples that were presented. The outcomes were different in each country, and the most tangible outcome was in Germany.

The industrial partner in Germany was Daimler-Chrysler. They not only made cars but built factories and research facilities. They therefore had a large construction activity, for which they engaged contractors. During the German workshop, the head of construction IT suggested that it could become a condition of getting a contract from Daimler-Chrysler that the contractors should take care of the human and organizational aspects of the technology that was going to be introduced. Clearly, only the client could have had the background knowledge to suggest this, and the design of the workshop had to provide the "transitional space" for it to happen.

He and a colleague later came over to work on this suggestion. During that session, we both—he and I—simultaneously realized that it was not a good idea to stipulate certain things that would have to be done in relation to human aspects of the system; much better to stipulate that review processes would have to be put in place with regard to these aspects.

We then went on to pilot the idea with three small contracting firms who work for Daimler-Chrysler, and this provided a mini-example of the unexpected and unplanned form that transitional processes can take, what Herbert Phillipson calls "the creative use of chance events" (Phillipson, 1989).

I had provided a check-list of "human and organizational issues". Although I speak German, I did not trust my German enough to translate this check-list from English, and it was done by a professional translator. However, when we started to work on it with the construction contractors, they were quite critical of the translation. They started to work on improving the translation, and in the process of doing this took ownership of the check-list and made it their own. It was both gratifying and fascinating to watch this happening and gradually retreat into the background in the course of it. It would not have happened if the translation had been good, and it would have been awkward if I had done the translation. The sensitivities of anonymous translators could be ignored.

CHAPTER 6

Freightliners Ltd

This is an example of a report to a client. Reports to clients are different from accounts of projects and are not often published. One difference is that one may not know what happened afterwards, which is the case here.

The project was about industrial relations problems in a traditionally "tough" part of the transport industry, focused at the London terminal of a national freight company. There was joint management/union recognition that the difficulties were hampering and possibly endangering the company's business: a senior manager (Mr "Brown") and a senior trade union official (Mr "Smith") had already carried out an interview study of people at shop-floor level. Now they wanted this to be followed up by an independent consultant.

In the industrial relations world of the 1970s, there were efforts to recognize both the need for the parties to collaborate for some purposes and the need for them at the same time to defend their interests, by institutionalizing these aims in separate systems. It was decided to focus the consultancy on the working of these systems. This paper was the final report on this fairly small piece of work, submitted and agreed within the organization in quite a complex way which reflects the situation itself. The emphasis is on the processes involved, not the various areas of content, which would in any case have been familiar to the readers. The company has agreed for the report to be published, including the company's name.

Industrial and human relations at Willesden Terminal

Background

In June 1979, a shared management/union concern about the quality and practice of industrial relations at Willesden Terminal led to an enquiry being conducted at the terminal by Mr "Brown", Industrial Relations Officer, Freightliners Ltd and Mr "Smith", Divisional Officer, National Union of Railwaymen (NUR). At a meeting in July to discuss their findings, two decisions were agreed:

(a) to set up a Joint Working Party (which later became two Joint Working Parties) at terminal level to work through the findings of the "Brown–Smith Report", involving someone from headquarters in this work;

(b) to make use of the services of an independent behavioural scientist from the Tavistock Institute of Human Relations.

A Joint Steering Group with representatives from Freightliner headquarters and the NUR was formed to review progress.

Methods

The terms of reference of the social science work were never very clear, and it was quite difficult to find a peg onto which to hang a "service". This is not a criticism, but as it is necessary to describe what happened, it is also necessary to describe the boundary conditions that influenced it. For example, I did not do systematic research at the terminal. "Research" was not the object of the exercise, and to carry out systematic interviewing or observation would have been costly and would probably have yielded a lot of the same information as the Brown–Smith enquiry. I did interview most members of management, because they had not given evidence to the Brown–Smith enquiry.

On the other hand, the work was not consultancy either, in the usual sense. Consultancy would have required a different kind of sanctioning process: in particular, my work was commissioned by the Joint Steering Group, and neither of the two terminal managers who were in office during the period in question had asked for help or had any say in the matter, but rather had my involvement wished on them. The chairman of the two Joint Working Parties, joining them as headquarters representative, had also not been asked whether he wanted a contribution from outside.

We are here at the boundary between long-established and highly institutionalized ways of doing things, and an attempt to try something new and different. It would have been inappropriate to be doctrinaire about how the situation should be handled; rather, I negotiated sanction as I went along and as opportunities presented themselves.

These were limited but real. Mainly, I joined the two Joint Working Parties throughout their deliberations, in the role of observer and consultant. As observer, I was concerned to make clear the distinction between content and process—the "double task"—in the work of such a group and fed back to them my observations of the processes and relationships they were engaged on. As consultant, I made occasional inputs to the content of their work, in particular when it concerned work organization and the content of jobs. These inputs were negotiated gradually, and became an accepted and organic part of the working parties' work. I was also invited to attend two meetings in the terminal, one where management representatives met with crane operators, and one where management met with the whole staff.

Feedback

The need not to offend too much against traditional procedures, while maintaining the integrity of one's own, also affects the question of reporting back. Originally, there was an assumption that a report would not be required, since the main input was to the ongoing work of the working parties. Towards the end, it was felt that a report would be useful, and there began a series of negotiations about who should see it and at what stage. Management felt that they had a prior right to see a draft report because they had paid for the work. The Steering Group felt that the project was theirs and the report should go simultaneously to management and the union hierarchy. I insisted that people about whom one is reporting have a prior right to vet what is being said about them.

In the end, it was agreed that I should report back first to the Joint Working Parties at the terminal, but verbally and not in writing. If they had no objection to what was being said, a report would then be written and submitted to the Steering Group, and I would trust the Steering Group to see that copies would eventually find their way back to relevant people at the terminal—that is, the manager and the members of the Joint Working Parties. The need for this kind of delicate walking-on-eggshells is, in fact, part of the original problem and will be discussed later.

Some observations

1.   My impression is that, between August 1979 and January 1980, the industrial relations atmosphere at Willesden improved somewhat, and the NUR's divisional officer has also pointed out that he was not called in during that period. It would be hard to say how much of this improvement is due to any one of a number of contributing factors:

(a) a new manager;

(b) the work done within and by the Joint Working Parties;

(c) the business situation, which has meant that the Local Committees and management tended to draw together a bit and fight the marketing department—which, it was felt, was not bringing enough business to Willesden—rather than fight each other.

In any case, I have wondered whether Willesden is "as bad as it is painted", or whether it perhaps serves as something of a scapegoat in the Freightliner organization, helping others to feel good when they look at themselves in comparison to Willesden. I don't have evidence for this, as I don't have evidence for my feeling that the previous terminal manager has also perhaps to some extent served as a scapegoat. It is simply easiest to put all one's troubles into one pot, and it is as unlikely that the new manager is "all good" as it is that the last one was "all bad". The trouble with this kind of dynamic is that, when reality breaks in and something, even something quite small, goes wrong, the pendulum is likely to swing too far in the other direction.

2.   The improvement, in any case, seems to me to be fragile and at surface level. The system of human and industrial relations at the terminal, even if bad (whatever that means—at any rate, there is no doubt that people feel aggrieved and unhappy) is in a kind of equilibrium. One is almost afraid to poke a finger at it in case the whole balance is upset and things get worse. Certainly, altering one element here or there does not change the system. This would require some very hard work and risk-taking, and my impression is that neither management nor the Local Committee representatives are yet prepared for this, generally preferring the devil they know—their familiar problems—to any devil they might not know.

   To give an example of what I mean: when I first visited the terminal, I was told about an issue that had been unresolved for two years, the question of whether the soap-dispensers in the toilets are functioning or not. It crops up repeatedly in committee minutes, and for both sides it provides evidence that demonstrates how unreasonable the other side is. (The issue is not that the soap-dispensers don't get repaired; the disagreement is about whether they need repairing or not.) But when the possibility was opened up of finding ways to resolve this issue, this was immediately rejected on the grounds that "our system (for dealing with such things) works".

3.   It is probably significant that the incident described happened on the last day of the life of the working parties, when the dominant theme was re-integration with the normal processes of the terminal, and the time for trying new things was over.

During the actual work of the Joint Working Parties, there was in fact considerable development. I have regarded the two working parties as "temporary systems", running in parallel with the business and negotiating systems of the terminal and working on matters that then get fed back into the mainstream systems. The purpose of a "temporary system" of this kind is to enable people to explore ideas informally, to experiment with new ways of behaving and relating to each other, without the kind of formal commitment that the mainstream systems involve. It should be possible to stick one's head over the top of a trench that one is occupying (or that other people think one is occupying) without having it immediately shot off! It is risky and it needs great skill, because at the same time one must not lose sight of one's interests or contact with one's "constituency".

The shift towards this kind of freer exploration was not very dramatic during the work of the working parties, but it was definitely there. There is therefore a very important question about whether the use of temporary systems of this kind should be further developed. Personally, I see no other way of working towards a change, if a change is wanted. One cannot move directly and immediately from *a* to *b* (consider the nine months of discussions about the shape of the table around which the Vietnam peace talks were to be held—that was a temporary system!)

4.   To an outsider, the handling of industrial relations at the terminal appears to be very formal and bureaucratic. The reasons are understandable: first, both management and the union side are not merely dealing with each other but are, separately and together, parts of larger systems with which they have to remain consistent. Second, the level of trust is low, and it is therefore safer—it is in any case always safer—

to have things carefully buttoned up than to leave anything to good-will and therefore to chance.

Nevertheless, the result is a quite extraordinary culture of working along precedents and formalities, of nit-picking about the precise wording of minutes, of fighting over whether something is a "minute" or a "note". Sometimes, enormous significance is given to shades of meaning in words or phrases that are really more a reflection of some-body's literary skill than of his motivation. It is this that gives rise to the mutual accusation of "point-scoring" to which the Brown–Smith Report draws attention.

The outsider has to tread a quite difficult path between, on the one hand, not offending so much against this culture that he puts himself outside the pale but, on the other hand, not getting caught up in it himself. I believe that the participants, too, sometimes feel themselves to be trapped by this culture.

5.   More attention could be given to the skills involved in human relations and industrial relations. People, especially managers, often feel that such skills should come naturally and that it is somehow weak or foolish to think about doing something to improve them. Certainly much "human relations training" is badly designed and a waste of time. Nevertheless, I think this is an area to which some thought should be given. In the first place, in many industrial organizations a unit the size of Willesden Terminal would warrant the employment of a professionally trained personnel officer. Again, there seems to be little or no supervisor or management training, particularly in the man-management aspects of supervision. For example, I was told, "We have a wonderful set of supervisors here; they are so keen to get the job out, they get down and do it themselves." Not least among the several difficulties about this statement is the lack of realization that any prob-lem-solving strategy produces consequences of its own. In fact, the supervisors have greatly resented doing the job themselves, and this resentment has been allowed to build up such a head of steam that it has become in itself an obstacle to working on a solution.

There is also a set of issues about the skills involved in face-to-face negotiation and consultation. It is clear from observing these processes that long experience of negotiating and defending one's interests has developed these skills to a very high degree. When there is a fight on, people know what they are doing. They have much less experience of working together to solve problems and are much less sure of them-selves when trying to operate in this mode. I am certain that, on some of the occasions when a row broke out in the Joint Working Parties, it was not so much because people wanted to have a row as because they resorted to skills and techniques with which they were familiar and about which they felt confident.

6.   The formal industrial relations system allows for two distinct modes of operation by differentiating between negotiation and consultation. In practice, however, there is no observable difference. Consultation meetings are just like negotiation meetings and do not provide a real alternative. It would be worth considering, as the alternative mode to negotiation, a process that would be called "joint problem solving", and providing some opportunities to learn and practice how to do it. The aim would not be to deflect people from fighting in the defence of their interests. Rather, it would be to widen the repertoire of skills that they have available and thus put them in a better position to select and control what they do.

BOUNCING
AGAINST THE CONTEXT

One of the complications in the practice of social science is that the context does not stand still. It changes from agreement about the ideas and methods to disagreement and back again, from an easy—even too easy—market to a difficult one, from an encouraging professional environment to a discouraging one and back again. It also encompasses cultural differences. The papers in this section reflect some of these shifts. As an individual professional moving through them, I have sometimes found myself engaged in skirmishes.

CHAPTER 7

Problems of application in the social sciences— contingency and organization structure, or "organization development"

There is a difference in approach that has dogged the "applied social science" or "applied behavioural science" scene for decades. I first came across it—indeed, experienced it—in a major way during my time in Esso, when the parent company introduced a team of American organization development (OD) consultants (chapter 4). The resulting controversy led to the ending of the Esso experiment. At that time I attributed it largely to cultural differences between American and European approaches, including an emphasis on normative rather than research values. Whatever the merits of that explanation at the time, it would not be accurate now. First, there is now a great deal of OD activity in Europe: for example, the seven case studies contributed by German collaborators towards the collection of cases in Klein and Eason (1991) were all of an OD type. Second, OD now covers a wider range of activities than it did at that time, some of them overlapping with an approach that includes structural or situational factors. And third, there is a good deal of research on OD itself.

Nevertheless, fundamental differences remain and need to be acknowledged. The controversy within Esso triggered a first attempt to set out the issues (Klein, 1976, chap. 13). The paper given below is adapted and developed from that discussion.

This chapter discusses, from both a theoretical and an operational point of view, one of the problems that arise in the application of social science, concerning the conflict and rivalry among social scientists that is nowadays part of the scene and for which organizations are providing an arena.

There are theoretical differences, and there is territorial conflict. It is important to know which of them one is talking about, and for purposes of discussion it is important to keep them separate; however, at an operational level this is not quite possible. A client who is buying one kind of application cannot or will not at the same time buy another.

Perhaps the main difference that has emerged can be polarized into two approaches, the one concerned with behaviour and the other with structure—the question being whether one regards behaviour or structure as the more important independent variable. On both sides of this fence there seem to be clusters of characteristics. Some hang together logically, others are there but for no apparent logical reason. On some aspects of the issue there is a true polarization, between irreconcilable views. On some, one postulates an "ideal type" view for purposes of discussion, though no individual social scientist necessarily holds it or holds it exclusively. Often the difference is merely one of emphasis, but this may be enough to have important consequences.

At the theoretical level, one can illustrate the two points of view by quotation. Thus on the one hand, Adam Smith first represented the structural or contingency orientation: "The understandings of the greater part of men are necessarily formed by their ordinary employments. The man whose whole life is spent in performing a few simple operations, of which the effects are perhaps always the same, or very nearly the same, has no occasion to exert his understanding or to exercise his invention in finding out expedients for removing difficulties which never occur" (Smith, 1776, bk. 5, chap. 1, art. 11). Marx demonstrates the same orientation: "Technology discloses man's mode of dealing with Nature, the process of production by which he sustains his life, and thereby also lays bare the mode of formation of his social relations, and the mental conceptions that flow from them" (Marx, 1867, vol. 1, p. 372).

The other orientation may be illustrated by the beginning of Rensis Likert's book *The Human Organization* (1967):

> All the activities of any enterprise are initiated and determined by the persons who make up that institution. Plants, offices, computers, automated equipment, and all else that a modern firm uses are

unproductive except for human effort and direction. Human beings design or order the equipment; they decide where and how to use computers; they modernise or fail to modernise the technology employed; they secure the capital needed and decide on the accounting and fiscal procedures to be used. Every aspect of a firm's activities is determined by the competence, motivation, and general effectiveness of its human organization. Of all the tasks of management, managing the human component is the central and most important task, because all else depends upon how well it is done.

Social scientists tend to identify more easily with one or the other of these orientations, and their choice will then have operational consequences. To illustrate: during the research project on soap manufacture, a situation was found in which there was a great deal of friction between the production and inspection departments. When the soap tablet emerged ready for packing, it was inspected for physical appearance—scuffing, clarity of imprint, and so on—and there were many borderline cases. The woman carrying out the inspection would decide against a tablet, ask the production manager to scrap it, and he would say "Oh no, that's all right" and have it packed. There were many disagreements, with the inspectors in a difficult position as they were junior in status to the production manager; to get support, however, they had to go to the organization's chief chemist, who in turn was senior to the production manager, and they were reluctant to do this.

There are a number of different things that social scientists might do in this situation, according to their perceptual set, training, and their professional biases: in a human relations framework, they might tackle the group-relations aspects of the situation in a variety of ways that would have in common the idea of getting the two functions to discuss their relationships; in the framework of social structure, they might notice first the disparity in status—the fact that these were not fights between equals—and tackle that. What I did first, as a researcher coming from a sociotechnical framework, was to say that, if it was to meet human relations criteria, the quality standard needed to be redefined so as to produce a minimum of borderline cases.

With greater experience of the politics involved, I can now see some reasons for not doing this. A structural solution such as this one merely removes a cause of difficulty. It does not give anyone a positive emotional lift; it does not lead to personal psychological growth; and it does not point out—let alone enhance—the role of the social or behavioural scientist as such. It does not signal directly enough that people are the stuff that one is dealing with and this is what the customers seem to want. If they want social scientists around at all, this is what they want them for.

Of course, there are problems of definition. A difference in status is a characteristic both of structure and of behaviour. "Behaviour" ranges from the flick of the eyebrow that suggests scepticism, through the obsessional way someone insists on a clear agenda for meetings, to the number of levels there are in a hierarchy or the size of managers' span of control. All are aspects of organizational behaviour, and it would be most helpful if we could use different words and discriminate.

But to return to the structure/behaviour controversy: in their research activities, both sides are busily collecting evidence, and, of course, as in the nature/nurture controversy of the psychologists, there is evidence on both sides. There has been a difference, however, in the strength of the ideological drive behind their researches, and this constitutes one of the sets of points in our clusters. A number of American behavioural scientists have been passionately concerned to reassert the superiority of man over "the system", or at least his freedom within it, without actually changing the system. Many have as their driving force the assertion of democratic over authoritarian values. The origins of this work lay partly in the wish to compensate people for what working in organizations does to them and partly in a strong need, especially in American society, and especially in the 1950s, the McCarthy era, to demonstrate that democracy is efficient.

"Participative management" is thus being propagated with missionary zeal, and it is a brave manager who expresses disagreement. Moreover, it has been propagated so widely that, whether they agree with it or not, this is what managers now expect from social scientists. It is therefore also a brave social scientist who says that social science is not necessarily about participative leadership. The intensity of the conviction about the rightness of these methods can paradoxically lead to some very authoritarian behaviour in applying them.[1] Indeed, the very language is coercive. If a manager disagrees with a particular technique or practitioner, how can he argue against something which calls itself "organization development", or a "change programme"? "Of course," comes the participative consultant's answer, "if you don't want to develop your organization, or if change frightens you too much, we are quite willing to withdraw."

The vocabulary may need to be explained at this point: in the United States the phrase "organization development" has come to be used for any kind of social or behavioural science intervention. In this country, the phrase generally referred first to strategies that a number of firms imported from the United States—notably Blake's Managerial Grid (Blake & Mouton, 1964)—and those social science interventions that are based on laboratory training designs, and then by extension also to any strategy that aims first at changing behaviour. It implies action rather than research. In both countries, the phrase must be rather galling to others, including other management scientists, who do things that develop organizations.

On the structural side, the greatest ideological heat was generated by Marx, who produced some of the best descriptions of different modes of manufacture and different levels of mechanization and their likely effect on attitudes and behaviour. He did not, however, predict the forms that technology would take. His ideological descendants were politicians and not social scientists, and tended to concentrate on the manipulation of macroeconomic structures. At the level of the enterprise, by a strange quirk it has been left to the cool, unemotional British to revive and continue the analysis of the interaction between technical and market characteristics and social behaviour. One does not associate Tom Burns, Eric Trist, or Joan Woodward with ideological passion (Burns & Stalker, 1961; Trist et al., 1963; Woodward, 1965, 1970). We must therefore add, to the differences perceptible among social scientists today, the difference between wanting first to reform and wanting first to understand.

On this issue there are really three role-orientations: understanding, reforming, and healing. The difference between reforming and healing is the difference between wanting to change a system and wanting to find remedies within it. It is an interesting question for the reformer whether the more "real", "basic", "radical" change is a change in structure or a change in behaviour. The healer, too, is faced with this dilemma.

It is probably true to say that, among current practitioners, the change-agent/OD/behavioural kind of social scientists tend to see themselves more as healers and the structural kind tend to see themselves more as explainers, even when in the action role. Partly this follows from the theoretical orientation—an item of behaviour in itself may be perceived quite quickly, and if it is not to be related to context, there is therefore not much need for research. Partly, however, it is also a matter of selection: social scientists who perceive themselves first as healers may select areas of subject matter where intervention can be rapid.

While there is therefore no logical reason why these roles should align with the behaviour/structure dichotomy, it is a matter of observation that, currently, they tend to do so. This is due to the differences in knowledge and experience available, the response of organizational clients, and the difference in the proportions of research and action. Certainly, the whole literature on change agentry—indeed, the very phrase change agent—implies that change or action is the dominant value on that side of the house. This has power implications as well: the change agent may be the most powerful person in a situation.

It follows, then, that another important effect of the difference in orientation is on the amount, and kind, and timing of diagnosis. This is another constellation of points in our clusters. On the one hand, one looks for problems in communication, behavioural styles, evidence of authoritarian behaviour, and so forth. Likert, for instance, did this with his core questionnaire. Others do it by observation of interpersonal behaviour. One may also assume that there is always room for improvement in this area and move directly into the action role. One change strategy assumes, for example, that teamwork could always be improved. A training course can therefore be formulated on the basis of a general, once-for-all diagnosis. What this therefore does not do is assess whether efficient teamwork is an important problem in a situation, as compared with any number of others.

Structural diagnosis, on the other hand, has to begin by looking at a very much wider range of factors, and it therefore requires a longer period of research with only a gradual zoning-down on problem areas. For clients who have overcome their hesitations and decided, at some personal and financial risk, to invest in a project, such delays before there is any action may be difficult to tolerate.

Strategically it is the difference between tackling general problems that may be presumed to exist in all situations to some extent, and therefore lend themselves to a packaged approach, and doing a specific diagnosis in a particular situation. In individual psychotherapy, the parallel is the encounter group, which is based on the assumption that all people have a degree of loneliness and could improve their personal relations, and which therefore skips individual diagnosis.

This also has some consequences for the "selling" of social science consultancy. The very idea of marketing implies that there is a product, something that is already formulated. It is hard to know how to sell open-mindedness or diagnostic skill. There is no doubt that an overwhelming proportion of what is being marketed in industry as social science is "OD programmes", concerned with behaviour. There is also little doubt that this has a greater and more immediate appeal for managers.

An identification with learning or with healing does not necessarily present an either/or situation, since they may merely be present in different proportions. It does, however, lead to either/or consequences. A very important one lies in the attitude towards the Hawthorne effect (see chapter 1). A "healer" will regard it as one of the most useful tools the social scientist has available to him, and try to maximize it; a researcher will regard it as a great scientific nuisance and try to minimize it. It really is not possible to do both, at least not in the same project! Recognizing this requires great integrity. There is work that appears to try to occupy not the top of the fence but both sides of it simultaneously.

Many social scientists would reject the maximizing of the Hawthorne effect as a tool for healing, except perhaps in cases of extreme emergency. At a conference of prison psychologists the point was made that during a riot the thing to do is to put on a white coat and walk around looking like a psychologist. There may be parallels to this in the situations that industrial sociologists get involved in, but mostly the situations are not of this kind. Assumptions about the "health" of an organization are likely to be influenced by the demand on one's services: it is not difficult to go and see what Johnny is doing and tell him to stop it. One can always find something to change.

Interventions at the behavioural level may be quicker and more immediately effective in an emergency, but their effect wears off and they have to be repeated or replaced. There was a department in a well-known company which boasted that it was undergoing its eleventh "change programme" in three years. Usually the turnover is not so fast, and managers are going to grow very old before they learn this lesson. While such a programme is going on—while, say, an enthusiastic trainer is fascinated with issues like leadership styles, communications, or attitude change—it is a thankless task to try to talk to him about budgets, or cost centres, or even role definition or task design.

The drive to change others can be very strong; one consultant in a training course was heard to speak about his "hit-list for paradigm change". Where it has this kind of strength, it also precludes the kind of understanding that starts from where the other is—exploring and learning about the forces, both conscious and unconscious, that impinge on the individual, the group, and the organization.

Basically, there are only two objections to "organization development" programmes, and both are to the label. First, there are very many ways of contributing to the development of an organization, and it is misleading to use this description for a limited activity that may lead people to think that it is comprehensive. Second, what these programmes often do is to provide opportunities for the personal growth of individuals. They may have nothing to do with organization, and they may therefore put out of joint the noses of people who do know about organization, but this is often the only opportunity that people in industry get of looking at themselves and treating their own behaviour and relationships as data. And, of course, personal development is an absorbing and endless process, which is why the appeal is so strong and so consistent. Perhaps one ought not to begrudge the opportunity, even in the name of greater reality and better applied social science.

Note

1. The paradox has a respectable ancestry. It is fascinating to read how the city state of Athens imposed democracy on her allies and in the process consolidated an empire: "The education which Athens gives to Greece is her own manner of life, her special kind of democracy, and the self-development and the self-respect which it encourages. This may be adopted voluntarily or it may be imposed by force, but in either case it is the most valuable thing that Athens has to give. Nor does the distinction much matter. What matters is that the Athenian example should be followed and all kinds of Greeks inspired to realize her ideal of the full life. Athens of course could not begin to set such an example unless she was unusually powerful. . . . Pericles [believed] that what Athens does for other cities is what no other power can do. In return for some diminution of independence, they are offered a wider and more glorious life. The empire awoke dormant powers and made cities conscious of their potentialities. Not all the allies welcomed either the claim or its implementation" (Bowra, 1971).

CHAPTER 8

Social science
as a threat to society

The excitement and growth in activities of the early 1960s had a downside. The social science establishment was not taking applied work seriously, and there was little consensus and no regulation about professional or ethical standards. One began to see signs of client organizations being exploited by the academic and consulting communities, and I felt that this needed to be confronted. The discussion may seem a little strange now, but the problem for the customer remains.

This paper was given to the Sociology Section of the British Association for the Advancement of Science in 1969 and later published in *New Society* under the title "Social Science: Customers Beware!" (Klein, 1969).

In the days when we were students and had time to read and argue, there used to be some elegant academic discussions about whether it was possible or desirable for social science to be independent of social values. One focus of these discussions was the concept of functionalism, and functional analysis: the analysis of a piece of observed behaviour, an institution, or a custom, in terms of its function in relation to the larger structure of which it formed a part, seemed to imply that anything at all—simply because it existed—must have a positive usefulness. Even the buttons on a coat-sleeve could be said to have the "function" of providing historical continuity in dress. So the functionalists came to be identified—perhaps identified themselves—with conservative forces in society. They were concerned with the statics of social structure, and not with structural change.

Then Merton (1957) came along and pointed to the possibility of classifying data as being non-functional or even dysfunctional. This took us, albeit in a very elegant and sophisticated way, back to where we started, with individual social scientists having to cope with the possibility that their analyses were merely the product of their own ideological position (and, of course, that their ideology in turn might be only a rationalization of their personal problems). Merton was—and so are the rest of us—left asking the basic questions, "How does one detect the ideological tinge of a functional analysis? To what degree does a particular ideology stem from the basic assumptions of the sociologist? Is the incidence of those assumptions related to the status and research role of the sociologist?"

At the same time as the theoretical sociologists were explicating this problem, empirical social scientists were discussing the problems of bias in research methods. They have not said much, incidentally, about bias in the selection of problems for investigation. How much of the work on race relations is done by members of minority groups? How much of the research on democratic leadership by people who are anxious about totalitarian systems? How much of the research on blue-collar workers by working-class, upwardly mobile researchers? Obviously a degree of personal involvement will make for a livelier study and without it many important insights would be lost. But there is a sense, too, in which the most convincing work is the most dispassionate and in which social science will become more credible as it becomes more boring.

However, that was a digression. It is reasonable to be selective in the problems one chooses to tackle, provided that one is then stringent in the methods used. Here the empirical social scientists—mainly psychologists—have been pretty thorough, and any student should be able, for instance, to answer an examination question on the forty sources of bias in an interview. Again, we have been fairly good at explicating the problem. But in many instances the best answer that the more sensitive social scientist can come up with is that one must take every possible step to become aware of one's own biases. Checks and replication are not always feasible (though with greater resources they would be).

Meanwhile, in another part of the forest, however, the social sciences have been clamouring for, and getting, power. Social scientists are rapidly moving into action roles, and all over the place—and particularly in organizations—are springing up as advisers, problem-solvers, and "change agents". It is the first part of my argument that this is happening without any of the earlier questions of value and bias having been satisfactorily resolved.

If this means that eminent (and less eminent) academics are imposing their value orientations—and with them their oedipal problems—on society under the authoritative mantle of social science, there would seem to be some urgent implications for democracy. Society can get rid of its politicians, but it cannot get rid of its eminent academics.

There are two factors that tend not merely to make this issue a subject for an academic romp but give it real urgency: one is the fact that social scientists are, in their action roles at least, extremely busy people. There is an inherent integrity in the subject which will be its own best safeguard, provided that people take time to think and read and discuss. But as social scientists get busier—and senior people in the profession are greatly in demand and very busy indeed—discussion of these issues inevitably takes a subsidiary role and may drop out of sight altogether. In the taxi between the directors' lunch and the government department, there is barely time to comb your hair and check to see which committee it is you are going to.

The second factor is the wide range of disciplines and areas of interest covered by the general phrase "social science". Social scientists who become consultants because they have specialist knowledge in one area will often be consulted on topics outside their own special knowledge. One does not often hear a social scientist say "I don't know". Moreover, and this is a point I shall discuss later, they are often not allowed to. People demand that they shall pronounce, and pronounce they do. It is not unusual, therefore, to hear judgements made with all the authority of the social sciences, which are as intuitive and fallible as anyone else's.

When we turn to the action role of the social sciences, and talk about the social scientist as adviser or problem-solver or "change agent", it becomes clear that we are no longer discussing theory or method. We are now talking about professional activities—a practice profession like accountancy, law, medicine—and then, in turn, about the theory and methods of professional roles. In the literature on these, the most frequent model used is that of the doctor, and perhaps the next most popular the psychoanalyst. (I shall be adding a third model, that of the priest.) As a matter of fact, none of these models is wholly satisfactory, but that is the subject of a different discussion and for some purposes they are useful. What I should like to point out here, as the second part of my argument, is that this is the only practice profession in which no control whatsoever is exercised over what goes on.

All the other professions have, for instance, some minimum standard for entry: we have none. We have not tackled, in this country, the question of what makes a bona-fide qualification. Has anyone any idea how many people there are coaching and interpreting social processes in T[training]-group-like situations simply because they have taken part themselves in such a situation and found it exciting?

Other professions have some sort of quality control through feedback. One can get some idea—admittedly it is not always easy—of whether a piece of legal or medical advice or intervention has been appropriate: if a severe error can be shown to have been made, it may be possible to get redress.

This is, of course, extremely difficult in psychoanalysis, and it is equally difficult in social science applications. You may realize in the long run that you were sold a pup, but the long run is usually very long indeed and often extends beyond the incumbency of the particular manager or administrator who commissioned the work. This leads to a very effective brand of consultancy, which consists of going to see what Johnny is doing and telling him to stop it. If they don't have a committee structure, you start a committee structure; if they do have a committee structure, you tell them that they are using committees as an alibi for management. Feedback is thus slow and ineffective. In the short run, a climate of enthusiasm makes it easy to identify with any change a consultant may suggest and so make it work, irrespective of whether it turns out later to have been appropriate.

Other professions have codes defining professional behaviour: we have none. When the social science community was small, there were some norms of conduct that could be taken for granted—that one does not, for example, do participant observation in secret, that one does not publish case material without the client's consent, or reveal identities without consent. Now, however, these standards cannot be taken for granted.

Institutional controls, however, can operate only in relation to the crudest and most tangible malpractice and cannot cope—any more than they can in other professions—with the irresponsibility and manipulation and abuse of power that I am here concerned about. For a history of the way in which the medical profession has abused its technical role and set itself up as an arbiter of morals and conduct (even now they decide who is "worthy" of contraceptive advice), I would recommend Alex Comfort's book *The Anxiety Makers* (1967). Compared with the creation of anxiety and dependence on this scale, some of the malpractices that are controlled seem rather unimportant.

By analogy, misconduct in some of the old-fashioned senses seems to me far less harmful than consultants' bamboozling of their clients, either to enhance their own role, or to further their own goals in some way, or simply because they are themselves confused. In the former case, the client at least knows what is happening and therefore retains some choice. In the kind of consultancy and social science bamboozling that is currently something of a growth industry, the client does not realize what is happening and is therefore denied a choice, and that, in my scale of values, is the sin against the Holy Ghost.

Perhaps I should define my terms here: bamboozling takes many forms, but it will always contain an element of inadequate or wrong information and an element of coercion, whether deliberate or not. I don't know which is worse.

It is the third part of my argument that social science as a practice profession has at the moment greater potential for abuse than the others because people are less sure what it is about and therefore less able to discriminate; because it is marketed competitively in ways that also confuse the customer; and because the roles of the practitioner are multifarious and ill-defined.

Let us look first at the practitioner's roles: researcher, trainer, sounding-board, designer of jobs or organizations, catalyst, adviser, therapist, problem-solver. All are valid in different situations, all are different; we are by no means all skilled at all of them; in particular, social scientists are frequently not skilled at recognizing and signalling which role they are in, and it is the resulting vagueness and ambiguity of the practice role that makes it so easy to abuse. We are involved not with the prescribed duties of the doctor, but with the unlimited potential of the witch-doctor.[1]

Sometimes the social scientist is asked to play the role of social conscience. There are mildly masochistic managements who rather enjoy being castigated and told they are doing things wrong. Others may deliberately look to social science as a barometer of the climate of opinion. Social scientists, in turn, may consent to take this role, since many people take up social science in the first place because they are idealistic and look to it as a means of channelling their idealism. If they do consent to act as social conscience, what are their criteria? Fre-

quently nowadays these have to do with a lessening of status differences and with participative behaviour. These values have nothing
intrinsically to do with social science—as neither does revolution,
which some others nowadays think it their duty to foster.

However, not all social scientists share these values of egalitarian-
ism and participation, and frequently those who do leave it unclear
whether they regard them as good in themselves or good as a means of
avoiding conflict and whether that, in turn, is good in itself. The literature about "change agents" is also very unclear about what change is
supposed to be from and to. It seems that change itself—any change—
has become the value, and the most damning label that you can
acquire is "resistant to change". Dislike the systems being promoted by
some social science consultants, get yourself labelled as "resistant to
change", and in some organizations you can literally write off your
career.

But to come back to the multiplicity of social science roles: the
practitioner is, in fact, frequently moving around between them, and
the ability to do this with understanding, and at the same time to
ensure that the client not only understands but consents, is perhaps the
greatest skill the practitioner needs and the biggest potential contribution he or she can make. What happens too often, however, is that one
role is used as an alibi for difficulties with another.

The dialogue then goes something like this:

Client: Help me.

Social scientist: I'm only a researcher, my concern is for knowledge.

Client: Then why are you so expensive?

Social scientist: Because I can help solve many of your problems.

Client: Then solve some of them.

Social scientist: You must learn to be independent and do that for
    yourself.

Client: How?

Social scientist: Aha!

It is not difficult to say "Aha!" but how many people really know what
they mean by it? From role confusion it is only a short step to the
deliberate creation of ambiguity, and it is this elusiveness and ambiguity that causes magical, religious characteristics to be ascribed to social
science. The power that then comes with the transition to the action
role brings rich rewards. It is sweet to be consulted, to dine with

ministers and directors, and to draw fees that by their size are a measure of deference rather than of actual work done. In this, there is collusion between society and the social scientist. The temptation to play God is very great because the need for God is very great, and industry is particularly susceptible to it. For generations, industry has come under fire for the awful effects that it has on people, and managers' guilt about making a profit is nowadays only exceeded by their guilt about not making enough profit. They cannot define the help they seek in this dilemma, and it is not to be wondered at that they clutch at social science when it offers equally undefined help.

Nor is it to be wondered at that social science projects are then decided on in nothing like the rational, discriminating way in which a decision over, say, an engineering project would be reached—that is, after careful deliberations, comparing tenders, and evaluating alternatives. Social science application at the moment is a matter of fads and fashions. What counts is the article, or book, or person who happens to make an impact when one happens to be in a receptive frame of mind.

One problem is that the notion "social science" covers not only a multiplicity of roles, but also a very wide range of areas of knowledge and of different possibilities of application. It is very difficult for customers to find their way around among all these activities, and it should be one of our first priorities to educate the customers, to make them sophisticated and discriminating. This is quite difficult in a situation in which we are all competing to sell our wares, but Caveat emptor is simply not good enough as a motto for the social sciences.

Practitioners have a very real dilemma of whether to keep at least in touch with the whole range of social science activities or to specialize in one technique or type of application. This latter has at least the advantage that people will then know what to come to them for, but there is a danger that they may then see that one technique or type of application as being appropriate to more and more situations.

There are some very limited solutions currently being sold as "social" or "behavioural" science. A number of them seem to follow a pattern: someone has a good idea that produces value in one situation. They become convinced that this value can be obtained in other situations, or even all situations. They have to convince others, which they do by publishing, lecturing, demonstrating, and so forth. They have to market their package, so they will train others to apply it or market do-it-yourself kits. In the process they acquire adherents or followers, and they all begin to close their minds to other possibilities. They acquire some of the characteristics of the narrower religious sects, with disciples, sacred texts, schisms, heresies and interdenominational bigotry, and salvation assured provided that you accept and believe. (There is a splendid PhD. waiting for someone who will make an anthology!)

These packages or "comprehensive" systems apart, the practical utilization of social science knowledge and methods takes, as I have suggested, many different forms. Each one therefore has its own potential for inadequacy and abuse. Note that there is a difference between inadequacy and abuse: manpower planning *may* get us into trouble through miscalculation (two points on a graph, and you have a projection); it may also cause problems by creating self-fulfilling prophesies, and thus unwittingly manipulating society.

The threats in my title are therefore many and varied, from the general dangers with which this chapter began, to some quite specific horrors: manipulation by manpower planning, ossification through selection and testing, castration through participative management, and torture by T-group.

Now let me propose some remedies.

I have already suggested that we need some institutional controls and that the customer needs to be educated. I want also to suggest a third approach.

We have become familiar over the past ten years with the concept of the sociotechnical system—we realize, that is, that any industrial situation consists of the interaction of a technical and a social sub-system. What we now need also to realize is that in any situation in which a social scientist is involved there will by definition be another sub-system: the helper sub-system.

In any situation except one in which the social scientist is only there to do pure research (and therefore actually takes steps to minimize his or her influence, in order not to distort the data), the helper sub-system needs to be taken into account; needs, indeed, to be subjected to just as explicit and systematic an analysis as the client system or systems. This means examining closely the needs and ambitions of the social science organization—its publishing traditions, its training needs, its needs for money and status, and all the other elements of its make-up that will inevitably influence the way it works. All these needs are perfectly legitimate. It is only when they are repressed, when they are not allowed to be an explicit part of the contract, that they emerge in undesirable ways.

We have, I believe, been working on a false—or, rather, an incomplete—assumption: that it is the client who has all the needs and the consultant who has all the resources, and that there is a one-way traffic between them. If we can correct this, and make the social science system and its needs a legitimate part of the contract, it will at least be less likely to fulfil them covertly.[2]

Notes

1. A well-known American social scientist, in a letter commenting on this article when it was published in *New Society*, appears to confirm this. He says: "you . . . fail to mention the worst sin of all for a professional: to fail to offer such help as one can to those who need it. Witch doctors at all times and places have had a salutary role, as we do now."
2. This idea is developed further in chapter 11.

CHAPTER 9

Problems of context: a fiasco

The book about working as a social scientist in Esso came out in 1976. It was a very detailed case study, and it seemed obvious that the way to take the subject further would be to document other attempts (of which there were by then quite a number) and compare them to see what could be learned. The writing of the Esso case study had been funded by the Social Science Research Council, and when it was published, the chairman of the SSRC wrote a very nice, unsolicited review. So I was optimistic about taking the subject further. I was working in the Tavistock Institute at the time; Ken Eason was a colleague and friend who had taken part in some of the Esso work and who was now at Loughborough University. Together we decided to try for a research grant to collect and compare examples of social science being applied in organizations. This paper tells the story of that attempt. It is the edited report to the SSRC on a feasibility study and has not been published before.

The attempt to get this work funded failed. Any researcher suffers bids that fail, and I have had my share of grant applications being turned down. But there is something different about this one and what it demonstrates about the institutional difficulties of relating research and practice. I knew that the climate among the academics on the SSRC's committees was changing, and that "usefulness" was going out of favour; but I did not realize just how far the change in direction had gone.

In the 1970s, it seemed clear that the subject of utilization needed further explicit attention, both research and development. As regards research, the Esso experience and book (Klein, 1976) had the disadvantages as well as the advantages of a case study: however valuable the experience, and however many ideas and hypotheses it might generate, if the subject of utilization as such was to be further explored the enquiry would now need to be systematized. The way to do this, it seemed to me, would be to collect a range of such experiences and compare them systematically. Considering the amount and range of work going on, it was no longer appropriate to limit analysis to the work of one person or institution.

Systematic comparison of cases, however, raised a number of issues. The first was that of access: we (Ken Eason, the colleague I proposed to begin work with, and I) knew that there were by now a large number of attempts going on to make use of the social sciences in organizations. We did not know whether access would be possible, especially in view of a second issue: the controversial nature of some forms and aspects of applied social science. We were known to prefer some types of application or utilization to other types, and we would need to demonstrate that we could be detached for purposes of research; we would need to design a convincing "detour via detachment".

As regards development, it seemed to us to be a contradiction in terms to treat a subject like "utilization" by merely researching it. It was one of the main findings of the Esso study that, in the social sciences, the "development" part of the "research-and-development" continuum was neglected, and it seemed essential that a programme about utilization should also concern itself with the development of the subject area.

One way to do this would be to feed back findings as they arose to those engaged in utilization whose experience was being tapped and to see whether this process, and the discussion that it generated, would help to clarify a range of professional issues.

A second, and very important, aspect of development concerned financial arrangements. The usual pattern was (and remains) that research is financed by public funds and consultancy by the clients who benefit from it. This basic funding structure creates boundaries that separate the worlds of research and practice and that are in many ways dysfunctional, the most obvious one being that most applied work never sees the light of day. This means, in turn, that it does not feed back into teaching and research. We wanted to explore whether it was possible to devise ways of joint funding whereby clients would pay for the help they received and public funds would ensure that the applied work could be analysed and published. Some form of partial public support was also necessary if young people were to be trained via apprentice roles that would not yield full "value for money" for a client.

This led to a third aspect of development, concerning training and training needs in utilization and application. It seemed to us that this was an area that also needed both research and development.

The feasibility study

I consulted the secretary of the relevant SSRC committee about the idea. His opinion was that the biggest hurdle would be getting access to other people's experience. He thought that referees would be very sceptical about us being able to find practitioners and their clients who would let us look at what they were doing. For me, that did not seem to be a problem at all, as we were already in touch with many such people. He suggested that we should apply for a small grant for a "feasibility study" to find such situations and that, if this problem could be dealt with, the rest would be straightforward. So we did that; it was 1977, and we succeeded in getting a small grant of £2,000.

The aim of the study was threefold:

1.   to conceptualize the issues involved;
2.   to explore the willingness of others to collaborate in a programme, the core of which would be the collection and comparison of experiences in utilization;
3.   to explore modes of joint funding.

For the first aim, we produced a theoretical paper.

The second aim, of finding collaborators, was easy to fulfil. The idea of learning from comparing experiences resonated with a lot of people and within a very short time we had thirteen offers. There were actually fourteen, but one later had to withdraw. Even people with whom we were likely to have differences of opinion wanted to take part and offered access to their work and to their clients. Because there were many types of work, and one would not know what the work was until one investigated it, we decided to sample the type of institution from which it was being done rather than the type of work: from in-house, from academic institutions, and from commercial consultancies.

With regard to the third aim, we tried to explore ways of designing a funding structure that would ensure that, on the one hand, clients who benefited from applied work were not subsidized by the taxpayer while, on the other hand, researchers could be assured some security and opportunity to write up work, and young people could be trained. We ourselves would, from then on, only take on work that the clients were prepared to have published. But it turned out that the SSRC could not—or would not—engage with the accounting problems involved.

The grant application

As a result of the feasibility study, we made a grant application for a programme of research and action research on the use of social science in organizations. The SSRC at that time funded "projects" and "programmes", a programme being a set of interconnected projects. So on the basis of our collaborators—what we had been told would be the most difficult aspect—we formulated a programme that should have three components: research into experiences of applying social science; adding a "research slice" to action-oriented work; and research into training needs and the possible development of training for applied work.

However, it turned out that getting collaboration was not really the most difficult aspect. The most difficult aspect was that the social science community could not at that time contemplate making applied work respectable. The more one dealt with any objections, the more determined became the search for new objections. "Feasibility", in that sense, was something quite different.

On reflection, and in the context of feasibility in the broader sense, it seems likely that this negative outcome was preordained. This impression began to form fairly early on, because of the way different objections and reasons for rejection succeeded each other. As soon as we met one, it appeared to become unimportant. Somehow, it seemed it was the *idea* of such a programme that could not be entertained, for reasons about which we can only speculate, especially as we only have part of the data. But we could see, for example, that if a particular point was met, this could increase rather than decrease a questioner's irritation.

Organizationally, work that was not clearly within the ambit of one particular SSRC committee ran into some special difficulties. Among them were differences in perception deriving from different disciplines and fields of study, about appropriate methodology. Some of the comments we received stem from a research frame of reference (the comprehensive literature review, the clear theoretical framework leading to the posing and testing of hypotheses) that seemed inappropriate to the problem area being tackled, one that was much more likely to lead to the development of grounded theory and was concerned with the development of the field. These were old arguments, which need not be reiterated here. The point here is that they were not arguments between "them" and "us". Some of "them", during the site visit, also said that they were not looking for a rigid, experimental textbook approach to research. (However, in the letters of rejection that we received, those were the reasons that featured predominantly, perhaps because they were easier to specify than some others.) The list of referees' comments received (see later) itself indicates the range of value systems existing within the same institution regarding research and development, not only of the kind proposed. Unfortunately, the effect for any proposed work of such a collection of comments is cumulative, suggesting that only work that does not offend anyone can pass, rather than work that evokes discrepant questions such as too much/not enough.

Again, it is possible that the function exercised by the SSRC secretariat in passing information between applicants, referees, and committees, and their perception of what it was relevant to pass on, exerted some influence. For example, the sum applied for was large for the time (£250,045 spread over five years). It is inconceivable that referees would not have commented on this. Indeed, at the suggestion of the secretary of the Management and Industrial Relations Committee, I had from the outset formulated the application in such a way that parts could be lopped off if necessary. The training research could have been omitted (this was suggested by one referee, but we were not able to respond to the suggestion—see later). In addition, we could have reduced the number of cases to be studied or debated the degree of depth at which they were to be studied. But at no point were we asked to suggest savings or ways of scaling down; it may be that SSRC staff thought methodological and theoretical comments more relevant to pass on.

In any case, it became overwhelmingly clear that by meeting specific theoretical and methodological queries we were not meeting the difficulty that SSRC itself might be experiencing in dealing with a proposal of this kind, or any other underlying problems.

The site visit

Major research-grant applications involved a site visit from members of the relevant committee. That immediately opened up a problem, since these committees were organized according to academic disciplines. Problem-oriented work cut across the boundaries of several disciplines. When a site visit was arranged for our application, it involved members drawn from three committees.

At a conference two weeks before the site visit, I met the professor who was to be chairman of the site-visit team. He said that he thought our ability to gain access to other people's applied work would need to be demonstrated. I asked if it would help if I invited some of the collaborators to meet the site-visit panel, perhaps over lunch. He thought that was a good idea—the panel could meet the collaborators informally over lunch and then, after lunch, formally ask them some questions about the experiences they could offer.

It was very short notice, but I was lucky. Seven of our collaborators could manage the date and accepted the invitation. They were (also a matter of luck) representative of the three types of institution: the head of the Behavioural Science Unit of the Greater London Council; the head of Psychology Services of the Post Office Corporation; the head of the organizational development function of Shell International; the managing director of an international firm of commercial consultants that did behavioural science work; an independent commercial consultant psychologist; a professor of industrial sociology; a reader in social psychology (the last two from different universities).

A few days before the site visit, a letter from the SSRC arrived, enclosing a list of thirty questions and comments from referees and committee members. The letter said: "You will have the opportunity together with your collaborators to look at the questions beforehand and formulate some replies in advance. . . .You may also find that some of these points are totally irrelevant and you would not wish to worry about those. . . ."

The questions were wildly disparate, and the antagonism contained in some of them came as a shock. The range of attitudes they showed made it unlikely that there would be agreement among referees and committee members. For example:

"What advantage would the Tavistock Institute provide over management schools or university departments?"

"Since all this work is centred on organizations, presumably there is an underlying view on the present state of organization theory. What are likely to be the important variables in a model of organizational functioning?"

"I read 14 pages of boring and pompous flannel illustrated with little pictures which were clearly designed for the epidiascope shows so beloved by management training experts. I know that this is the style of pseudo-science often found in large organizations but I thought it had gone out of fashion at the beginning of this decade."

"How do the statements in the programme relate to the ongoing debates in sociology, as to whether the social sciences are of the natural science type aiming for testable, generalizable propositions, or whether the social sciences merely develop a particular interpretation of the world, which cannot be claimed to be more 'true' than others? Since there is a whole range of positions in between one would hope that this programme might contribute to this discussion, especially insofar as utilization is concerned."

"It was thought that there were a number of gaps in the conceptualization of this programme: (a) insufficient attention was given to the 'skill diffusion' model, (b) no mention seems to have been made of yet a different role for the social scientist, i.e. the one of the social critic, the maker of alternative realities. . . ."

We did a great deal of work to prepare responses to the points made. However, when people had gathered for the site visit, the chairman opened it by saying that we should not be too worried about the questions of committee members which had been sent to us, since the panel members would prefer to ask questions of their own. Not only had they put us to a lot of unnecessary work; more importantly, an eventual decision would be made by the committees from which the panel members were drawn, and none of the people who had sent the questions would ever know whether satisfactory answers to their points had been available.

A common factor in the questions the panel itself asked related to methodology. We had written some working papers on methodology but had decided not to include them in the application because the document was getting long. I said that if methodology was felt to be such a problem, I could get these papers into shape within two or three weeks and circulate them as a supplement to the proposal. This angered the man who had led the questions on methodology: these issues were much too difficult to be dealt with in two or three weeks, he said; they would need several months of work.

By lunchtime, there had not been an opportunity to mention the people and institutions who were prepared to collaborate with us, and I asked if I might do this. The chairman said there was no time, and the panel members did not seem interested. Rather desperately, I asked if I might at least explain who was coming to lunch, which I was then allowed to do very hastily. It was at this point that I began to recognize the hopelessness of this exercise. To have obtained collaboration in this work from a rich range of experience was probably our biggest asset, and I had been told that doubts about it were the main stumbling-block. It was as if they did not want the stumbling-block removed.

This impression grew when, during lunch, the chairman said that there was still so much to do that there would be no time to talk to the collaborators. In a short speech, he thanked them for coming and explained that they would not be required. There was an awkward silence, then the university professor, who presumably did not feel as overawed by a panel of eminent academics as some others, protested: "Aren't you even going to talk to us?" The answer was a polite no.

After lunch, the site panel wanted to meet on their own for a time, which gave us the opportunity to apologize to our guests. Some of them were very angry, and some showed us the notes they had prepared about their work.

In the afternoon, the panel concentrated on Ken Eason, asking whether there were any aspects of the programme that interested him especially. He mentioned one, almost at random—the search strategies used by people who experience problems. They suggested that this would make an interesting research project on its own, and that he should develop a separate application about it from Loughborough. I, on the other hand, was advised to apply for a personal research grant to enable me to write up more of my experience. We were strongly advised not to go ahead with the programme application—it was bound to be rejected.

We could abandon the development aspects of the programme and restrict ourselves to a research project. But splitting up, and obtaining a personal grant to write up further personal experience, seemed crazy when the main reason for wanting to do this work was to broaden out personal experience into a more general and professional body of thought. We formulated a research proposal that was greatly scaled down and paid a lot of attention to methodological issues. The chairman of the site-visit panel offered to vet it before submission and declared that his concerns had now been met. It failed. In the letter from the SSRC announcing the rejection, there were a whole lot of new objections that had never been mentioned before, as well as renewed attempts to split us, with insulting remarks about Ken's role. Having been told that we both had excellent track records, and that I was a "centre of excellence" in the subject, we did not get even the smallest support to pursue it.

Discussion and conclusions

What follows is the final section of the report on the feasibility study.

Discussion

I should like to attempt to understand why we failed so completely, by posing a series of questions:

- *Was it the money?* This is the most obvious and attractive explanation, but on closer examination it begins to look unlikely. True, the amount was large. But money and scale were never discussed with us, and we were never asked to suggest savings. And not even a very small grant was made.

- *Was the subject matter considered unimportant?* In general terms, given the origin and raison-d'être of the SSRC, this is out of the question (Heyworth Committee Report, chap. VII). Specifically, for any particular generation of decision-makers, it may be the case.

- *Was the subject matter too important?* At the time our applications were being processed, the Management and Industrial Relations Committee had a sub-committee on research utilization working and, in one sub-division of the field, a working-party on work organization. There may be a question about what to do if initiatives at the centre are concerned with the same problems as initiatives taken in the field.

- *Were we not considered competent or experienced enough?* I have to allow for the possibility, but it seems unlikely. We were both said to have good "track records", I was described as a "centre of excellence", Eason was encouraged to make a separate application.

- *Were we too competent or experienced?* Disregarding the immodesty of this possibility, there is a real policy question about setting up centres of excellence and the effect this may have on others interested in the same field. What is certain is that we were repeatedly told that we would stand a better chance if we split up.

- *Was it problems of organization?* Some of the organizational issues have been discussed. It is certain that they affected the outcome to some extent, but it is impossible to judge to what extent.

I need to make clear that I in no way dispute the SSRC's right to use its collective judgement and reject a proposal *on whatever grounds*. I do, however, dispute two things:

1. The right to undermine confidence and damage reputations where that is not warranted—where, that is, theoretical or methodological criticisms are substituted for the real reasons for rejection. Even personal dislike could be a reason, but it should not be cloaked in "respectable" objections on scientific grounds.

2. The right to waste the time of professional colleagues frivolously. Towards the end of this saga, an administrative officer of the SSRC said that, in the current situation, there had never really been any likelihood of a programme being set up. "Then why did they give us the money for the feasibility study?" I asked. The answer was that "the Committee thought it would be interesting to see what you had to say". This disregard for the use and value of my time is the only aspect that leaves me angry. It shows as well as anything the difference between the worlds of academic research and of those who are engaged with problems in the real world.

In Germany, I am a member of a committee of the Ministry of Research and Technology with somewhat similar functions to those of the SSRC, the disbursing of research grants. Grant applications are circulated to committee members, and then the applicants present and defend their work in person to the committee. If a committee member cannot attend and sends an opinion in writing, or if opinions are collected from other sources, they are signed.

Obviously, every system has advantages and disadvantages. The advantages of the German system are:

- Simple misunderstandings can be cleared out of the way [there were several in the list of comments we received from the SSRC].
- Objections as well as proposals are subject to the scrutiny of peers.
- One can distinguish clearly between research issues and non-re-

search issues [some of the SSRC comments seemed, for example, to object to the Tavistock Institute rather than to the work; this should have been explored—if there was a serious objection to the location of the programme, I would have been prepared to move].

- One can distinguish clearly which questioners have more and which less experience of and concern for the subject in question [this was unclear from the SSRC comments received].

- Most importantly, in the course of clarification and discussion, people quite often change their views [this seems to have been precluded in the SSRC process].

Conclusions

1. It was possible to conceptualize the issues involved in the utilization of social science in such a way as to provide a basis for further research and development.

2. It was possible to obtain the collaboration of a wide range of people and institutions engaged in the utilization of social science to contribute to such research and development.

3. It was possible to design partial funding but not—in the limited attempt we made—in a way that realistically reflects the relationship between research and practice.

4. It was not possible to get research on this topic off the ground within the framework of the SSRC.

5. It has proved possible to get the research off the ground in a different framework. We have received a grant from the Anglo-German Foundation for the work, which began on 1 June 1980.

Postscript

After the SSRC had been re-formed into the Economic and Social Research Council, and no doubt against the inclination of many of the people involved, the climate slowly began to change. In 1996, almost twenty years after the débacle with the SSRC, I was commissioned by the ESRC to look at the relations between researchers and users in one of their programmes (see chapter 10). In 1999, I was at a workshop that the ESRC organized about the general issue of relations between researchers and users. Someone said that it would be a good idea to collect case studies of applied social science. The book resulting from our research (Klein & Eason, 1991) was, of course, by then out of print.

Studying the relationship between researchers and users: The Nation's Diet programme

By the late 1970s, the Social Science Research Council appeared to have forgotten its original remit, though that was probably not the reason why it was nearly abolished under the Thatcher government. In any case, a funding institution for the social sciences survived and re-emerged as the Economic and Social Research Council. In 1993 a White Paper on Science, Engineering and Technology affirmed a "customer–contractor principle" for research sponsored by the research councils (Cabinet Office, 1993). It is not the same thing as a concern for utilization, and was not the best frame of reference for the social sciences, being limited to the "knowledge-into-use" framework. But it was better than what had been there before and allowed for the possibility of evolution. After decades out in the cold, the utilization of social science began to experience a slow turning of the tide. In 1994, the ESRC's Chief Executive, Professor Howard Newby, published an article strongly urging that the social sciences should be of use in society. I wrote to him, but with exquisite timing my letter reached him two weeks before he was due to leave the ESRC. However, he briefed some of his senior colleagues about a response. I was asked to give a seminar to ESRC staff about the history and issues of utilization, and afterwards there were to be discussions about how to follow through.

The Esso experience should have taught me that a large tanker cannot change direction quickly. The change must have been painful and difficult for many people, and it took an enormously long time for these discussions to happen and then to lead to anything; I began to wonder whether I would live long enough. Eventually it was decided that I should look at one of the ESRC's research programmes from the point of view of the relationship between researchers and users. The programme selected was called "The Nation's Diet", and it happened to span the time before and after the publication of the 1993 White Paper. The report on the study led, eventually, to a presentation on the broader issues to the ESRC's Research Priorities Board.

In formulating a contract for the study, the question had arisen of whether it was to be regarded as research or consultancy. When it emerged that consultancy attracted VAT, the contract was formulated as research. So the report given below is in the public domain, although it was commissioned and not carried out with a research grant. It has not been published before; the text was cleared with the people who took part.

Introduction—background to the study

This report describes a study of the relationship between researchers and users in one of the ESRC's research programmes, "The Nation's Diet".

Because I have a history of concern for the utilization and application of the social sciences, both the ESRC and I thought it important to emphasize to the researchers involved that this study was not intended to be normative about user engagement, but simply to "map the territory" and understand it: whom do the researchers regard as actual or potential users of their work, at what stage do they engage with them (if at all), what is the nature of the engagement? Is there a spectrum of user engagement that can be defined, and if there are variations in it, can they be explained? However, what neither the commissioners of the study nor I realized was that such reassurance was not necessary in a situation where the researchers had not heard either of me or of the earlier work on utilization!

Staying in role, in the sense of not conveying a normative approach, proved not to be difficult. None of the researchers had objections on principle to the idea of user engagement. This could be due to the nature of the topic, to the original selection of which researches were to be funded, to shifts in the climate of opinion, or to chance. In any case, no one took the line that I once heard put forward by a professor of psychology, that "you should fund geniuses and leave them alone."

What was difficult, on the other hand, and at times impossible, was to refrain from all discussion in the course of these interviews, where a large number of fascinating issues, both of method and of substance, were being discussed. Twice I found myself even venturing a suggestion; the report will make clear where this happened.

The study

Interviews were held with researchers from fifteen out of the sixteen studies in the programme. It needs to be noted that I did not see the whole teams. It also needs to be noted that the interviews took place at a particular point in time; a good deal will have happened since then. Listed below are the studies, their location, and the researchers interviewed, in random order and with a code letter that has been allocated for purpose of the analysis. Item H includes two studies.

A. Ambivalence about health-related dietary change. Leeds/Reading, Dr P. Sparks.

B. The effects of life stress on food choice: an ecological study. St. George's Hospital Medical School, Prof. A. Steptoe.

C. Food consumption: social norms and systems of provision. School of Oriental and African Studies, Prof. B. J. Fine.

D. A longitudinal study of food choices made by mothers on behalf of infants and young children. Nottingham, Dr E. Murphy.

E. Constructing the consumer interest: retailing, regulation, and food quality. Hull, Dr T. K. Marsden.

F. The marriage menu—food and diet in transition after marriage. Glasgow Royal Infirmary, Dr A. S. Anderson.

G. Teaching and learning about food and nutrition in educational settings. Warwick, Prof. R. G. Burgess, Dr M. Morrison.

H. Concepts of "healthy" food: a comparative anthropological investigation. Goldsmith's College, Prof. A. P. Caplan (two projects).

I. The role of the media in the emergence of food panics. Glasgow, Prof. J. E. T. Eldridge, Dr J. Reilly.

J. The psychological determinants of children's food preferences. Bangor, Prof. C. F. Lowe.

K. The decision not to eat meat: an analysis of changing preferences. Manchester, Dr T. Young.

L. Dietary change among South Asians and Italians in Glasgow. Glasgow (University and Royal Infirmary), Dr R. G. A. Williams, Prof. M. E. J. Lean.

M. Eating out and eating in: households and food choice. Lancaster, Dr A. Warde.

N. Consumption, diet, and ageing: the construction of food choice in later life. Nottingham, Mr R. Silburn.

Interviews were also held with the programme director and with the chairman of the Programme Steering Committee. A good deal of published material from the researches has also been collected. I share the dilemma expressed by most of the researchers, of having more data than can be handled in the available time.

The code letters are attached to the projects for convenience, they do not make them anonymous. Much of the time it will not make sense to try to keep the origin of the information anonymous. The report has been circulated to the respondents in draft for checking and correction. Full and systematic accounts of outputs from the programme are available to the ESRC in the normal reporting framework.

The programme

The programme was in two phases, with eight projects in each phase. In addition, two Programme Fellows were appointed for a year. At the time of the interviews, a number of projects had already been completed for some time, while in others analysis was still going on. All the projects had produced material that had the potential of keeping the researchers writing beyond the finishing date—estimates of how far beyond ranged from a few months to ten years. Whether the researchers would actually be able to do this would depend on their institutional positions, types of contract, involvement in new work—and, of course, funding.

The projects cover a wide range of topics, disciplines, and approaches, with virtually no duplication. One wonders if this diversity can be due to chance or was in part the basis of selection. As two respondents pointed out, it does not necessarily mean that what comes out is (or is intended to be) a coherent body of knowledge; a broad spread does not imply coherence. Its meaning is more that the social sciences should have demonstrated that they have a contribution to make in this field; indeed, one respondent felt that this objective somewhat overshadowed the topic itself. In selecting the projects, there was some attempt to cover the food supply chain from beginning to end, though with rather more emphasis at the consumption than the production end. One of the researches (C) points to this vertical perspective as providing the most likely framework of explanation.

The weighting at the consumption end is probably related to a particular characteristic of this programme, its normative element. There seems to be policy consensus about what constitutes a "healthy" diet (only one researcher suggested that current views about this might be transient), and some of the projects are explicitly about finding out why people eat what they do, in order to influence and change it—"If people know what is healthy, why do they eat the other stuff in such quantities?" That brings particular sections of the public, as well as their doctors and other advisers, into the frame as potential users.

A second characteristic of the programme is the universality of the topic. Everyone is interested in food; so everyone could potentially be a user.

There is a third characteristic of this programme which is relevant when one looks at it from the point of view of user engagement: the programme was originally launched before the 1993 White Paper on Science, Engineering and Technology (Cabinet Office, 1993), which had such impact on the ESRC's strategy and policies. It therefore straddles a period of major changes within the funding body, including administrative changes and considerable periods of uncertainty. Policy relevance was not new as a criterion, but engagement with users was. For the researchers, "the goalposts shifted" in the course of the programme: user engagement had not originally been part of the deal. So, "one reason if they are grumpy about users is not because they are against users but because they thought they were doing something else". I did not, however, encounter "grumpiness" about users; what I encountered was the problem that whatever "user engagement" meant, whether in terms of writing, meetings, presentations, or whatever, it meant extra work.

The reader as user

The overwhelming output is publication. This, after all, is the unquestioned hallmark of research: the received wisdom is that if it isn't published, it isn't research. So the dominant category of "user"—or even characteristic of a user—is someone who reads.

Two of the programme's characteristics mentioned earlier present questions of how and where to publish. Its normative element means that there are practice-oriented professions—for example, in nutrition, healthcare, home economics—whose journals are appropriate for some of the output. In relation to the general public, these professionals are "gatekeepers" in the sense in which Havelock uses the term (Havelock, 1969). Many, but not all, the researchers have published in this practice-oriented press. Not all the work is suitable for that kind of publication, although some could be scanned for elements that might be—"if one was that way inclined or had the time, there would certainly be things that one could incorporate . . .".

The universality of the topic means that aspects are of interest to the popular media: newspapers, radio, television. This can be appealing to social scientists, who do not often find themselves the object of media attention—it is very rewarding to see one's research described as "ground-breaking". It can also very quickly become a burden, taking up too much time and energy, and carrying the risk of being misrepresented. There seems to be a band of tolerance below which one wishes one's work was better known and above which the attentions of journalists are too demanding. There had been one serious incident of distortion, where a journalist had got her information from another journalist's account rather than from the researcher and had written a very snide critique, leading to formal protests and editorial apologies. Dealing with the press: "(a) it's unpredictable, (b) it's not very satisfying by and large, and (c) it is very time-consuming".

Getting media attention can be a matter of serendipity. In H, the researcher's presidency of the Anthropology and Archaeology section of the British Association presented an opportunity to convene a panel on "Food in Britain", which attracted a lot of media attention. For M, the British Sociological Association's annual conference provided a similar opportunity, the association having its own PR apparatus that circulates abstracts of papers to journalists and brings them to its conference.

One can also be proactive in contacting the media. M developed a dissemination list for publications, which includes journalists. This led to a considerable amount of activity, including commenting on a radio station's own survey. I is a research group with a lot of substantive knowledge and experience of this field, and it has been consulted by several of the researchers about their relations with the media.

But research has to be interpreted for journalists, and this is laborious: "So I sat at the word processor and spent a couple of hours turning thirty-two pages into four pages of useable text, and whether that's a good use of my time. . . ." Writing at the level of popular journalism also takes skills that some researchers acknowledge they do not have. Sometimes it is delegated to junior staff who may be better at it. But research assistants often move on after the funding period, and this leads to the question of when, at what stage, the popular writing should happen.

For many of the researchers, it is crucial that the professional output happens first; until that is done one does not know what the findings actually are and a project cannot be said to be complete. Other writing and dissemination can only be based on this sense of completion; before that, the researchers do not feel confident about what it is that is being presented. In one project, workshops, both in the United Kingdom and internationally, will be set up "when we've got all the data together and we've published a reasonable amount and we know where we're taking it forward." For another, "I'm a little uneasy at the moment about [publishing in practice journals] right now, but once we've settled it in our minds, about how the data is going to work . . . ." Or another: "We started by giving conference results at an academic level because they have to be academically secure before you can pass them on down."

It can also be a question of worthwhileness, of values rather than intrinsic need—"the science should come first, for me it means that the sociology should come first. . . . Once I get the sociology right, it's then that I should be publishing in an accessible way to a wider practitioner audience. . . . I think that the practitioner publications will be infinitely more worthwhile if they reflect theory in that broader sense than if they simply recounted empirical facts."

In this phased approach, the later, more applied or practice-oriented writing and dissemination may by that time be competing with work on new projects. In the same way, unease about writing popular science may be linked with not having the researchers any more by that time. Who is to write the popular stuff if one is not used to writing in that mode oneself?

This sequence is to some extent a function of the particular discipline and the kind of data it produces. The above examples came from psychology and sociology, although the sociology example indicates an element of choice. In both sociology and anthropology the empirical data, the descriptive case studies, may be seen as worthwhile and written up in their own right before higher-level analysis and conceptualization have taken place, thus reversing the sequence.

The Research Assessment Exercise

Clearly, the Research Assessment Exercise (RAE)[1] is an important factor in this tension around how much and what kind of written output to produce. That there is an issue around the RAE is well known; there is no need to labour it here. But it may be worth spelling out what it is:

For the researchers in this programme, the issue of science-related or user-related output was not a question of either/or. All of them were keen to contribute to academically respected knowledge and to theoretical and methodological development. All had, or were working on, outputs of that kind. But some wanted or felt under pressure to do other things as well. It is then that the different demands made by funding authorities create conflict.

So for those who only saw the scientific community as their audience, there was no conflict. Of the others, two did not appear to have problems: in one case, there was little difference in the level of writing needed, so that it was possible to meet both sets of demands; in the other, there was a kind of division of labour, with practice-level writing being delegated to junior staff. All the rest experienced conflict of varying degrees of severity, some explaining at length how the problem affected them in their particular discipline or institution. In some cases, this was very severe; in one, it had nearly led to disaster. The majority view is probably summed up in this comment: "The ESRC and HEFC are both government-funded, they need to get their act together so that what's valued in one sphere is valued in the other."

Some trajectories

This section attempts to present a selection of thumbnail sketches of what may be regarded as trajectories—the route taken by a piece of research along its way to outcomes, impact, and influence. While all the projects inform the body of the report, only seven of them (projects A, B, E, I, J, K, and L) will feature as examples in this section.

A piece of research may have multiple outcomes, with multiple trajectories, and these are generally not linear. One may think of them along two dimensions:

- The first concerns degrees of immediacy and directness: some findings may have immediate relevance for application, while the most theoretical or methodologically oriented research may be regarded as simply taking a longer, more indirect route.

- The second dimension concerns degrees of "applicability". Research may simply serve to enhance understanding, with no specific relevance for behavioural or institutional change. And it must be remembered that the most useful, applicable, and user-friendly findings still present their recipients with problems of implementation. It would be fascinating to take these trajectories further, to track the researches beyond where the original researchers lose sight of them. But that is beyond the scope of this study.

While I have found it helpful to think in terms of trajectories, the concept also has limitations. It implies that the work/results/output start at the point where a grant is awarded. But the antecedents of a piece of research are also very important: researchers themselves are in a context and have a history, and this affects not only the work but their relations with users. Some researchers have pre-existing relationships with professionals who may be considered users, or with members of potential user organizations; some begin to set up such relationships when they know they are getting the grant. The research then has a ready audience or can become a collaborative effort from early stages, and there is virtually no detectable "handover" of results. Others do not consider such relationships until the work is done and may then be frustrated in their efforts to form them.

These are the kinds of categories that emerge in the sketches that follow. The sketches themselves clearly do not do justice to the richness and complexity of the material. They are selected to illustrate a variety of situations.

Project A

In this project, the route to an eventual end-user is indirect. The research (on ambivalence) has suggested modifications to theories and models of attitude and behaviour change; thus a concept has been enriched, rather than a "finding" produced. If, from a policy point of view, an end-user is considered to be the person trying to change his or her diet, an improved model may eventually, via a number of intermediate stages, lead to more appropriate pre-conditions being recognized and set up. Meanwhile there have been a number of other outcomes.

The conceptual advance has helped to explain data from a different study. It is influencing several other projects currently going on and will no doubt do so in the future. The effect of conceptual advance is pervasive, as ambivalence is relevant to many topics.

The project has demonstrated relevance for other social science disciplines. Economic psychology has an interest in motivation and behaviour change, and the conceptual developments have been presented at a conference that these researchers would not normally have attended. In turn, economic theories of choice have influenced the researcher. So links have been established with other social science disciplines (but not, apparently, within the programme).

But researchers don't only give out, they take in. Someone at a conference mentioned a statistical technique that suggested to the researcher a better way of comparing groups. This led to different ways of looking at regression coefficients, interaction effects, and multiple regressions. This then spread into other projects.

The main audience for this researcher's publications is the psychology community. If they are to see the work, it has to go into the prestigious international journals, and some parts of the output are aimed at these. Other parts will be aimed at the food and health-promotion literature. Papers have been and will be given at conferences. The researcher's colleague has been lecturing about the work in American universities. The researchers do not write for the popular press. The professional output has to happen first; until that is done, the project cannot be said to be complete.

The main long-term orientation is towards health promotion. There are links with the National Food Alliance, a confederation of different consumer groups.

Project B

There are four studies in this project: a methodological one, two of diet changes among populations under stress (students under examination stress, shop workers under occupational stress), and the fourth an eight-week food-diary study of two occupational groups.

The project is embedded in the context of a range of related researches, forming a broad programme on the relationship between stress and health. Some of these are more user-connected than others. There is research funded by the British Heart Foundation on work and cardiovascular disease risk; two pieces of research for the Medical Research Council, one on gender, occupation, and health risk, and one on health in family life relating to infectious diseases; work for Leverhulme on blood pressure and working people; work for the Arthritis Research Council; and work for the R&D Division of the Department of Health on lifestyle changes. Unlike the ESRC project, this one is action-oriented, involving a programme of behaviour counselling in groups, to modify diet and exercise behaviour.

All these pieces of research except the one for the Arthritis Research Council concern different aspects of the same area. It is quite difficult to know exactly which findings relate to which studies, and therefore what the specific dissemination products are from any particular study. So results from the ESRC research are, along with others, incorporated into the programme for the National Health Service on counselling for dietary change. This concerns the use of behaviour-oriented counselling in general practice for modifying diets and for exercise. A randomized controlled trial of twenty general practices is currently going on.

There was some direct feedback to the subjects of the studies, who are also a category of user. The students were given written feedback about other physiological factors as well as the dietary data. The store workers had individual verbal feedback and an offer to come back to a half-day workshop if they wished. Very few took this up, possibly losing interest because of the passage of time, or possibly because the session had to be outside working hours. In a few cases they were advised to seek help from GPs. The store's management, though they had some health-related policies in place, were not interested in getting feedback from the study. This could be because of lack of continuity in management: by the time the study was finished, key personnel in management had changed. The subjects of the diet diaries also received quite extensive feedback.

The work feeds into the researcher's teaching. Being within a medical school, there is quite a lot of interface with clinical groups who are not research scientists but may use the work in practice. The researcher also acts as a consultant to a food manufacturer, on the subject of their own research. The more junior researchers have moved on, one to a post in the closely related subject of eating disorders, and one to a post in social anthropology.

But these routes—to students, to the subjects of the research, and to clinical colleagues—are "spin-offs". The main findings are subtle and complex and are not susceptible to immediate or simple application. Publication so far has been in academic/professional journals, as the researcher is uneasy about premature writing for popular science— "The popular journalists and popular scientific journals are always interested in eating behaviour and stress anyway, so it's not difficult in that respect, but in fact I've been rather diverting people from that approach."

Project E

This research concentrates on the "why" of the topic at institutional level. The study examines the relationship between the national state and corporate food retailers, and how these relationships are translated at the local level between the local authority enforcement officers, whose job it is to ensure food safety, and individual retail outlets. The method was to track two pieces of legislation, the outcome of the Food Safety Act of 1990 and the Food Hygiene Directive of 1993. The analysis is at the level of policy implementation; the aim is to develop more generic models.

User engagement was built into the research design. There was an element of participative observation of local professionals (accompanying environmental health officers implementing food policy). Arranging this and getting agreement from their organizations itself involved engagement and a commitment to report back. Interviews with government officials led to expressions of interest and to regular contact "backwards and forwards".

The organization of the project was to allow output and dissemination from the end of the first year. So "from the word go [the project] was interactive with the policy community and the private and public sector." Research papers have been circulated to some key respondents in draft for discussion. There is then a need to go back at the end with findings, to close the circle. There are other implications for use—for instance, in training—but "there's a limit to what you can do".

For non-academic users, a series of "research briefing papers" is being produced, "a kind of user's guide to the results of research", and is being widely distributed to key groups of representatives, officials, and professionals in the food sector. Others will be produced that are aimed at particular target groups.

Project I

This project is concerned with the media treatment of "food scares": why some issues about the health and safety of food (salmonella, listeria, and BSE) receive publicity, whereas others (coronary heart disease) do not. It has three components, concerning the production of news, the content of news, and the public understanding of news. I only have detailed information about the third.

The aim was to study differences between different food panics and between those and coronary heart disease in terms of what the public understood from the media. Twenty-six focus groups were presented with sets of photographs from which to make a news story, and this was to lead to a discussion. The groups spontaneously took the method further and set themselves up as news teams. One output was the confidence of the subjects, who "suddenly became aware that they knew what they were talking about". When there was a new public announcement on BSE, half the focus groups were reconvened under a supplementary grant, to see how views had developed.

So the method was itself an output and has been tried in Germany and France. Beyond the boundary of the session, people "just wouldn't stop talking" and also projected expertise onto the researcher, who had to be careful to resist. When a new food panic arose recently, people who had taken part even years before phoned for advice, assuming that advice had been given, which it had not. So the method itself was very engaging.[2]

The researcher's growing expertise on how the media handle things means that she is consulted by a range of professionals when media-related questions arise for them, including other researchers in the programme. She has done media training for Unison and other trade unions, particularly with the aim of making women more confident in relation to the media. Her colleague has been consulted by an advertising agency, and their material has been requested by the Department of Health and MAFF (the Ministry of Agriculture, Fisheries and Food). Articles have been requested by newspapers and then shelved because other things happened. They have appeared at various times on Radio Scotland. The researcher has a page on the Internet and has attended many conferences and presentations. As well as this formal dissemination, there is informal help to a number of local "café-projects".

Project J

This is an experimental, problem-oriented programme designed to influence the food choices of children in the direction of fruit and vegetables, which they had previously been refusing. The method focuses on the individual child, combines peer modelling with rewards, and is carried out in the children's homes and administered by their parents. It has been very successful and has been replicated on a larger scale in schools after the ESRC project, mainly funded by Unilever Research.

Initial work in this area was already going on, funded by Unilever, before the ESRC programme. When the ESRC programme appeared, it seemed to fit in well with what had already begun, and Unilever continued to contribute to the funding. They had originally approached the researcher because of a broad interest in consumer psychology. An important feature of the relationship is that there has been continuity: the Unilever scientists have been alongside from the start ("the first faltering steps") and have seen the whole programme develop.

The researcher's theoretical interest, the mainstream research which is his "main love", is in the language development of children, and this has influenced his more problem-oriented work. The first study was in the area of dental care—trying to influence children to brush their teeth—and it was during this study that the present methodology was developed.

The contract with Unilever does not impose any restriction on publication. Indeed, the research team's "champions" within Unilever are actively encouraging them to publicize the work. They want the findings to be used by government and health-promotion agencies and are helping with relevant contacts—"Basically all we would like is to present our findings to . . . whoever's really concerned about the health of the nation."

"National Veg-Out Week" was an event where schools across Britain were encouraged to use fruit and vegetables, using a system drawing on this group's methods. The packaging of Bird's Eye vegetables was modified to fit in with this event. The objectives of health promotion and of the manufacturer are in this case congruent, and there is much advantage in working with a large manufacturer rather than, for example, health-promotion agencies. Influencing the market and the practices of a large company like Unilever has much more impact.

The researchers held back on publicity until they were confident about their methods and results and were ready to move on to the next stage, which would be a systematic study of a large region—say, all the schools of a major city. That would require extending methods to working with education authorities and government agencies, and training others to use the basic methods. Publicity is now substantial.

Feedback was given to the children's parents, who were also interviewed and are in some cases now also being interviewed by the media. Local health-promotion agencies in North Wales are picking up the findings, which provides a local base for further dissemination and development.

Project K

This project is studying decisions about meat purchase (both whether to purchase and how much) at the level of the household by statistical analysis of data from the Family Expenditure Survey and the National Food Survey. So the method is secondary analysis of data from large data sets. To establish how these decisions have changed over time, data sets over twenty years have been analysed. Work has also been done on the effect of BSE on these purchasing decisions through looking at media interest in the subject. The sample is a very specific one: households with single adult heads.

The researchers see their work as informing people about the functioning of the market and how people respond to various incentives. They have been working in the area of meat demand for some time. They send copies of their articles directly to officials in the Meat and Livestock Commission (MLC) and MAFF, and also to the Vegetarian Society. Some of their earlier work has been quoted by the chief economist of the MLC, which sees itself as a significant user. The officials here and in MAFF are regarded at the level of professional colleagues, and relationships with them have been built up over time. They often attend the same conferences.

The main contact in MAFF is very well qualified, was an academic himself, and had had primary responsibility for the National Food Survey—"technically he can cope with our stuff". In the MLC, the people were more concerned with a broader methodological approach. Since they are not in a competitive situation, they see price changes as less significant and less under their control and socioeconomic factors as more significant in helping them predict the market or direct their marketing. This is new for them, as it is to some extent for the researchers; researchers and users are to some extent moving into new areas together, or at least in parallel.

As well as publication they use the Internet, publishing their results in a "Food for Thought" discussion network. This led to enquiries from academics in other fields. A piece has also appeared in *MIDAS*, published by the Manchester Computing Service, which gets national distribution. There has been interest from other econometricians in the modelling aspects. It is an advanced method; the researchers did not invent it but are among the early users.

The long and well-established relationship with users gives rise to some anxiety. "User involvement is in part accountability . . . [but] . . . users have quite short-term issues they're interested in. MAFF and MLC have particular fires they're interested in fighting . . . sometimes it is good to step back from that and do more long-term things which present users may not be interested in at all". Over the long term, one becomes aware of the pressures that users are under, which can make them "very much geared to the flavour of the month".

Project L

This research is multidisciplinary, involving medicine (both clinical and public health, as well as human nutrition) and medical sociology. It set out to study the food habits of two different immigrant communities (first- and second-generation) in Glasgow to see if they related to their differing rates of coronary disease. Numerous papers have been given at conferences, in the United Kingdom and abroad. There are audiences—mainly from the social sciences—who are interested in migration, and audiences from a wider range of disciplines, including epidemiology and human nutrition, who are interested in the interplay of migration, diet, and heart disease. Otherwise, "it would be fair to say that this project is much more interesting to the run-of-the-mill medical sociologist than it is to the run-of-the-mill medical person. The run-of-the-mill medical person might like to see a catchy version in a one-page editorial but wouldn't like to read a paper." The researchers have developed considerable interest in and understanding of each other's disciplines.

Papers will be placed in the journals of practice professions, but the scientific results need to get into the academic journals first. One output is a very large database of detailed information about the social background, food choice, and nutritional intake of their subjects. This leads both to needing more opportunity to do analyses and, at the same time, to wanting to do more research on the subjects from the biomedical point of view. Another output is the development of methods for analysing diets. Yet another is the development of a skilled researcher, who has since then been doing a review for the Department of Health of the whole area of nutrition among all the main ethnic minorities in Britain. This was facilitated by the programme director. It will include recommendations about what future interventions should explore, what would make better-designed future interventions with ethnic minorities, and what should be future research priorities.

The findings will feed into work such as the intervention programme on heart disease which the Department of Health is funding at Newcastle. This includes service initiatives targeted at South Asians. Understanding the dynamics of migration helps to explain what is happening. But "findings" are not stand-alone entities susceptible to independent application. It is when they are integrated with other knowledge that they can affect, for example, the advice that doctors give their South Asian patients. Among other things, they will help this advice to be more differentiated.

There are potential applications in the training of doctors and in health-promotion and disease-prevention policy. These are not yet formulated; in the meantime the clinician in the team feels it has coloured his practice and made him understand better the issues behind what he encounters. It does not necessarily mean "Ah, I therefore have to tell him such-and-such or . . . do such-and-such . . .", but understanding the context of the patient is very important in making links that make advice or actions relevant. It has fed into his teaching, but there remains the problem of how to transfer understanding of this kind into the understanding of other doctors.

There also remains a sense of not enough time to make the most of the data that has been collected, and to synthesize and integrate what has been learned, turning it from project findings into knowledge—"the best stuff comes out later, and it comes out on someone else's money".

Factors that influence the pattern of user engagement

From these sketches, and from the other studies not summarized, one may derive some of the factors that influence user engagement. A number of them are linked.

- *The discipline and the type of data it produces.* In some disciplines, the data do not yield findings until aggregated; in some, an individual case study can be used to highlight an issue. Some findings are not directly applicable for a user but serve to unpick or differentiate a subject; their users are other researchers. Some are useable even in a tentative state, for others this is dangerous.

- *Time aspects.* This is linked to the previous point. Some types of finding are immediately useable; some need a long process of digestion, or to be combined with others, before their meaning becomes clear, or replication before one is confident.

- *The antecedents of the project.* Engagement is more likely where there are pre-existing institutional or personal links: with user professionals in nutrition and healthcare, with administrators in user organizations such as government departments, with researchers in user organizations. Two of the researchers also have consultancy arrangements with the research function in user organizations. One has pre-existing relationships with medical and health journalists.

- *The general orientation and values of the researcher.* In some projects the trajectory is towards further research and does not involve users. Conversely, in one project (E) an element of user engagement is built into the research design.

- *The nature of the research topic.* Two of the studies (C and K) are mainly concerned with secondary analysis of existing data. Nearly all the others, in various ways, study populations (of children, mothers, the newly married, people in particular locations, immigrants, older people, etc.) around a topic where some practices are seen to be "healthy" and others as "unhealthy". So in a more specific sense, the researchers have had to deal with the issue of their own detachment or commitment, and this in turn affects their attitude towards dissemination. One (F) used a finding to pinpoint a target group who are at a stage where they are establishing dietary routines, and it linked up with a supermarket to run health clubs for them.

- *The context of research careers.* Some researchers stay within a subject area, accumulating expertise, while others move on to other topics and have to leave the subject area behind.

- *The institutional context.* In G, there is a Centre with a well-established methodology for running short courses and workshops, to which workshops on a new topic can be added ("But it's finding the time!"). B and L are wholly or partly in medical schools, with access to the teaching and training of doctors. D and F also have teaching access to gatekeeper professionals. Teaching in general is a route to dissemination, but not all the researchers are teachers. Multidisciplinary work may include people from disciplines with which users can identify, and who can act as "ambassadors". The institutional context also includes other relevant research going on in the institution. It also includes the RAE.

Discussion

Transitional systems

It is often not possible to move directly from *a* to *b*: design attention needs to be paid to the vehicle for getting there. The concept of "transitional systems" derives from the work of D. W. Winnicott, who showed how toys and other forms of play help children to explore possible futures (Winnicott, 1971). In the utilization of knowledge, prototypes, pilots, workshops, and conferences may have this quality of facilitating transition, provided that certain conditions are met, including some incompleteness. Two of the researchers had, in fact, devised transitional systems in the form of "working papers" (H), or reports circulated in draft (E), which did not have the finality of findings being presented *and with which users could engage*. In case studies of social science utilization (Klein & Eason, 1991), transitional systems were found to be a key element, and there is much scope for their creative use. Publication is not the only possible vehicle.

The (first) Nation's Diet Conference[3]

It had to be explained to me that this should not be called the "Flora Conference", for that was how the researchers had referred to it. Variously described as "a fiasco", "lunatic", "a mess", criticisms of this event were so many and varied that it would be easy to write a piece of knocking copy. I have no wish to do this, and I understand the reasons for at least part of what happened. But there is a broader point to be made. Applied social science is not just about conveying specific findings from specific studies to specific users. It is about certain skills and methods and a general, more diffuse, understanding of the behaviour, development, and dynamics of individuals and institutions. In that framework, conference organization and design are applied social science and convey a message.

First, the term "Foundation" carries associations of Nuffield, Ford, Leverhulme. These foundations disburse funds in a way that is distanced from the products that generate the income, so that the recipient is not under pressure to promote cars or soap. There was a need to clarify or perhaps negotiate with the Flora Foundation exactly what the relationship between product promotion and the funding was to be, and then to convey this to the researchers. Instead, they had to interpret the relationship for themselves—"Not that someone thought Flora would tell people how to do their work, but how they would use or interpret the results." People did not know whether they were endorsing the company; some felt that if there was to be sponsorship, there should have been more than one sponsor. There is quite a lot of research sponsorship in the food industry, and it is a sensitive area.

Second, it was felt that the conference was premature—the wrong audience at the wrong time—and that the audience had been misled. Apparently two hundred people were invited before any papers had been agreed. Some who were asked to present were from Phase 2 of the programme and had barely started. "I don't think it's bad to present work in progress, but when I saw the letter that had gone out. . . . This impatience to have something to show for the programme to practitioner or applied audiences actually means that what they're getting isn't good enough, they're being sold short." This was thought to show a lack of confidence, and "if you're constantly being pushed to anticipate on a short timescale and with very little evidence, you can end up with egg on your face." On the other hand, people from Phase 1 who were ready and had findings and had agreed to present them were then not asked.

Third, people were not consulted. The subject was brought up in one of the programme workshops; some people were wary about it and were then told that the decision had been taken anyway. And they were not in the picture: "The letter had gone to the people who were invited, several months before I heard anything about it or heard that we were being asked to present, which actually made it clear that our project was going to be presenting." "So I said to this young woman, 'will you send me information'. 'Yes', she said, but she never did. I heard subsequently that it went ahead. . . . To this day I don't know who was invited and why. . . ."

The conference experience itself appears to have been difficult. I have no information on how the audience experienced it, except that one member telephoned one of the participants to "commiserate" and to complain about jargon.

The frame of reference

This issue already emerges in the discussion of the Nation's Diet Conference. From the beginning, I have felt a slight unease about the frame of reference for this problem area being defined as "engagement with users" rather than "use" or "application". It seemed churlish to quibble, because the framework is so nearly right. But the unease has not gone away, so I need to try to understand and explicate it:

"Engagement with users" focuses on entities defined as "research-ers" and "users", and on the relationship between these parties rather than on the value or utility of the research and what needs to happen to it. Focusing on the relationship between the parties can lead to ignor-ing the point of the exercise, the research and its utility, whereas the converse is not true: focusing on the research and what to do with/ about it does not lead to ignoring the relationship between the parties, it encompasses it.

That may sound like a small difference, but it has important conse-quences. This is illustrated by the workshop on researchers and users convened by the ESRC and reported on by Dr Elizabeth Shove (1997). A range of researchers was invited to unpack the issue of their relation-ships with users. After many interesting accounts and stories of such relationships, they conclude that "user" should not be interpreted just as individual users or persons, and they express the professional di-lemma as: "How far should researchers get into all this?" and "Where does the job end?"

Thus the framework has constrained the discussion to the roles of the parties, and it continues to do so even when one of the parties apparently turns out to be mythical, for the overall conclusion from the workshop is a paradox: "In some ways the most striking feature of the workshop was that we were able to spend a whole day talking about the qualities and characteristics of users *while at the same time acknowl-edging that the 'user' is a mythical beast.* As we agreed . . . utility is a function of context. It therefore makes as little sense to talk of users as a category of people, as if they shared some fixed 'user' attribute, as it does to say, in some absolute way, that research is or is not relevant. *Yet still we talked of users.* . . . To get much further we would need to develop a more sophisticated vocabulary which captured the range of relationships involved and so got us out of the trap of unwittingly contributing to the fictional construction of personified users . . . " [my emphasis].

There is great integrity in an account that sets out the dilemma so honestly. It is, however, not a more sophisticated vocabulary that is needed, but a change in frame of reference. Short of that, some strange connotations can be given to the term "user". In the effort to make the concept fit the need, language gets distorted. I have heard the term "user" taken to mean anyone who is not a social scientist, anyone who is "them" rather than "us".

In this report, I have deliberately avoided the quagmire of trying to define "users". The question to which the "engagement with users" framework leads in the present study is who wants/needs/should *read* these findings, not how do you use, what do you do with, these researches. So, for example: one of the respondents was discussing forms of publication and different audiences. He has an interesting finding about the key role played by school dinner-ladies in influencing the food choices of schoolchildren. The implication seemed so obvious that I suggested: "So are you holding workshops for dinner-ladies?"—and the idea came as a complete novelty. That was the second time I fell out of role.

The question is one that I have discussed elsewhere: that of internalizing a finding and turning it to use (Klein & Eason, 1991, chap. 2). This is a different process from conveying it to someone else. Also, knowledge diffusion is not a question of simply presenting the results to the right people. In turn, it is set within and influenced by the context of research careers, the various stakeholders, and so forth.

Thus it would have been wrong to ignore the slight niggling unease, because the difference between the two frameworks really turns out to be important: "engagement with users" traps people (see above) and prevents them from being able to give attention to other ways of looking at utilization. The converse is not the case: "utilization" by no means precludes paying attention to the relationship with users, which, of course, remains important.

And finally . . .

For some people, engagement with users was a new experience, the first impact of which was about the resources it requires. Those for whom it was not new were discovering a whole new set of issues that it brings: users are not neutral recipients of "science" but are themselves under changing pressures about which they may want only short-term help. They have views of their own about scientific methods. A relationship with a user organization requires continuity of its personnel. And so on. User engagement means you can't get away with things; it makes stringent demands on professional competence and confidence and requires new kinds of skill. As one respondent, shaken by the experience of the Nation's Diet Conference, put it, "There has to be a mechanism for getting lots of social scientists to think about that." If user engagement is to be handled seriously and professionally, it needs to be undertaken with the relevant knowledge, understanding, skills, professional support systems, and infrastructure.

Notes

1. The Research Assessment Exercise is a process by which the Higher Education Funding Council (HEFC) assesses the quality of research in every department of every British university. Members of staff submit their research grants, details of research students, and their four best publications in the previous five-year period, and departments present their research achievements and plans. These are assessed by subject panels (e.g., psychology, management, chemistry, etc.), and each department is given a rating. Based on this, research support funds are awarded to departments for the five years following the exercise. This could mean up to £30,000 a year per member of staff, and with this core funding such departments can limit the number of students they teach.

2. The method triggered associations with the work that Kurt Lewin did on food choice in the United States during the Second World War; so I fell out of role and supplied some references (Lewin, 1942, 1943). It is interesting that none of the researchers referred to Lewin's work in their project applications.

3. The programme was funded in two phases. As studies in the first phase were nearing completion, the ESRC had organized a conference intended to present findings from the researches to users. Some funding towards this conference had been obtained from the Flora Foundation, whose logo was apparently prominent in the conference hall; all the researchers who mentioned it referred to it as the "Flora Conference". I actually thought that was its title and used the title in the first draft of this report A second "Nation's Diet" conference was held later and was better received.

CONCEPTS,
REFLECTIONS, METHODS

The papers in this section begin to put the experiences of the earlier papers together into a more coherent theoretical frame- work, to combine the use of knowledge and the dynamics of action for the utilization of social science. The first three are cumulative, moving from the learning to be gained from the Esso experience to the learning from the wider range of experiences in the case studies collected in Putting Social Science to Work (Klein & Eason, 1991). *The fourth adds an explicit component from a psychodynamic perspective for action and application.*

CHAPTER 11

On the utilization and diffusion of social science

This paper was produced about 1980, but I cannot trace for what occasion it was produced! It brings together much of the material from the discussion in *A Social Scientist in Industry* (Klein, 1976) at a more general level, without the Esso-specific illustrations. In part, it was a response to the issues discussed in chapter 8. Although the paper in some places refers to "industry", the discussion and the models have been broadened out to apply to other kinds of organization.

The dynamics of utilization

A few years ago there could be detected a growing excitement among social scientists, who were beginning to feel increasingly confident that there really were substantial contributions to be obtained from the social sciences in tackling, and even sometimes solving, social problems. At the same time industry, in particular, began to show an interest in using this contribution. Social scientists were invited, in various roles and with various kinds of assignment, to see what they could do, and there have undoubtedly been a number of successful episodes.

Why, then, is there a vague, intangible sense of disappointment, among both social scientists and their industrial clients? Were expectations unreal? Was excitement the only criterion of success? Was there not enough practitioner training for social scientists?

A reason could be found in the nature of the models that were in use, concerning the utilization of social science, and their applicability in a new situation. I want to look, therefore, at theories of diffusion and utilization in the light of the experience of the last few years. Two kinds of model of diffusion were available to social scientists: the healing or helping model, derived from the practice of medicine and psychiatry, and models of the diffusion of scientific knowledge, which have been developed in a number of studies, particularly studies of the diffusion of agricultural innovation.

In the medical and psychiatric worlds, a contract is postulated between doctor and patient in which help, treatment, or advice are exchanged for payment—direct or indirect—so that both parties gain from the transaction. Menninger (1958) summarized the doctor–patient relationship pictorially, as shown in Figure 4. Where the relationship is between patient and psychiatrist, the kind of help given is different and may extend to other relationships of the patient. The patient's contribution still consists, on the one hand, of co-operation and information about his or her problems and, on the other, of payment for the service and skills he or she is receiving (Figure 5). Where the relationship is between a patient and psychoanalyst, the contribution of the patient is more active and that of the analyst less active than in the other two instances (Figure 6).

Obviously, there are assumptions in these models about "sickness" and "health" which are not necessarily appropriate to the situation that

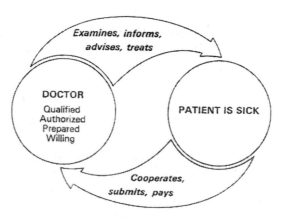

FIGURE 4.   The doctor–patient relationship (Menninger, 1958).

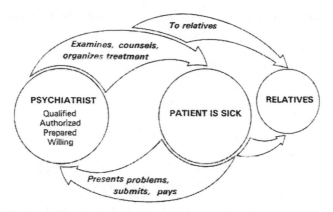

ΓIGURE 5.   The psychiatrist–patient relationship (Menninger, 1958).

we are considering—that of the utilization of social science in an organizational situation. What constitutes "health" is much less clear with regard to an organization than with regard to an individual; many contributions can be made there that have nothing to do with "ill health" and "therapy" but, rather, with goodness-of-fit and with development and design.

The other kind of transaction that has therefore been thought relevant is that of the diffusion and utilization of knowledge. Here, too, there are a number of models in the literature. Most of them have in common the notion that there is an action system and a resource system, and that what needs to be understood, or, according to the

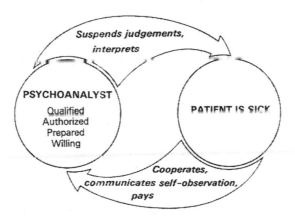

FIGURE 6.   The psychoanalyst–patient relationship (Menninger, 1958).

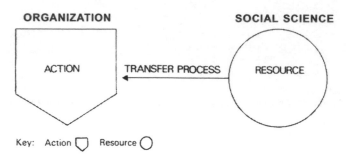

FIGURE 7.   Movement of resources—basic model.

writer's particular orientation, enhanced and developed, is the process of conveying the one to the other (see, e.g., Cherns, 1968; Havelock, 1969; Lazarsfeld, Sewall, & Wilenesky, 1968).

Thus where an organization is the action system and social science the resource system, the general model would look as in Figure 7. Many of the models are much more sophisticated than I have suggested here, but they almost invariably assume that resource is conveyed—somehow—from a resource system to a user system, and that what is conveyed in the other direction is information about needs and feedback about the usefulness of solutions.

There are some aspects of the reality that are not accounted for in any of these models:

1.   First, an organization already contains resources for coping with its own problems, including those that are the subject matter of social science. Every individual in it has some knowledge and experience. Some of organizations' resources for coping with their problems have become institutionalized—for instance, in management service departments. The trade unions and the personnel management function can be seen as institutionalized resources for coping with some of the human problems of industry. A first modification of the model should therefore be as represented in Figure 8.

Put in such a summary way, this may sound obvious and simplistic, but it has important consequences for the dynamics of utilization:

(a) Help may be a threat to the regard of individuals for their own resources, and the preservation of autonomy and the integrity of the resources they already have may be more important to them than the help that is being offered. That is the explanation of "resistance".

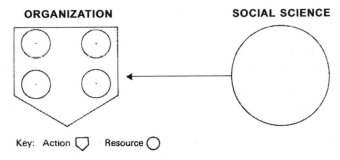

FIGURE 8.   Movement of resources—first modified model.

(b) New kinds of help may be a threat to existing kinds of help and may create difficulties for those who are already in helping roles.

2.   Second, social science is not merely a resource; it has needs of its own. Among other things, social science institutions need money, they need field sites, they need social recognition, and they need autonomy. Individuals within social science, in turn, have needs for security, for training, for career development, for recognition, for opportunities to work, for autonomy.

Thus social science is not merely a resource system; it is also an action system in a different frame of reference, and there are resources going in the other direction, as depicted in Figure 9.

This, too, has consequences for the dynamics of utilization:

(a) In the relations of social scientists with their clients. The financial needs of institutions and individuals in social science are recognized and have become part of the contract with clients. Although they haggle, they haggle openly. Their other needs, however, have

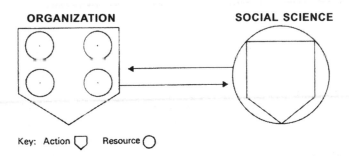

FIGURE 9.   Movement of resources—second modified model.

not become part of the contract. Social scientists don't generally ask their clients for help. Their needs may become repressed and emerge as disguised bids for power or other kinds of exploitation.

(b) In the relations of social scientists with each other. When they are in an action role, social scientists are competing in a market:

- Theoretically: a problem may be researched from a dozen different frames of reference, and each will shed some light on it. But when it comes to giving advice, one direction has to be arrived at, and different solutions compete for acceptance.

- Territorially: once they have invested in a direction of career or work, social scientists or their institutions cannot change that direction after every assignment. They have to find other assignments, and work loads have to be evened out. It turns out, therefore, that the problems of visibility and possibly even of advertising and selling have to be faced with regard to social science as they do with regard to products and services; as the numbers of social scientists have increased, the problem of competition with colleagues has to be added to the list. It is a most difficult confrontation for a professional. There are currently no means of codifying or regulating it, with the result that some people withdraw from the scene from shyness or distaste, while others may become more commercial or business-like than the business firms who are their clients. In either case, the level of business skill is something quite distinct from the level of social science skill. This is not allowed for in the medical and psychoanalytic models, which assume that one waits for clients to come.

Behaviour in this area will at least in part depend on the long-term or short-term nature of financial support. This also leads to complex political relationships between those who have long-term support and those who do not.

A model that does not carry the implication of "haves" and "havenots" is one in which "applicable social science" is regarded as a product, with some institutions collaborating in its generation and support (e.g., work organizations, universities, independent research organizations, etc.) These institutions are then collaborators in research and development rather than consultants and clients. The question of who has needs and who has resources, with its political implications, then only arises when they want to pass the results of their work on to another generation or to other institutions, who become the users.

Having suggested a way of looking at these transactions, a great deal more can now be said about the characteristics of user systems and resource systems, as these affect the dynamics of social science utilization.

User systems

There is a kind of logical sequence in which industrial activities and their attendant problems develop. First, there is a scanning of the environment to see what needs doing or what available knowledge suggests might be done. This is the exploration of markets and resources. Next comes the question of how to do it. This is the stage where the primary task is most clear-cut and interest focuses on the engineering, the medical techniques, and so on. Then comes the question of how to do it in such a way that one can go on doing it. Emphasis shifts from how to build a motor car that works to how to build it economically; from how to prevent polio to how to ensure the availability of vaccine and trained staff. In other words, criteria based on values begin to operate in a more explicit way to determine what happens. The first explicit criteria that emerge in this way have generally been welfare criteria in social administration, and economic criteria in industry, where engineering has been closely followed by scientific management methods and where cost consciousness is an intrinsic part of engineering training. As these first criteria are met, however, it is generally discovered that there are unanticipated consequences in other directions; other criteria turn out to have been neglected and become important. Industry has to come to terms with various kinds of social implications; welfare agencies have to cope with the economics of welfare.

The cycle does not, of course, take place in this kind of simple order or clear time sequence. For one thing, each problem-solving activity itself goes through the cycle of examining needs, developing methods, and seeking to meet economic and other criteria. More importantly, the time sequence has become shortened. Nowadays, when a new need or market is being explored, even the earliest considerations are likely to include at least such things as distribution problems, or the availability of the appropriate skills, or the reactions of organized labour. Very gradually, too, the secondary criteria (economic considerations in welfare, social considerations in industry) are entering into the discussion, not merely as necessary evils but as accepted parts of the institutional value system.

As each problem or generation of problems is recognized, so ways of responding to it have evolved, some in quite early stages, some later. Problems of lag and conflict therefore develop between different generations of solutions. Long before the methods of social science were explicitly turned towards industry, industry had some responses to its human and social problems. These lay not only in the personal knowledge and experience of individuals, but had become institutionalized. The activities of trade unions and personnel management contain not only the elements of caring and concern, but also those of systematizing various methods of dealing with problems, even if it is only a supervisor disciplining himself to ask why people are late before bawling them out.

Any kind of helping agency becomes attached to its own methods of problem-solving (and therefore also perhaps—dare one say it—to the continuing existence of the problems it knows how to handle?). Within social science, too, there is a process that has been called the hardening of the categories. Probably the biggest current difficulty therefore lies in relating the various resources to each other. Frequently it lies in relating social science and personnel management. It would be important to find out more about this, and to find out what happens in organizations when Operational Research succeeds Work Study, and Corporate Planning succeeds Operational Research.

More concretely, individual industrial organizations also go through different phases of organization, in which different needs predominate; some of us in the social sciences may have assumed too readily and on the basis of limited research what these needs are.

I have suggested elsewhere (see chapter 2) that industrial management involves three distinct phases of activity:

(a) the setting up of a workable system, for production or service;

(b) maintaining the system by planning the work, co-ordinating the materials and services needed, keeping quality and costs within acceptable limits, and so on;

(c) improving the performance of the system and improving the system itself.

In many organizations all three phases will, of course, be going on concurrently. But firms in different technical and market conditions use the energies and skills of their staff to different degrees in different parts of this schema. Insofar as organizations engage with social science, the kind of social science that is relevant for them, or appeals to them, quite possibly also varies according to where they are in this schema.

(a) Organizations in the first developmental stages rarely make much use of social science. In the developmental stages of an organization, during the phase of creativity, building, and shared difficulties jointly overcome, the more obvious problems of morale and alienation among staff tend to be least acute. And yet it is during this phase that much of the knowledge would be most relevant, since it is at this stage that the seeds of future problems are frequently sown into the design of organizations, roles, and equipment. Attempts of this kind are likely to be realistic—that is, there is a good chance that the latent functions of such social science activities are not too different from their manifest function.

(b) The second phase, of coping with an on-going situation, is probably most characteristic of the state of many organizational situations in the recent past.

It is in these phases of organization that much of the social science research has been done, much of the knowledge built up, and many of the social scientists' expectations about what constitutes organizational problems developed. Problems of the division of labour, of payment systems, of role and task definition, of conflicting demands made on middle management from above and below, of relations between departments and functions, of reconciling the demands of quantity, quality, and cost; conflicts of interest, centralization versus decentralization, technical change, integrating new methods with existing methods, fluctuating conditions in the product market, the money market, and the labour market, the effects of control systems—this is the stuff of organizational problems that one learns about in research. Sometimes organizations with these problems ask for help from social science. Often it is when the problems have become intractable.

Here, too, there is likely to be a high degree of realism. The main difficulty arises from the fact that engaging with social science itself takes time, thought, and energy. Cherns (1968) postulates a "crisis theory" of social science utilization. In my own experience, it is not in times of crisis that people make most use of social science. Crisis may be the time when they need or even want it most, but it is not the time when they have the spare capacity needed to engage with it. What does seem to work is having a relationship that is developed during a time of non-crisis and is there, ready to be drawn on, if a crisis later develops.

(c) However, there is another trend. Many of the organizations that have engaged with social science appear to be in the third phase, where the attention of managers is less involved in coping with problems on a day-to-day basis and more in looking for improvements in the long term. The mere fact that social science exists in the environment will then mean that it is considered. Many factors, including fashion, will play a part in the process. Sometimes, also, it is not so much a matter of looking for improvements as looking for new stimuli.

In that case, social science may be engaged in answer to the question "What shall we do next?" which is very different from the question "How shall we deal with this problem?" and it is a different kind of social science that meets the case. Designing a situation so as to prevent problems, for instance (and it is the dearest wish of many social scientists to be allowed access to situations at the design stage), conflicts directly with the exhilaration to be gained from overcoming a problem or from gaining a new insight. Cultural norms, however, make it difficult to admit that one likes to have some problems, and this may lead to a lack of reality appearing in descriptions of what is going on.

At this stage, also, when the situation is not dominated by acute problems, other latent needs may emerge. It is an old truth that travelling hopefully is better than arriving. Starting projects is more interesting than reaping their results on a long-term basis, and it is likely that a proportion of projects have this kind of stimulus as their main function. In a culture that values innovation and change, the excitement of innovation and the utility of its outcome may become separated. Cultural norms, or perhaps the Protestant ethic, again do not permit stimulus and emotional excitement to be the expressed aim of activities for which organizations pay. Here, too, there is therefore the danger of lack of realism entering into the situation.

Thus the needs that organizations express and to which social science may provide a response vary with some organizational characteristics, and in some circumstances the difference between manifest and latent needs will be greater than in others. Social scientists whose expectations develop in relation to one set of circumstances may not respond in the way that meets their clients' wishes in a different set; if they do realize what is happening, they may need to re-think in a very basic way the role they want to play. There is a social scientist who says explicitly "my aim is to bring poetry into the organization". It is no bad aim, but it is different from using the findings of social science to help with organizational problems.

The gatekeepers

However, the characteristics of organizations in an aggregate or socio-logical sense must not be confused with the characteristics of individuals within them. Social science is not engaged by "industry" or by organizations, but by individuals in gatekeeping or sponsorship or client roles. The outcome, therefore, is also mediated through the needs, resources, and roles of such individuals.

People in organizations have a need for autonomy. In relation to social science, this essentially means that not only organizations but the individuals within them have resources of their own and are not merely users of resources. An important resource is an individual's accumulated experience of living and working. People may genuinely believe themselves to want additional resources, but they may in fact have a greater need to preserve the integrity and standing of what they already have.

Part of individuals' resources in relation to social science is now also very often their earlier contacts with it. Any previous experience they have of social science will colour their views and expectations and will need to be explored.

Second, it is an obvious characteristic of both sponsors and clients of social science in organizations that relating to social science is not the only goal they have. Career goals often mean that people move around. The medical and psychoanalytic models postulate some conti-nuity in the relationship between consultant and client. Where indi-viduals are getting help with their role problems, they can continue to relate to the same consultant when they move. But the problems of a function or department have to be left behind, and this discontinuity between incumbents and problems affects the kind of help that can be used. There is also frequently discontinuity in the role of sponsor, which substantially influences the political context of social science.

Third, obvious and simplistic as it will again sound, people cannot use or introduce resources they don't know about. This immediately confronts social scientists with the problem of visibility and information flow. It is one aspect of the business relationship mentioned earlier. The absolute—and for many professionals the preferred—position is not to take any propaganda or sales initiative unless invited. The fact is, however, that there are clients who need and want help and who have no means of finding out what help is available or how to get it. Medical or psychiatric consultants do not tout for business, but general practitioners have some systematic knowledge about the specialisms and know where to refer patients. The knowledge of people in gatekeeping roles in organizations is generally not so systematic. There is a real need for systematic but non-coercive means of making information available.

Where people bring in consultants explicitly for their own departments, they are both sponsor and client. Frequently, however, these two roles are carried by different people. In that case, the consultant must, in some sense, be seen as an extension of the sponsor. Where there is a political problem between sponsor and client—for instance, between a training department and line management—the consultant brought in by the training department becomes part of the problem. He or she may be brought in to do something to the client that the sponsor cannot do himself; in turn, he or she may be rejected by the client as a way of rejecting the sponsor.

A consultant who remains based outside the organization can confront the organization with issues of this kind more easily than one who has joined it. Even where there is no political problem, there is a political relationship. A consultant introduced by person A is an extension of A and not of person B. No matter what his or her qualities, B is not likely to relate to him/her in the same way as A does, and B may wish to introduce his or her own consultant. The need for autonomy includes autonomy in the search for help, and the wish to innovate includes innovation in the kind of resources that are sought.

People who act as sponsors of social science may have strong wishes to change some situation or person, frequently rooted in what to them is idealism. A common stereotype is that social science is brought in by someone who wants "to make the workers more cooperative". Experience seems to show more frequently, however, that it is brought in "to make my colleagues more participative". This, too, will of course affect the kind of social science that is brought in.

People in organizations need to make sense of their environment. Sometimes this leads to a search for knowledge and understanding, sometimes it leads to the search for a formula that will reduce uncertainty and complexity. There are many examples of ideas or techniques currently being propagated in this way, because they offer to reduce complexity. Sometimes this is not necessarily the intention of the originator of the idea—people who knew Douglas McGregor say that he would be far from happy about the way in which his concepts of "theory X" and "theory Y" are sometimes used (McGregor, 1960).

Sometimes the ideas or techniques are valuable in themselves but are extended to encompass over-confident promises of salvation or claims to comprehensiveness. When an idea or method has this function for its proponents of reducing complexity, they are likely to carry it with them from the situation in which it was developed, and to which it may have been appropriate, to others. The idea then becomes an ideology.

People in organizations need to feel worthy. Everyone needs, to some extent, to relate his or her own activities to the values of the society around him or her. There are questions, however, about whether an organization as such needs to be normative—that is, whether it needs to go beyond its legal obligations and set some kind of pace and, if so, in what directions and according to whose opinions. There are also questions about whether all roles in an organization carry its concern for human and social values, or the top policy-making roles, or whether some staff roles (e.g., a human resources or a public relations department) are designed to carry them. Sometimes human resources management is perceived in this way. On the other hand, some human resources managers are positively anxious to avoid the label of do-gooding and, instead, to do "hardnosed" things unrelated to welfare.

The dilemma is rather similar in relation to social science. Both in the client and the social science communities there is confusion about the normative function of social science. Social attitudes about the responsibilities of industry have in some instances outstripped legislation or have extended into areas where legislation is not appropriate, and some people look to social science to fill the gap and tell them what is right. They ask from social science guidelines to social values, sometimes down to very simple instructions in common courtesy, which are to be bought in some management-training packages and are labelled "behavioural science". People who do not feel that they need such teaching understandably resent it.

Social scientists vary in their readiness to fulfil this normative role. Many try to avoid it. They want to make clients aware of what they are doing, and of whether it meets their own values, presenting them with alternatives for choice rather than telling them what choices to make. Such refusal may be resented, too. There is simultaneously a wish for exhortation and guidance, and resentment of exhortation and guidance.

For social scientists themselves, the mere fact that they are dealing in human systems means that they cannot operate in a normative vacuum. How they handle this varies greatly, and the fact that they do not all handle it in the same way is one aspect of the great ambiguity that social science presents. The other is the large range of ideas, methods, and kinds of knowledge that are often not given a specific name but are put together under the huge and vague label "social science". This vagueness, combined with the central importance of the subject matter, means that hopes of many kinds get projected on to social science: hope for certainty, for simple answers, for life to become easier, for values to become firmly established. These, too, will affect what kind of social science is brought in. The most difficult task for users is to keep their balance between exaggerated hope and unreasoning rejection.

Social science as a resource

We now come to the characteristics of social science as a resource system, its institutions, its content, and its practitioners. In case sight is lost of the fact, there really are substantial resources: what the human and social sciences have to offer are, first, concepts and ideas that may lead to looking at familiar things in a different way; second, there are research methods; third, there are some empirical research findings; and fourth, there are research and consultancy skills.

Knowledge and institutions of knowledge

In the course of research, ideas and knowledge tend to be developed not separately but in linked sets of items. This is our first manifestation of the fact that resource systems are also action systems in a different frame of reference and have their own needs: there is a need to put some limits on the infinite complexity of knowledge and ideas—hence the grouping of ideas, and the development of research traditions and academic disciplines, and schools of thought within them.

If part of the development of an academic discipline itself arose from a felt need, the discipline may provide an adequate description: problems of learning may be described fairly comprehensively in terms of psychology, though other disciplines may contribute to explaining their origins. On the other hand, needs are not necessarily experienced in the terms of academic disciplines: industrial disputes cannot be described comprehensively in the terms of either individual or social psychology, or sociology, or economics, or anthropology. Each will have its own description, each description adds to an understanding of the situation. At this level of description, it is merely confusing to attempt multidisciplinary work.

If a complex situation (e.g., a shareholders' meeting) has been habitually described in the framework of a particular discipline (e.g., law) it may be very illuminating merely to have a different description (e.g., from anthropology). This general principle applies over a wide range of possibilities: it would be interesting to have an economist's description of a T-group session, a social psychologist's description of the stock exchange, a sociologist's description of a selection process. There may also be competing sets of ideas, or schools, leading to competing descriptions within the disciplines.

However, the interest of situations such as organizational problems, both intellectually and in their social relevance, and their consequent intensive study, has led in recent years to the emergence of a number of research workers and schools that are field-oriented rather than discipline-oriented. At professional meetings of sociologists, organizational sociologists will find people who turn the particular kind of spectacles that are the frame of reference of sociology onto a variety of fields—education, politics, religion, and so on—and may find that they have lost contact with this way of operating. The intensive study of the problems of organization will have led them to draw on the concepts and frames of reference of other disciplines, and they find that this has also happened to people whose original academic roots were in anthropology, psychology, and the like. There is a new hybrid of single-field multidiscipline research worker. This leads to questions of professional identity, which may be raised at one level when such research workers submit their theses to their home universities for examination, and at another level when the functions of new university departments (e.g. "Behaviour in Organizations") are being defined.

More recently still, there can be discerned something of a feeding-back at a more general level into new quasi-disciplines. The kind of knowledge produced by the single-field, multidiscipline workers (e.g., organization theory), is being taken back to be tested in a wider range of fields, such as church organization or medical organization.

There is, therefore, a trade-off between breadth and openness on the one hand and the power of illumination provided by descriptions from a particular discipline on the other. To revert to the earlier example, the most powerful description of a shareholders' meeting in terms of anthropology is likely to come from an ivory-tower professor whose only fieldwork has been with primitive tribes and who has no knowledge or experience of shareholders' meetings. The more he or she is aware of economic or historical or other factors at play, the more the observations in his or her own frame of reference will be weakened.

While all contribute to the sum of knowledge, these different descriptions, and disciplines, also compete with each other for limited resources of attention, prestige, and finance.

Thus we have reached the second manifestation of the needs of the resource system: the development of ideas has led to the development of a variety of institutions. The moment these exist, they have needs to do with continuing to exist: they need money, they need some security and development for staff, they need recognition, and they need autonomy to continue developing ideas.

Aspects of knowledge

One important characteristic of the social sciences is that they deal with two kinds of knowledge: that which comes from "inside" and that which comes from "outside" the learner. "External" knowledge can be demonstrated and therefore passed on; knowledge that derives from personal experience cannot be passed on; in order to acquire it, others have to enter into the same experience.

Most phenomena involving people can be investigated in either way. One can observe management or shop-steward behaviour, or one can become a manager or shop steward and find out how it feels. If the purpose of the enquiry is in-depth understanding, then some degree of sharing the experience or empathizing with it is important. If the purpose is to make comparisons and see if there are consistencies and patterns, then the researcher cannot go through the experience repeatedly, and some external manifestation has to be found that can be used as an indicator. Intelligence is something internal that has external manifestations, and we have devised ways of eliciting these and arranging them so that they can be observed and compared. Grief is something internal that we have not treated in the same way. There seems to be reasonable agreement among researchers about which kind of enquiry is best treated in which mode, and many investigations contain elements of both.

What has become more controversial, among both social scientists and their clients, is which kind of feedback or learning experience is more valuable at the receiving end. Do you learn "better" or "more" by some intellectual input such as reading a book or getting the results of a study, or by some form of experiential learning? Opinions about this often carry over onto the material that is being learned, so that those who value only one kind of learning tend to think that only one kind of knowledge is worth having. It is as incomplete to say that peoples' feelings in a situation are not part of the "real" data as it is to say that feelings and experience are the only worthwhile or relevant data, and that every generation must experientially rediscover the wheel. Where the emphasis is put is often a matter of belief or ideology, rather than of appropriateness to the needs of the occasion.

The strategy of feedback is, of course, different in the two cases. One has to do with evidence and demonstration, and the other with sensitizing the learner to experience. What is certain is that at least something of both elements needs to be present. The most formal proof and the coldest statistics will not register without the "click" of understanding that says, "Ah, yes—that figures". Conversely, the most intuitive apprehension about one's internal dynamics, with or without the intervention of an outsider, must have something to do with evidence. Not, "you reject uncomfortable information; I, your consultant, say so", but "this or that in your behaviour suggests that . . .".

Thus one aspect of social science knowledge is the "internal" or "external" nature of the way it is learned. Another is the whole area of "fact" and "interpretation". In one sense, it is a question of consensus. Things about which there is agreement are generally regarded as facts, sometimes for generations without being tested, and the higher the consensus the "harder" and more incontrovertible the fact.

In another sense, it is a question of frame of reference. Social scientists may feed back to the client data perceived in the same frame of reference as the client's: "x people left the organization last year." This is fact-finding. They may collect the data in the same frame of reference but arrange it in distinctive ways: "Turnover rates among young people are increasing, turnover rates among older people are not." This organizing of the data is beginning to impose a frame of reference.

They may take this further by processing the data through some framework that produces not only facts but meanings: "Turnover is a form of withdrawal and expresses something about the organization."

Sometimes merely freeing data from a habitual frame of reference is enough to shed new light on it. In a small group, the consultant may feed back facts that are easily accessible, such as the number of times someone has tried to intervene and been prevented. Merely freeing these facts from the habitual frame of reference of the client ("Mr X is a nuisance") may allow new aspects to be seen ("Mr X might have a contribution we are missing"). Or the consultant may go further and interpret them to produce meanings that are less accessible ("We have been afraid to have our agreement and cohesion challenged").

It is the same in the larger organization. Hard, statistical facts about how people spend their time, freed from a habitual frame of reference, may allow roles to be seen with a new kind of reality or interpreted in a new way. Or the facts may be processed through a more dominant frame of reference, leading to a greater degree of interpretation.

The practitioners

Just as organizational needs are mediated through individuals in gatekeeping roles who will influence what happens, so the same is true of social science. It is not social science that is utilized but the knowledge and skills of its practitioners. While it is possible to define fairly precisely what is an attitude scale, or an unstructured interview, or a psychoanalytic interpretation, or a controlled experiment, or participant observation, it is not possible to define what is a social scientist. All of them have a different mix of the skills and the available knowledge. One result is that the work has become rather personalized. The individuals concerned may do a greater variety of things than is generally attributed to them and may dislike being thus categorized. However, so little of the knowledge is codified that the resource is transmitted not only via this mix of knowledge and skills in the broadbrush sense, but also via personal style.

One result is that sophistication in social science is very much a matter of knowing who does what. Another result is that the practitioner has to make a painful choice between being versatile and anonymous or specialized and identifiable. This issue is less of a problem in research, where the output is published and generally available; but it is a serious problem in application, where the output is only available to the immediate client.

Another result is that the new or potential client has no way of knowing what to expect or, indeed, what to come to a social scientist for. The irrationality that is at work in many situations where social scientists are engaged, sometimes on very slight whims, is therefore supported by the real situation in which being rational and systematic about it is very difficult.

The situation presents another kind of problem for the user: the more versatile the social scientist, the more diffuse is the threat he or she presents. Any individual who had really mastered all the potential there is in social science, or even a large part of it, would be a very great threat indeed. The only imaginable position for such an individual in an organization would be that of owning it, or owning its owners! The more diffuse the social science, the greater the fears that one might be taken over. (However, the diffuseness of social science, while creating difficulties for clients, also has its uses: if you want to reject a social scientist, you can always point to some skills he or she does not have, for there will always be some. If he is not "talking jargon", he is "only talking common sense".)

The way to cope with this is either to limit the potential value that can be obtained in order to ensure that one is at least getting some, and engage social scientists in a limited capacity for limited and defined purposes; or to reduce the threat by using those who are based outside the organization; or to give the relationship the opportunity to develop on a long-term basis, so that the reality of the threat can be tested. If one finds that one has not, in fact, been taken over, one can then extend or change the area of subject matter and take further risks.

All this presupposes, however, a body of highly versatile and experienced professional practitioners, about whose training there is some consensus. In fact, there is in Britain almost no recognized training route by which people arrive at action research, or other forms of applied work in the social sciences. It is one of the main obstacles to utilization. It means that there are no recognizable people available to whom organizations can turn when they develop an interest. The gaps are filled in a number of ways, some of them a little bizarre, and this is not merely a matter of professional qualifications. The professional qualifications themselves are varied and ambiguous. The product of a first, or even a second, degree in social science is by no means prepared for practice.

In medicine, general-practitioner training is academically respectable; in social science, it is not. University social science departments are ambivalent about whether social science should be useful, and the training that they provide for practice professions is limited to social workers and personnel managers. Young people entering organizations with academic qualifications in social science have great difficulty in knowing how to operate. If they go into personnel departments, they are unsure how they differ from personnel managers; if they go into operational research, they are unsure how they differ from other operational research people. In either case, they generally express surprise at how little what they learned at university has to do, in an immediate sense, with their new situation. There is great temptation for them to pick up quickly one or two of the more easily acquired intervention techniques in order to achieve some identity. In the process, they may abandon their research and knowledge base. There are counselling methods that succeed in evoking material, although they do not give any guidance about what it means or how to use it. These are now widely used, simply because they are easy to learn and because they are distinctively "behavioural".

Towards a model of social science utilization

Applied social science is not about an abstract entity, knowledge, being conveyed to another abstract entity, a client's needs. In both institutions, it is mediated through a series of filtering processes and link-roles, each of which has both needs and resources, as have the institutions themselves.

Thus social science in application involves a continuous interplay between the content of the work being done and its context. Indeed, utilization is about relating the content of the work to the context. Context here means those aspects, both of the client and of the resource system, that are not part of the immediate problem. It concerns, on the one hand, the on-going aspects of the client organization that are not the immediate subject of the work and, on the other, the needs of the resource system which must be met so that they do not impinge on the work being done.

This is not meant to imply that there is one best way of doing that. Utilization can be successful when the work and its context are distinct, as in some clear-cut, definable projects with a beginning and an end. The project in that case is a temporary system, which helps the client make the transition from one phase to another, and the important test (not of the quality of the social science but of the quality of utilization) lies in re-entry and re-integration. It can also be successful where overlap between content and context is almost complete, as when a

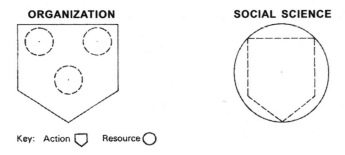

FIGURE 10.   Action and resource—content and context.

specialist or specialist department is accepted and trusted and has become part of the furniture.

Utilization is unsuccessful if the problems of context (frequently the political problems) dominate the situation so that it becomes impossible to get on with the work. Contrary to appearances, it is also unsuccessful if work goes on unhampered, but only for the reason that the context has been damaged or eliminated—that is, the client has in some sense been taken over.

Schematically, success in utilization depends on successfully regulating the relationships between the system described by continuous lines in Figure 10 and the system described by dotted lines.

CHAPTER 12

Elements of practice 1: vision and competence

This was a joint paper with Ken Eason. After the fiasco described in chapter 9, a study of social science utilization was funded by the Anglo-German Foundation.[1]

It was this project that made it clear to us that there are two distinct frameworks involved in the practice of social science in organizations—knowledge-into-use and the dynamics of action—and that the practitioner needs to have both. We collected case studies consisting of the following:

- Fourteen cases in organizations—passenger and freight transport; banking; electrical products; precision engineering; confectionery; food processing; freight import and export; oil (marketing); motor components; motor industry (guest workers in Germany); motor industry (supervision); distribution; news technology; rubber.

- Five practitioners—a research assistant in a trade-union research department; an in-house OD adviser; an organization theorist; a psychoanalytically oriented organization consultant; the manager of psychological services in a public service organization.

- A government programme—The Commission for Economic and Social Change was set up in Germany to advise the government on "what economic, social and educational policy options are available for furthering technical and social change and for fashioning it in the interests of the population, within the framework of a market economy".

This paper and the next one originally formed a chapter in the book resulting from the study (Klein & Eason, 1991) but have been edited to make them stand alone—where particular cases are referred to, the reader does not need to know their content. They also draw on experience outside the particular case studies.

In reviewing all the case material, its analysis, and our own experience, the most significant lesson for us is that the utilization of social science requires four things:

1. *Vision*: in particular, a sense that things are not immutable. Social science, if it is to be valuable, has to bring insights, perspectives and methods to bear on situations that bring with them the possibility of change and development.

2. *Competence*: a range of skills, knowledge and understanding. Practice requires a repertoire of skills which have their own unique characteristics and are not simply, for example, research methods on the one hand or management consultancy on the other.

3. *Infrastructure*. to fulfil its potential, social science practice needs enabling and supporting practical arrangements and resources.

4. *Institutionalization*: valued outcomes and processes need to be embedded in the client system concerned.

When things have gone less than well, it is because of some imbalance between these. We find that any one, or two, or even three of them by themselves are not enough. The present chapter will consider the first two.

On vision

Vision, in the social sciences, concerns system change and hope. In the engagement between client systems and social science systems, clients generally have some vision of a desirable future before they ever approach the social scientists. It may be a future state that is different in level of understanding, or different in some tangible sense, or the mere hope that it may be so. Sometimes the main result of an intervention may be to effect a loosening-up in the client system so that alternative futures may be envisaged, or that there may be a vision about a route as well as about a goal.

In all this, scale is a crucial factor. There used to be an advertisement for shaving-cream, which showed three faces: one disappearing under lather, one with almost none, and one with the amount needed for shaving. The caption read: "Not too little, not too much, but just right." It applies to the visionary aspects of the social sciences.

Where there is "too little", situations may not be seen as containing any potential for change or development, or the system being considered for change may be within very tight boundaries. These are some of the arguments that take place between ergonomists and other kinds of human or social scientists. An episode during the Esso work may be helpful in clarifying them. There were, by chance, two teams of researchers working on projects for the company's marine department: a team of ergonomists, carrying out studies of human factors in ship design and contributing to the redesign of a ship's bridge; and a team consisting of an anthropologist and a social psychologist, studying problems of "life and work at sea". Both used system terminology; both were concerned with relating human and technical aspects of the system to each other and, in the process, giving greater primacy to the human aspects; both were working on Esso's oil-tankers, so that many technical and organizational factors were constant. Yet it was hard to see any connection between the things they did, which seemed to be completely different. This raised questions about the meaning of systems concepts.

When the teams were persuaded to meet in a seminar, the differences between them could be articulated along two dimensions. The first concerned the different parameters—all of them within the definition "human"—that they tackled: on the one hand, such things as human ability to judge distance, speed, and acceleration and to see objects in the dark; on the other, such things as the concept of "shipmates" and controlling relationships in a confined space, and the ship as a 24-hour, total institution. The other dimension concerned how they defined the boundaries of the systems they looked at—that is, what they considered to be "the system" (and subject to change), and what the environment (and given). The ergonomists took the organization and its general policies, as well as the ship and its basic technology, as given. The other team took nothing as given except the continuing need to transport oil.

While this could be described in terms of a difference in the definition of system boundaries, both in the sense of scale and in the sense of degrees of openness or closedness, it was debated in terms of values: the social scientists accused the ergonomists of accepting too much— that is, of having too few values—while the ergonomists accused the social scientists of being so airy-fairy that nothing practical could, in fact, be done.

"Too much" vision, in this sense of system boundaries, means that the whole world must change before anything at all can be done. Another form of "too much" is to put the vision so far into the future that there can be no testing of its validity. No one is in a position to contradict the pronouncements of futures-oriented "visionaries" of this kind. In fact, in either case, whether the grand design concerns the world system or the far-away future, its main characteristic is that it cannot be tested. So the first question to be confronted is: "What system?"

The second question is: "Whose system?" There is much need for care about powerful visions concerning systems in which one is not a stakeholder. Within organizations, too, the vision of one group may be the constraining environment of another. There is much discussion in professional circles about the dynamic of transference—that is, a client transferring onto a consultant hopes, expectations, and feelings that have been developed in some other situation. But social scientists also need to explore the converse—the countertransference—and ask themselves, "What am I trying to do to them that I have not been able to do to my family/colleagues/political masters?"

It is not enough to say that one guards against the danger of using clients for one's own needs by making sure that they become actively involved. It is not so much *whether* stakeholders in a client system are actively involved in a project but *how* they are involved—specifically, whether they are involved in the role of objects or subjects—that provides clues about any countertransference that may be at work. A very strongly held vision can become a "mission", which may then be thought to justify the use of power and even a disregard for damage that may be done in pursuit of the mission.

When a vision is relatively bounded, interventions are often successful in their own terms but the effects may be marginal, not extending in time or affecting much in the organization. There is also the possibility that accepting such a narrow frame makes it possible to avoid addressing or calling into question wider issues.

The grander vision can avoid these dangers but carries with it other dilemmas. The grand vision is very tempting for the client. When you are beset with problems, the prophet who offers hope, ultimate solutions, or panaceas can seem very attractive. The grand dream, however, often leads to disillusionment. Too often, it is either found to be a partial solution, unable to recognize many other realities in the situation, or the "prophet" had neither the will nor the wherewithal to turn the dream into operational practice.

Sometimes a client's vision is stronger than or different from that of the social scientist. Looking at the case studies, we see a range of ways in which social scientists and clients have negotiated their visions and collaborated to develop an appropriate vision around which work may take place. It may be that the generalized "vision" of a piece of social science theory can be made specific to the client's situation. It may be that diagnostic studies provide findings that are the raw material that can then be used to build the vision. It may be that social scientists provide a process by which client staff engage with one another, with the problems, with the person of the social scientist, or with concepts and findings.

In some of the organizations involved, activities of the kind described were fairly widely diffused; in some, they were one-offs; and some have dissipated. Where they fell short of the vision, the vision was nevertheless necessary to make them happen. In all of them, the professionals involved and sometimes also their clients would have liked to see more—or more systematic, or more sustained or consistent—outcomes. This then brings us to the other three components.

On professional competence: practice as a discipline

The professionals in our study showed much variety in their approaches to practice. However, there is also great commonality in the issues practitioners face and even in the ways in which they face them. Dealing with people, work, and organization in an attempt to support and help tends to trigger similar issues, whatever route takes you into the situation. It has been salutary, for example, to meet practitioners with an OD perspective who nonetheless (and perhaps with some feelings of not staying "pure") deal with design and other structural issues. Similarly, practitioners whose starting-point may be structural change have to deal with the dynamics of situations and take on facilitating roles that would fit a process-oriented OD approach. Situations frequently pull one away from the "pure" teaching of a discipline or methodology; it gets modified in collaborative action research. One of the most difficult issues a practitioner has to deal with is deciding when this becomes inappropriate collusion.

This section attempts to synthesize aspects of practice as a discipline by putting together what works that seems common to many or all of the case studies: what are the common roles that are played, what are the common methods employed, what are the common issues faced, and so on. By this means we hope to give a focus to what is distinctive about the emerging practice, what it has to offer, and where development is still needed.

It may be useful to begin by summarizing the ways in which there is broad agreement that social science practice involves unique characteristics. For example:

1. It is different from social science research. In research, one investigates a particular topic, maybe tests a hypothesis, perhaps pursues an interesting line of enquiry. In practice, while the methods of diagnostic investigation need to be every bit as rigorous as those of research, the investigation has to be client-centred and problem-centred. It may involve problems one has not studied previously, it may need conceptual tools and models from a number of different areas, and in the investigation it will be necessary to take heed of the action timetable within the organization that the investigation is designed to serve. At the same time, it is valuable to help the client system acquire a hypothesis-testing way of working.

2. It is different from some other forms of practice. When the subject matter is inanimate, a discipline that translates scientific findings directly into practice may be possible. Engineering practice has given us this model, and there appears to be widespread expectation that a "mature" social science practice would do the same. However, in social science practice the "what" cannot be separated from the "how". On the one hand, structural change is not useful unless the people in the roles involved learn to understand it, own it, and equip themselves to work within it. The subject matter is the people who must internalize and work with findings and who, in the process, will develop their own versions and modifications. On the other hand, a process that develops individuals and groups is not valuable or lasting if it is abstracted from consideration of environment and task. For this intimate link between content and process, engineering practice has not provided the language.

These characteristics lead social scientists into adopting roles that are subtly different from the role models with which many professionals and clients are familiar, and this may itself be a cause of uncertainty and conflict. If the practitioner engages in an investigation that does not fit the model of "research", it may be seen as low-quality research. If the practitioner engages in an action role but does not deliver the firm recommendations expected from the model of the "consultant", the judgement may be that this is a poor consultant. To avoid these interpretations, we need a statement of the specific character of these roles in social science practice against which a practitioner might more appropriately be judged.

In this section we make an attempt at such role definitions. We summarize them as *diagnostic roles* (including *evaluation*), where practitioner and clients are endeavouring to understand a situation, and *action and development roles*, where an attempt is made to engage with the client in work. The "diagnosis/action" paradigm is a useful distinction, but it should not be assumed that all practice divides neatly into these phases. Some forms of intervention take place without explicit diagnosis. Also, as the cases show, episodes of intervention can contain within them many short problem-solving cycles which involve diagnosis, action, and sometimes evaluation. The diagnostic activity is part of the action programme. The separation is therefore to demonstrate the nature of the function and role, the methods that support them, and the issues that surround them, rather than to imply a neat sequential phase-structure to practice.

In diagnosis or in action, an important factor is whether the practitioner is a member of the organization or comes from outside. The practitioner in the motor components case was able to do what he did by virtue of his detached and neutral role as an outsider, more than because of any specific professional background. In fact, he deliberately kept professional knowledge about payment systems out of the picture at first. But the inside/outside dimension is not so simple: there are insider-insiders, like Mr B, who grew into the role from inside the company, and whose strength derived from familiarity with the business, its people, and its politics; and outsider-insiders like Mr E, a professional psychologist who became manager of a large in-house unit, and whose strength derived from his professional knowledge and frame of reference. In the latter case, the existence of a whole department helped to keep the professional culture going, albeit in a modified and adapted form. Where there is no such department, a network of professional colleagues becomes very important. A professional needs a reference group and needs to maintain contact with it.

Diagnostic roles

Diagnosis needs to be seen in the framework of development. This means that the institutions that will "hold" the concern for development should be in place before, during, and after any explicit data-collection phase, and appropriate links agreed. Institutional aspects include: agreeing the brief, the methods of work and methods of follow-up, who is to be involved in steering groups, and so on.

Not all applied work includes an explicit diagnostic phase; where it does, the diagnostic activity has a number of functions apart from the manifest one of collecting and analysing data:

(a) a familiarization function, enabling clients to test out the professionalism and way of working of the practitioners, and enabling the practitioners to get to understand the client situation;

(b) an education function, showing how familiar information may convey different meanings when presented systematically, or in a detached way, or processed through one or more different frames of reference;

(c) a development function: the feedback and working-through phase may take on the characteristics of a system that facilitates transition, in the course of which issues, conflicts, and differences in perception come to the surface and can be worked on.

It follows that diagnostic studies, even those that most resemble research, require some action skills. If there is a written report, practitioners need to frame it in language that is comprehensible to the readers, in categories that are relevant to the problems they experience, and with a minimum of methodological ifs and buts. They may also, minimally, need to advise on how the report may be handled. They may need to present in meetings the essentials of what comes out of the study and to be able to handle the reactions provoked not only by the study, but by their own role and behaviour. An action role means constantly, on one's feet, having to decide between options about how to proceed. The only tool for doing that is one's self, and what one has genuinely internalized; formal models are fig-leaves and are likely to be recognized as such.

Engaging in an explicit diagnostic exercise involves a range of agreements with the people concerned, and these have to be negotiated. Considerations include the following:

1. *The rights of those who give information.*   Contributing to an investigation has to be voluntary and should be on the understanding that confidentiality will be protected in reporting findings. In circumstances where this is not possible—for example, where the population involved is very small and everybody knows the individuals—what is reported must be cleared with the individuals. For many, good practice includes checking with individuals what has been learned through them, in order to confirm the findings and also to offer some benefit in return. It is an important part of the professional role of the practitioner to establish this kind of "contract" with the people taking part and to maintain it whatever the subsequent pressures to reveal sources. Practitioners who are junior in status to those exerting the pressure may find this difficult. It is important, therefore, that the support of senior levels of the back-home institution is somehow visible. There are, in fact, many ways in which it makes an important difference whether a practitioner is seen as working solo or as part of a team or institution.

2. *The process of reporting information.*   Ideally, the maintenance of a non-partisan position should be supported by reporting findings to all parties concerned. There may be reasons why this cannot be fully achieved, but the practice of getting findings that originate from a particular source back to that source can and should be sustained. The process of reporting findings may include the formal preparation of a report, but this by itself is not enough. Engaging client staff with new perspectives on their situation involves working through with them the nature of the findings and their implications, if the diagnosis is to act as a vehicle for sharing knowledge and as a bridge to action.

3. *The role of the client in data-gathering for diagnosis.*   The process of internalizing the findings within the client organization is greatly helped if client staff are themselves involved in the data-gathering and analysis. Such a collaborative venture also institutionalizes the research methods and reduces dependence on the practitioner. In the transport case, two members of staff were assigned to work with the social scientist. In the oil-marketing case, the marketing

staff undertook the diagnosis themselves in a process designed by the social scientist.

However, there are two restrictions on this general principle. First, some client roles are incompatible with diagnostic ones. Anyone in a power relationship with those taking part in a study, such as most obviously line managers with their own departments, cannot suddenly take on the role of detached data-gatherer: they cannot "forget" the data when they get back to their previous roles, and they cannot forget who supplied it (if, indeed, it was supplied in such a situation).

Second, if the organization is to gain from the theoretical perspectives the social scientist can bring to bear, there must be a point at which the social scientist plays a role in interpreting the findings. Otherwise, the organization may get the benefit of the process or method, but not the frame of reference.

There are many options with regard to project strategy, and each has benefits and costs. The benefit of the involvement of members of the client system has to be traded off against the value of a detached input. This is one of many instances of strategies needing to be chosen in knowledge of their consequences.

4. *Scale and duration.*   In research methodologies the size and nature of the sample is crucial to the extent to which findings can be generalized, hypotheses tested statistically, and so on. This may demand large samples and studies of long duration and may not be appropriate in a diagnostic study. In this kind of study, the practitioner often uses his or her knowledge, as well as intuition based on experience, to make the best use of limited time and resources. It is better to offer possibilities for later testing than to devote time to validation and miss the time-scale when action would have been possible, or miss the opportunity to share insights with client staff.

Adapting in ways like this to the circumstances of action does not mean that one abandons or denies a previously learned set of standards or values. It means that they get overlaid with another set and that the trade-offs are understood.

Action and development roles

The action and development roles taken by practitioners also have a number of functions simultaneously:

(a) They are a vehicle through which knowledge informs action.

(b) They involve collaborative action with clients so that the decisions belong to the client.

(c) They facilitate development opportunities for individuals and groups.

(d) They act as receptacles or containers for the anxieties evoked by change.

(e) They create a safe space within which the organization may review its situation and decide on next steps.

(f) Valued knowledge and methods should become institutionalized, so that the withdrawal of the resource leaves a more competent client system.

One perennial dilemma for the social scientist practitioner has been that direct application of (a) in the form of knowledge inputs and recommendations precludes some of the more developmental functions, while methods that emphasize learning from experience often leave no room for the contribution of substantive knowledge.

The types of contribution may be discussed under two headings: process design and direct intervention. Practitioners may be involved in designing a process by which the client can move towards action, and they will then be involved in this; or they may be involved directly without such a vehicle.

Process design

The design of an action process has elements of designing a learning experience and elements of designing an institution in which planning decisions, technical design decisions, and the like are taken. It was a common feature of those cases where the practitioner was helping the client work on a particular problem. Although the practitioners did not recommend specific solutions, they recommended processes by which a solution could be found and implemented. In doing so, they created the necessary space for the work to be done. This might involve a temporary institution with temporary roles for members of client staff (and for the practitioner), goals to be achieved, activities to be pursued, and methods to support. The temporary institution might be a working party, committee, conference, negotiating system, or some other organizational form to which people either belong in addition to their normal roles or to which they are seconded temporarily from their normal roles (in that case, re-entry may become an issue). Depending on the background, membership is drawn from the client organization to include those with a stake in the outcome, who have to live with the consequences, and those who have relevant knowledge and expertise to contribute (which may include the practitioner). The design of such a structure—who is part of it, how selected, what roles they are asked to adopt, the way in which they interact with the rest of the organization—is vital to success. There were many such temporary structures in the cases, with different design characteristics: in the motor components case, the practitioner's diagnosis led him to conclude that relations between groups of staff were so poor that they would not be able to work together in such a temporary structure. He therefore created a structure in which groups at first worked separately. When common problems had been identified and exchanged, joint problem-solving groups became possible.

Temporary systems, such as training courses, negotiations, and working parties, will have the function of facilitating transition if they create an environment where options can be explored in safety without later repercussions, where people can experiment with roles and behaviours beyond their habitual ones, and where issues can be worked on that the normal working culture may not encourage to surface. The temporary system then takes on the quality of transition in the sense of permitting exploring and testing-out, in order to move on (Winnicott, 1971). Thus not all temporary systems facilitate transition; for them to do so, some conditions have to be met.[2]

In such a system there may be a phase in which the group works on the findings of diagnostic studies as a means of developing shared perspectives on the topic under consideration. There will probably be a phase of searching for solutions and testing them against goal criteria before a specific plan is agreed, developed, and implemented. These activities have the simultaneous function of problem solving and developing team-functioning. This is where the temporary system takes on the function of facilitating transition. Techniques and exercises will not facilitate transition if they only present the issues intellectually and do not enable the work to be done that deals with the anxieties involved and develops the necessary inner resources.

The characteristics of such temporary systems obviously vary. If they are training courses, they have to provide opportunities for people to test out new approaches in an environment where they can take risks without punishment. Negotiating systems generally put some limits to conflict by involving a high degree of structure. People may then co-operate in operating the structure where they cannot co-operate on substance. Progress may be made by moving between the two.

When the task involved concerns design, there is a particular set of such methods by which people can be supported as they create and evaluate alternative futures. In such cases, it proved particularly useful to create a physical representation of the future, as when a factory layout was created out of Lego bricks for the confectionery factory. Sometimes a working prototype can be tested or given a trial implementation as in freight-forwarding, when a trial system was introduced into a branch as a "vehicle for learning". When a concrete manifestation of the future scenario is not possible, it seems important to create at least a paper representation that is sufficiently objective and "out there" to be the focus for debate and analysis. Such structures may be as simple as cardboard-box prototypes of workstations and control-rooms or as sophisticated as computer-based working simulations. What they must be is sufficiently flexible to permit alternatives to be demonstrated and sufficiently real for informed members of client staff to be able to imagine the consequences of such alternatives. They must also incorporate the human and social, or "soft systems", aspects in a realistic way—that is, in a way that is not merely the result of wishful thinking. They may then simply support a freewheeling discussion of consequences, or support an experimental programme that indicates outcomes.

Action and development

Practitioners may provide a number of kinds of direct contribution. One will be their frame of reference. Whatever they are doing, or even if they are not "doing" anything, they will convey by their own behaviour, implicitly as well as explicitly, the frame of reference within which they are operating. This may be about the strategic interdependence between an organization's environment, its primary task, its values and culture, and the technical and other arrangements to meet that primary task; or it may be about the interdependence between technical and social aspects at the level of the primary work group, or about the interdependence between task and process in the life of a group, or about the links between the inner and outer worlds of people occupying organizational roles; or any others. Whatever it is, this framework will inform any diagnosis they may undertake, the design of any transitional system they suggest, the issues to which they draw attention, and the interventions they make; it is, in any case, likely to add a perspective that is different from the ones already in use.

The practitioner who holds such a framework is in a position to convey it. Once clients have internalized it themselves, they apply it to their own data and come up with syntheses that would not have occurred to the social scientist. This is very different from refusing to make a contribution for dogmatic reasons.

A second possible contribution is to bring in relevant empirical research findings. Sometimes empirical research will have a direct relevance to the situation being considered; more often it is likely to need re-interpreting and translating. The process is one of internalizing and translating into use. In this way the use of empirical research enables the contribution to be a proactive one. Much research in the social sciences has been concerned with *post-hoc* analyses of things that have gone wrong. Knowledge of earlier research may be turned into predictions of how to set things up so that they are less likely to go wrong, or at least so that their consequences are faced knowingly: "If you set it up in this way, there are likely to be consequences of that kind—is that what you really intend?"

A third kind of contribution is process facilitation, supporting individual and group development. In the case studies, this involved supporting specific developmental needs—for example, management style, language needs, team building, and so on. It may also be of a general character—when groups, teams, or individuals explore their own dynamics. It is a process that often follows the same structure as that described above in relation to "transitional systems": suspend normal business, reflect, examine goals and values, consider and evaluate alternatives, and so on.

Within the process orientation, too, there are roles that permit knowledge transfer. This may, but need not, lead to drawing consequences in the form of recommendations. As a group works within the "transitional" process, there are spaces and times when an input may be appropriate. When future possibilities are being considered, there may be room for teaching to enlarge the number of options that can be considered—for example, by referring to particular concepts or bringing in relevant experience. When options are being evaluated, there may be opportunities to include findings from research studies that inform the evaluation. The practitioner will need to have the capacity to adapt to the learning style of a particular professional group.

Evaluation is, indeed, a fourth kind of contribution. When trials or experiments are undertaken, one of the roles often adopted is evaluator of the outcomes, a role that can be extended after a change has been introduced. In the knowledge-into-use framework, evaluation of policies or experiments by detached outsiders may be carried out systematically, and there is a large literature on evaluation research. In the framework of dynamics, the cycle of evaluation and consideration of next steps is much shorter. It becomes more a matter of reviewing and considering next steps on a continuing basis.

Once a transition has been accomplished, it may be appropriate for the practitioner to withdraw. The objective at this stage is to institutionalize the learning. Sometimes this means that the process of creating a "transitional system" itself has been learned and is used in other circumstances. It may be embodied within the management procedures of the organization or in the way it undertakes change. Commonly, training events are taken over by the institution and offered as part of the development process offered to staff.

Issues associated with practice roles

There are a number of themes that emerge from consideration of the practice role and that are relevant to the further development of practice.

The first of these concerns staying in role. The role that we have elaborated is not easy to describe and does not relate easily to other role models that may be familiar to client staff. It is therefore important that practitioners are able to signal clearly the nature of the role so that expectations are realistic and are fulfilled. There is also a heavy responsibility on the practitioner to stay in role at all times.

Clients may invest a great deal and take on big risks when they commit themselves to social scientists. They are likely to test out how safe they are in having taken these risks—that is, whether the professionals both know what they are doing and will not exploit clients or abuse their own position. Attempts to trip the professional out of role may be quite unconscious testing of this kind. They may seem to offer rewards that, on the surface, appear very reasonable and appealing, such as a special relationship or access to information that could not be obtained otherwise. But there is always a price to pay: things that go wrong can very often be traced back to a consultant having fallen out of role. In a seminar for young researcher/consultants, the members of the group were asked to think back to an occasion when they had found clients inexplicably angry—that is, angry in a way they could not understand. When some of them had located such an occasion, they were asked to think back to what had been going on before that particular episode. It turned out that some form of falling out of role had generally been involved.

One defence in the face of this risk, for the consultant, can be to draw very formal, distancing boundaries round the role. It is a viable strategy, but it brings with it a greater likelihood of fantasies being projected onto the consultant, and this in turn has consequences. Such distancing is not essential; it is perfectly possible to be informal and stay in role. Staying in role is, however, a total commitment, without any let-up. As a non-partisan resource, the practitioner cannot, for example, while having a drink at the bar, appear to join in the general denouncement of absent colleagues. In a role that supports the development of others by not providing specific recommendations, it may be dangerous to announce views on related issues. Staying in role involves reacting in role to things that happen or are said, rather than merely reacting to them. It also means being able to cope with expectations, assumptions, hopes, and fears that may be projected onto the practitioner, including when these are unrealistic. (It is useful to explore what earlier experience of social scientists a client may have had, since this may well have influenced such expectations.) It becomes clear that, to be able to maintain their capacity to stay in role, practitioners themselves need a professional support system.

Establishing and sustaining a role may also be affected by age and gender stereotypes. Relatively young social scientists, no matter how competent, may have difficulty gaining acceptance among senior and probably older members of the client organization, and it has sometimes been necessary to "match hierarchies": to field an older and senior social scientist (whose involvement may not have been functionally necessary) at a time when senior client staff were directly involved. Gender by itself needs to be recognized as having an influence. In some organizations, accepting that a young woman may have knowledge and skill that an older man does not have can be problematic for the client staff. Establishing and holding a professional role under these circumstances can tax the poise of even the most mature practitioner.

A second theme concerns the management of resources. The practitioner task is not a closed one and, once it is seen as valuable, tends to expand in many directions. The initial group of people with whom one works may engage progressively more attention as they grapple with difficult issues. It may become obvious that there are others who are relevant. There will always be a reason to extend one's own understanding by deepening and widening the diagnostic or exploratory efforts. As will be seen in the next chapter, there is also a continuing need to monitor and work on the structures that support the practice within the organization. If the fruits of the work are to be disseminated and institutionalized, work will be required away from the main focus of practice. Given limited time and resources, these conflicting demands make it difficult to establish priorities, and many of the problems encountered in the cases arose because practitioners had chosen some avenues and neglected others. The strongest temptation appears to be to continue working closely with those who demonstrate that they need you. Individual or group development may then continue, but at the risk that the organization becomes a progressively more inhospitable place for those individuals or groups. There is also a temptation of becoming over-invested in some kinds of innovation or experiment because they are interesting or because one does not see the institutional constraints.

A third issue concerns withdrawal. This can be very difficult to manage. In one of the cases, a client explained frankly that he was so afraid that his own dependency needs might turn out to be uncontrollable that he would rather not risk getting involved at all to the extent needed. One way in which clients in the case studies managed this risk was to create a "ghost" consultant in the place of the real one ("What would he/she say under these circumstances?"); another was by relating to the consultant indirectly, via the supervision of a student. Another common problem is when the client begins to feel able to manage the process and wants to act independently but the practitioner does not feel the situation has made sufficient progress for this to be effective. At the same time, practitioners also need to manage their own dependency on the client: practitioners depend on clients for a sense of being needed, for a sense of contributing to worthwhile activities, for continuing learning, and indeed for income. Dealing with these issues as matters of professional judgement, when they obviously also affect the contractual position and funding of the practitioner, is obviously difficult. It is yet another reason why practitioners need a professional support system.

A related issue is when and in what form client staff take over these roles or functions. To institutionalize the learning, many of the functions should remain within the organization. Some of them can sensibly be taken on by people operating within their normal roles: groups can suspend business to review progress, individuals can build in time for reflection, in-house trainers may be able to take on more topics for training. Some of the activities, however, require the full practitioner role—that is, the ability to be independent, impartial, maintain confidences, and so on—and this may not be possible for people in normal organizational roles and positions. It may indicate a need to institutionalize the practitioner role within the organization. Aspects of the contribution that may then be lost are, first, "stranger value" and, second, the knowledge-into-use element that depends upon the social science training of the practitioner. This may also be achieved by recruiting, by sending staff for appropriate training, or by establishing links with research organizations.

Action research

We have dissected these roles and functions, in order to be able to spell out some of their attributes. Together, they form the pattern of activities that is generally called action research. There are many forms of action research, but they have in common three elements. Action research aims:

- to make a contribution to problem-solving or development;
- to make a contribution to knowledge;
- to involve the people in the system in active roles rather than the passive ones of only being the subjects of research.

Where there are differences between different kinds of action research, they are likely to be differences in the proportion of these three elements.

One characteristic of action research is that the situation is changing while the work is going on, and this can trouble academic researchers. The difference between action research and consultancy is that consultancy may not have an explicit research objective in addition to the problem-solving one; also, some forms of consultancy do not involve the participation of members of the system in active roles. Another factor is that in-house practitioners, while generating important knowledge, may not have the time or opportunity to publish it. One result of the splitting that has occurred between the world of research and the world of practice is that research has not fed into practice. It is at least as regrettable that academic research and teaching have not been informed by the experience of practice.

Action research can and should be totally rigorous. There are likely to be "working hypotheses" that are jointly explored and may be jointly modified as the work proceeds. As regards methods, it is not a matter of intervening in an *ad-hoc* and uncontrolled way, "letting it all hang out", but of selecting and agreeing strategies (a) in a way that fits the problem and (b) in knowledge of their consequences; generally documenting them; and staying in role.

Even if, for example, the agreed strategy is only to provide a feed-back report, there will still be different consequences according to whether this is done in writing or verbally; with or without the opportunity for discussion and revision; with all interested parties together or different parties separately; reporting only what has been found; including analysis and comment; or including inputs from other research and experience. All of these have different implications, and rigour in action research means selecting and agreeing the strategy with some understanding of the likely consequences.

Implications for the development of practice skills and competence

The processes described above are difficult and demanding. They demand knowledge, maturity, and professionalism from those in practitioner roles and from those in client roles who engage and support them. There are implications for the development of people in all of these roles; indeed, there is a need for "matching competencies" as well as hierarchies.

1. *The professional development of practitioners.*   The description above requires practitioners, first, to be knowledgeable about theories, methods, and empirical findings of social science if they wish to operate as "general practitioners" rather than specialists in a particular area and, second, to be skilful in managing the processes involved in practice. The first capability could and should be developed in social science teaching. The difficulty there is to avoid transmitting the value that research and research methods are good and practice is less than good. Ideally, the teaching should convey what is characteristic and worthwhile about practice, to prepare would-be practitioners so that they hold realistic expectations about the rewards and frustrations of practice. They need to recognize, for example, that it is difficult to undertake doctoral studies in practice because the conflicts between the academic research-centred thesis and the client-centred practice may jeopardize both pursuits.

Most disciplines teach their particular research methods, at least at postgraduate level. It may be possible at the same time to begin the process of developing the skills necessary to manage the dynamics of change and getting knowledge into use. It is possible, for example, to undertake supervised diagnostic studies and to develop some of the diagnostic methods. It is difficult, however, to see how the full repertoire of skills can be developed except in a kind of apprenticeship with a mature professional. The development of these skills is so dependent on experience and review of the experience that real engagement with practice is essential. Such experience is not easy to organize, since the process often calls for client staffs to put themselves at risk by having their values, purposes, and behaviour questioned.

2. *The development of in-house practitioners.*   Some very able practitioners have developed from in-house positions where they have had managerial or technical responsibilities. It is important not to preclude this kind of development by establishing a closed profession in which membership depends on formal routes to qualification. The strength of in-house development is that the perceptive individual may develop a deep intuitive understanding of organizational dynamics and behaviour from experience in organizational roles. This is the weakness of the academic route, which provides only limited exposure to the realities of organizational life. By contrast, the weakness of the in-house route is that student practitioners come late to the formal acquisition of knowledge and the skills of supporting change and development processes. There has been a tendency for in-house practitioners to attend experiential courses to acquire the skills for managing processes. This leaves them possibly unable to contribute the knowledge-into-use element and serves to reinforce the divide between contributions about content and structure on the one hand, and process and dynamics on the other. One possibility of bridging this gap lies in the area of diagnosis and the teaching of diagnosis.

3. *The management of competition.*   One situation for which no amount of professional training prepares the practitioner is how to cope with competition. When an organization throws several consultants at the same problem, this may be a way of avoiding commitment to any of them or to the change effort involved; or it may reflect conflicts and competition within the organization itself. The best response is for the professionals together to confront the issue with the client and explore its meaning. But the anxieties of the competitive situation may make this impossible. To throw competing solutions at a problem, leaving their proponents to fight it out, may appear to be in some sense "fair".

If it is genuinely intended as a rational strategy for finding the "best" solution, some evaluative mechanism needs to be put in place to which the practitioners can relate.

4. *Informing clients about social science practice.*   Much of what social scientists do in organizations has an educational function. The aim, after all, is for members of organizations to be aware and take account of the human and social aspects of systems as a normal part of what is going on. There is also, however, a specific need for clients to know what they are taking on if they engage with social science practitioners, so that realistic expectations are promulgated in the client community. If the expectation is direct transfer of knowledge into usable practice via direct recommendations, there will be disappointment. If the expectation is that social scientists will use the opportunity to conduct academic research, the engagement may not even begin. If the belief is that the social scientist will quickly wash away the frustrations and dysfunctions of existing organizational life, there will be disillusionment. The cases demonstrate many ways in which social science practice has been valuable. This section has shown the nature of the practice that leads to successful outcomes. It has its own distinctive character and requires distinctive competencies. It is this value and this distinctive character that needs to be conveyed to prospective clients.

Structured methodologies

Clearly, the skills involved are complex. One consequence has been the development of structured and "packaged" methods, which aim to take some of the complexity out of practice and systematize and prescribe how to go about it.

In many instances there is a discernible trend from open-ended, grounded diagnosis and action formulation to a more prescriptive and formalized approach. It seems natural that, having invested heavily in a learning and development activity, the organization should then want to disseminate and institutionalize the outcomes and not repeat what may have been a laborious and expensive process. As a result of a project, therefore, the results may be encoded in a set of standards for others to follow. The standard may refer to the outcomes or to the process by which the outcomes are to be achieved. Codifying knowledge so that others may use it without having to go back to first principles has been a basis for much development and obviously serves a purpose.

But there are dangers. A standard and even a process can be applied automatically and the person applying it may learn nothing. This may result in inappropriate application. It also does not further one of the principal objectives of practice—that of development and learning. The challenge is to produce forms of institutionalization that provide appropriate opportunities for development and guard against inflexible and inappropriate application, but do not require everybody to rediscover the wheel.

We have both been involved in major programmes of R&D of information technology: the Alvey Programme of Advanced Information Technology Research in the United Kingdom and the European Strategy Programme of Research in Information Technology (ESPRIT) programme of the Commission of the European Communities. A technical feature of these programmes is attempts to encode research findings into products, software tools, and methodologies. This model of "research into practice" may be appropriate to computer science, but there is an expectation that it also applies to social science. It is a major challenge for social scientists to respond without being drawn into inappropriate models of practice. At present the social science community is accused by many technologists of "not getting its act together" and of expecting technologists to wait while fundamental research is undertaken on the implications of new technologies. What the technologists want are "user models" and "enterprise models" that automatically embody human and organizational issues so that designers do not need qualifications in social science, and systems can be designed without elaborate organizational research. The challenge for the social scientist is to respond with methods and tools that encourage exploring and learning strategies in technologists and users. The outcome should not be a product that can be applied without understanding, but a process that leads to the development of appropriate understanding.

Notes

1. Case studies in Germany were contributed by Dr Edith Rost-Schaude and Mr Rolf Kunstek, of the Forschungsinstitut für Arbeit und Bildung in Heidelberg.
2. For more about the concept of transition, see chapter 14.

CHAPTER 13

Elements of practice 2: infrastructure and institutionalization

This is the second part of the joint paper with Ken Eason. As a result of the complexity of the skills involved in practice, practitioners—including ourselves—have been preoccupied with the need to explore the nature of these skills and develop them. They have tended to neglect the other two essential elements of successful practice, namely infrastructure and institutionalization.

Infrastructure

We believe that the issue of infrastructure has so far been missing in discussions of the subject of practice. It is important, not because our pet concerns are otherwise not as successful as they might be, or because the world has to be kind to social scientists, but because of the waste that is involved when genuine attempts, jointly initiated, turn out not to fulfil the hope and promise that launched them. This may be the place to point out that there is a distinction between the system of entry and the system of continuing work or intervention. It is at the stage when the shift from entry to intervention is taking place that matters of infrastructure begin to be important.

The topic divides into two aspects:

1.   The supporting infrastructure that will help sustain the work.

2.   Strategic issues involved in the management of social science practice.

There may be appropriate vision and skill, but the undertaking will not realize its full potential unless attention is also paid to these aspects.

Infrastructure support

It would seem to make sense, if an organization is going to go to the trouble and expense of engaging with social science professionals, that both parties should pay some attention to the necessary infrastructure. It may be simply because this is so obvious that it has tended to be neglected, or it may appear too mundane a concern in the euphoria surrounding a new venture. At any rate, those of the case studies in which care was taken of it—whether through policy or by accident— tended to be those where success was more demonstrable.

We can distinguish six aspects of supporting infrastructure:

1. *Funding structures.*   Funding structures not only have practical consequences but are also at the same time an important part of the dynamics. The main—if somewhat obvious—issue is that the funding structure should be appropriate to the needs of the work. No one's funding these days is totally secure, but some funding bases have a longer time perspective than others, and this will affect the kind of work undertaken.

An in-house practitioner does not have to worry about day-to-day funding but may need to negotiate on an annual basis the scale of what is being done. If client departments fund the projects they engage with, this is an indication of commitment. On the other hand, one can be too purist about this when, in the early stages of an activity, other aspects are in the forefront of people's minds, and some central support may be valuable. In the first model, there is more chance of client departments really owning and taking responsibility for the work; in the second, there is more chance of adventurous, untested activities being tried.

Funding in a day-to-day sense is also not a problem where the funding base is the state, either because the work is being done from an already-funded university department or from a funded programme. The client, one might say, is paying indirectly through the tax system, but it creates a problem for the relationship and raises the question of who, in fact, is the client. In such cases, there have always been conflicts about the freedom of academics versus their responsibility for useful outcomes, and whether the quality of the academic output that has been bought at the cost of usefulness has been high enough to warrant the sacrifice. Recognizing practice as an intellectually respectable discipline would go a long way towards solving this perennial problem.

When researchers or consultants are publicly funded, a long-term grant may require manpower estimates to be firm at the beginning, allowing no flexibility for later changes in circumstance. Academics whose income does not arise directly from the work done may lack a sense of commitment to getting usable results; also, client systems will in general be much more committed to use work for which they are paying. On the other hand, consultants whose only source of income is project work may be tempted to use projects to generate more projects by encouraging dependency. As before, the concept of "not too little, not too much" applies: the work needs to be protected from the immediate financial worries of those who are doing it, but not too much so. We tried originally to propose a model of dual funding, where public funds would pay for the research component and clients for the action component of work. We still believe that this would be valuable: the costs of work to client organizations would be reduced, in return for opportunities of making valuable knowledge available to the research community.

Where assignments are funded directly by a client organization, an open-ended per diem arrangement—that is, charging explicitly for every day's work—is suitable for occasional consulting, but it was not helpful in the confectionery case, as the consultant did not feel able to propose visits and activities. Budgets estimated for whole projects or phases leave greater flexibility.

It is generally thought better if clients rather than sponsors pay for the work (we take sponsors to be those who bring social scientists in, while clients are those for whom they actually work). Where sponsors and clients are not the same, the funding structure becomes a function of the relationship between them. In-house, there was one situation (oil marketing) where the client departments were charged for the practitioner's work, and one (Mr B) where they were not. Both worked well, which indicates that the sponsor departments had good relationships with the client departments. A "seeding" arrangement, where the first exploratory part of work is funded centrally but local clients take on the cost of taking it further, has been found to be a useful model.

2. *Continuity of key people in post.* Obviously, one cannot expect other systems—such as career-development systems or the election of trade union officials or, indeed, political elections in the wider system—to be accommodated to project activities (of whatever kind, not only those involving social science). Nevertheless, the evidence by now is overwhelming, and the instances too numerous to list, that enormous waste of resources—including those of skill and enthusiasm—results from these discontinuities. Knowing this should therefore at least influence the timing of the beginning of projects, as well as strategies concerning timing when projects are being designed. In addition, the terms of reference of project committees, steering groups, the members of joint teams, and so on should include paying explicit attention to the issue of individual or collective handover where that becomes unavoidable.

Social scientists who have not learned this lesson the hard way, as we have, need to know that they will have to spend at least as much, if not more, effort with those who enter a project activity part-way through as they did with those who started it off. Client organizations need to recognize the demands this makes on the social scientists' resources. It needs to be allowed for in money and time budgets. Sometimes, if the project activity is taken seriously, one might even suggest considering some adjustments in the timing of other systems.

3. *Links with the organizational environment.* The links between a project activity and its organizational environment need to be considered, in two senses: first, social science activities have often been undertaken in a framework of "demonstration project". If such a project is successful, and its participants enthusiastic, this is as likely to put others off as it is to encourage emulation; demonstration projects tend to become encapsulated.

Second, most worthwhile project activities are likely to have systemic implications. These need to be considered, strategies for dealing with them designed, and linkages built in, from the outset. Social scientists often point to the broader systems implications of what they observe. In many of our cases, systemic links between different levels are clear from the accounts. Some of the issues encountered could only be dealt with at higher systems levels. The problem about working at the higher systems levels, however, is that one might never get among the nuts and bolts. In the freight-forwarding case, the practitioners thought this a reason to discontinue the work. The problem about working among the nuts and bolts is the lack of connection with higher systems levels. That is why, very soon after an activity begins to look as if it is taking root, an institutional framework that links it with the wider system is needed.

4. *Institutional change.*   The three items above were concerned with infrastructure support to on-going work. But there is also a need to consider from an early stage the infrastructure that will be needed to support institutional change as the work comes to fruition. One of the most significant findings, when the German government's Commission for Economic and Social Change reviewed the state of existing economic and social research, was that those researches were most likely to have been taken up and used whose boundaries aligned with existing institutions. Similarly, one of the difficulties in the way of making use of the Commission's own work was that it was problem-centred and cut across the boundaries of discipline-based ministries.

5. *Institutions for review.*   Both at the level of individual projects and at the level of the total social science activity, there is a need for a locus where progress can be reviewed, difficulties worked on, next steps discussed, and strategic objectives held in review. Such a "locus" may be a single senior individual, as in the transport case; more often it is likely to be some kind of steering committee, with appropriate representation. If the internal dynamics of an organization make that impossible, there may be a need for parallel bodies.

Some practitioners encourage institutions such as steering committees to evolve as and when it seems appropriate in the course of the work. Others insist on a pattern of institutions to be agreed—if not put in place—at the beginning, even using them as a kind of trademark. The danger of the latter strategy is that it may seem to be artificial and dogmatic; the danger of the former is that it may not be explicit enough or taken seriously enough.

6. *Structures of authority and power.*   Linked to the previous point, it is important to identify the power structures in the client system, so that there is some understanding of where the critical decisions are going to be made. Discussions about participation and consultation are gener-

ally about involving those at junior levels in the system in decision-making. But it can also happen that key individuals at senior levels have not been involved, or not soon enough. Mechanisms for steering and review need to include the stakeholders in the undertaking and need to be linked appropriately into the power-and-authority structure.

Strategic issues

We have been discussing project work in terms of a supporting infrastructure and links with the project's environment. But there is a serious question about whether a "project" is in any case the best mode for engaging with social science, or whether project activities, if they occur at all, should be less strongly defined and be seen more clearly as stages on a path of continuing development. We said earlier that a consultant may have the function of containing (in both senses of the word) the anxieties evoked by change processes. This may also be true of entities called "projects". Indeed, it may be a reason why there have by now been so many projects and so little matching change in basic assumptions. There is a need for strategic thinking on the part of both clients and the social scientists they engage with.

Possible strategies will depend on the extent to which a "project" is in phase with the surrounding culture. In the development of new plant or systems, there are many things going on simultaneously. If one of these is an attempt to develop ways of working that are more participative, there will nevertheless be decisions needed in the other streams before these methods are learned, practised, and become part of the culture. Where the culture is already participative, it will more easily be extended to include technical matters. At the level of organizations, a project may have the function of mutual exploration and testing out, but a number of organizations by now have got beyond this. This shows in the way in which strategy featured in the reflections of some of the individual practitioners included in the collection of cases. The three who were working in-house all discussed strategies designed to develop a practice, like a medical or legal practice, which would bring something new while remaining congruent with the values and culture of the organization. For the two with professional qualifications in parts of the social science spectrum, the "something new" was the knowledge and methods of their disciplines, adapted so as to be need-oriented. For the one who was "home-grown", the something new was the sanctioned role of process facilitation, cutting across normal departments and hierarchies. In all three cases, it seemed likely that values and culture might, in turn, eventually be affected.

For client systems, strategic questions arise about whether to engage with social science sporadically, as and when a need is felt, or systematically, and what parts of the social science spectrum to engage with. It is clear from the case material that the application of social science to practical affairs can come in many forms, and the forms it takes can be influenced by many different factors: political context and goals, the desire to disseminate the benefits of one's experience, different skills, experience, and training, and so on. The range of inputs and of types of skill, knowledge, and approach is very great, and practitioners have different mixes of them. There is also the question of to what extent to rely on external professionals or grow the skills and knowledge in-house; whether to develop and deepen relationships with known and trusted professionals or "play the field".

Institutionalization

The final question concerns institutionalization: what should be put in place by the client system to enable the system to retain what it has gained and continue with its learning and development?

To institutionalize something is to build it in. Once the excitement of doing something new simmers down, the less exciting, but possibly more important, task of making it go on happening has to be confronted. Only individuals learn. For institutions and societies, although the term "learning" is frequently used, it is only a metaphor. Institutional "learning" depends on whether it is possible for individual learning to pass from one person to another.

In societies, the constant overtaking of generations, and the dynamics between generations, mean that much learning is lost. Those learnt things that are institutionalized in laws or artefacts have the greatest chance of surviving. Thus in the legal, engineering, or medical professions, in all of which there is much institutionalization, one generation builds on the achievements of the last.

In the field we have been considering, there is much less institutionalization. What there is takes different forms. When something is formulated as a standard, that is a form of institutionalization. Where it is integrated into technology, such as computer dialogues that provide genuine options, or counters on a machine that provide feedback, that is a more powerful form. In some situations, the remedy becomes costly or even impossible if the value is not thus structurally embedded. An example is pacing: if people doing a job are inappropriately paced by the equipment they work with (being coerced by it into a pace that is too fast, too slow, or, most importantly, too inflexible and out of their control), this is one of the most powerful sources of frustration and discontent and, at the same time, one of the most difficult to undo.

On the other hand, there are other values whose whole point will be lost if they are structurally enforced. One cannot force people by dictat to learn, to explore, to work through differences. The data suggests that people for a time are playing with new concepts. Some developments are less of measurable institutional change and more of conceptual growth. Such efforts require enabling institutions rather than structural ones, and the enabling institutions then need to be provided with the means of making use of them.

To give an example of an enabling institution: a resolution was passed by the European Parliament, saying that applicants for grants under the various technology development programmes of the European Commission should be required to state, as part of their grant applications, what effect they expected the developments they proposed to have on "employment, the nature of the work, skills, health and safety at work and older workers for whom retraining is no longer possible". It would not be expected that applicants would get such predictions right, nor were they required to pay specific kinds of attention to these factors. But they were required to think about them seriously, and this, in turn, might have a knock-on effect on the education of technologists. (At the time of writing, however, this resolution has not been implemented.)

The general idea of institutionalization may be illustrated by a rather simplistic example. Society has made a policy decision, crystallized in law, to restrict driving to one side of the road. This apparently simple decision is supported by a surprising number and range of institutions: the assumption that it must happen is built into the design of vehicles. It is built into the training of drivers, as well as into their legitimation (licensing). It is built into the formulation of codes and standards (the Highway Code, standards about the width and layout of roads, and so on). Then there is the continual reinforcement of seeing that others do it and, finally, sanctions (punishment) if it does not happen. These institutions, in turn, are supported by funds, training establishments, staffing, and monitoring (traffic police).

Together, these institutions are very powerful, and they have been in force for a long time. In addition, a breach of the policy is generally clearly visible and unambiguous. As a result of all that, the policy is mostly carried out: drivers are not in the position of having continually to decide on which side to drive.

Clearly, many of these institutions are of the mandatory kind, which is not appropriate to our topic. But some have more of an enabling character, and when one considers their whole range and mutual reinforcement, it is little wonder that the project activities that have featured in our study, relying as they did mainly on small teams or even single professional practitioners engaged with the topic for a limited time, tended to lose force as they moved out from the small-scale, bounded area.

Towards getting the best of both worlds?

The issue is about balancing development and institutionalization. In comparing the German and the UK cases, we pointed to a tendency in Germany to institutionalize early—that is, to try to capture "proven findings" in legislation and standards—whereas the UK tendency was to avoid institutionalizing altogether—that is, to treat each development in a unique way—and we said that it would be good to get a little nearer to having the best of both worlds. Well, the research does now point to such a possibility:

1. Start in a developmental, exploratory, learning way; don't begin by formulating regulations or structured packages, or there will be little learning and, eventually, a reaction by those who feel they have been manipulated. When the processes of entry shift into the beginning of a system of engagement, start taking care of elements of infrastructure. Then, when a project or other form of work appears to be gathering momentum, build in a review activity for selecting those aspects that should become institutionalized and begin to build those institutions.

This phase was mainly left out in the UK case studies. One of the weakest aspects of current practice appears to be the tendency to achieve some of the necessary elements of institutionalization but not others. There may, for example, be a training scheme that develops individuals but no change in control structures, so they are unable to use their new capabilities. A policy to operate enriched job structures may not be supported by changed career paths, and so on. Attention to the various elements that have to come together to sustain a change is what matters.

2. Institutionalize reviewing and evaluation and "hypothesis-testing". But beware of continuing the rituals and procedures associated with, say, reviewing and evaluation, as if they were the essential core.

3. Institutionalize "permission" for roles, relationships, and dynamics to be a normal part of the agenda. This is sometimes taken to mean merely that people should express their feelings: "I feel angry" is not a contribution. But "I feel impossibly squeezed between the demands of department X and those of department Y; I think they are loading their difficulties onto me" is a valuable contribution and a potential growth point.

4. Include institutions—that is, transitional systems—for handling the outcomes of possible research loops.

5. In the design of transitional systems:
    - avoid splitting, by involving all stakeholders;
    - provide the data/experience that will facilitate internalization ("knowledge-into-use");
    - provide the "space" for reality-testing;
    - provide the "space" for personal and group review and development, and relate to the infrastructure that sanctions and supports this;
    - provide the basis for subsequent institutionalization/wider dissemination (the "vehicle" may be a large part of what is institutionalized).

6. Slant the institution-building towards processes rather than content, so that the institutions that are created are enabling ones that will ensure continuing learning, rather than ones that merely require conformity.

7. However, express in structured ways the values that are declared in policy: in budgets (time as well as money budgets), in the criteria on which members of the organization are assessed (e.g., where job satisfaction is an expressed value, job design and work organization should feature in the training of management, and department managers should be assessed on the job satisfaction of their staff),

in the factors that have to be included for consideration in technical and organizational project proposals, and in the training of those who shape organizational life, such as systems designers, production engineers, and accountants.

It will be seen that there is a limit to what can be done in this direction through projects or even strategies within organizations. The splitting between professions—for instance, between the engineering and social science professions—is deeply embedded in the institutions from which succeeding generations of professionals emerge. Projects in organizations are therefore not enough.

We have no sense of omnipotence on behalf of the social sciences and are very conscious of the criticisms that may be—and have been—levelled at the professional worlds both of academic social science and of organization development. But much has also happened that has been valued in client systems, and that has contributed to the aim that we have expressed, of synthesizing and integrating different value systems. It is a vital part of the task to try to secure the institutionalizing of the good things that have happened. This set of perspectives and approaches needs to become integrated as a normal part of what goes on. It helps people to gain understanding of their own operational settings and thus, in turn, equips institutions to relate in a strategic and integrated way to their environments.

CHAPTER 14

Three examples
of transitional interventions

This paper is adapted from a chapter in *The Transitional Approach to Change* (Amado & Ambrose, 2001). The story of "Henry" has been shortened from the original to bring it in line with the other two, and the consultant in the second example has been identified.

When I initially told some colleagues about the first of the examples, the story of "Poor Old Henry", I had to be nudged to write it up in this theoretical framework. With regard to the other two also, although they had been written up, it was in a project framework and not as illustrations of transitional thinking. But my colleagues were right—there is a conceptual message to be pulled out.

This chapter describes three experiences of transitional systems or roles. The first was devised by members of a client system, without any overt contribution from the external consultant who was working in the organization at the time. In the second, the consultant spontaneously began to take on the role of a product and, in doing so, loosened the log-jam of a design discussion that had become stuck. The third, by contrast, was a highly structured and formal experimental design. They are presented here in reverse chronological order: the first is the most recent and happened during my work from the Bayswater Institute as a consultant in the National Health Service. The second happened during my earlier nineteen years in the Tavistock Institute. And the third took place before that, while I was social sciences adviser in Esso Petroleum Company.

The notion of "transition" in human life was first put forward by the psychoanalyst D. W. Winnicott (1971). He pointed to the function that toys and forms of playing have for small children in facilitating experimentation with new and unknown aspects of the world and the working-through of anxieties and conflicts. The fundamental learning from this observation can be extrapolated to other aspects and phases of life, with very rich and creative consequences. Throughout the last decades, there have been massive and repeated discussions about the problems of technology or system implementation, how to cope with "resistance to change", and so on. The concept of "transition" (as distinct from the "management of change") helps to understand that it is very often simply not possible to go directly from a to b; at least as much thought and creativity needs to go into designing the vehicle for getting there, and ensuring that the vehicle has the requisite characteristics, as go into designing b.

In the design and implementation of technology, there are many forms of simulation, prototyping, and piloting that may be used. But for these to have the function of facilitating transition, certain conditions have to be met. They must be sufficiently flexible to permit alternatives to be demonstrated, and sufficiently realistic for the operational realities involved to be experienced or at least imagined. They must also therefore incorporate the human and social, or "soft systems", aspects in a realistic way—that is, in a way that is not merely the reification of wishful thinking.

In policy implementation, there is a similar need to provide a space for people to explore who and how they are in relation to the new situation. Institutions such as training courses, steering groups, and working parties will have the function of facilitating transition if they provide some "transitional space"—that is, if they create an environment where options can be explored in safety without later repercussions, where people can experiment with roles and behaviours beyond their habitual ones, and where issues that the normal working culture may not encourage to surface can be worked through.

Example 1:
The patient and the ward as aids to integration—
the story of Poor Old Henry

Background

This story concerns the use of scenarios about a fictitious patient and an imaginary day in a ward to aid integrated working in a hospital. In 1990, a London hospital with 700 beds became one of three National Health Service pilot sites in the United Kingdom for installing a large integrated computerized Hospital Information Support System (HISS). I was working there as consultant at the time but was not involved in this episode.

Although the information system selected was "off-the-shelf", there was a good deal of detailed design work left for the in-house project team to undertake. This team was drawn from different professions and departments in the hospital; as members of the team developed work in their own areas, they became increasingly aware that they were having to make assumptions about things outside their own specific knowledge. These were assumptions both about what happened in the hospital and about what would be happening in the information system. The nursing officer:

> "We   wrote the Operational Requirement for a lot of disparate systems—the nursing system, haematology, the labs, etc. I could understand the individual bits and what they could do but, not being IT-literate, I had a problem fitting the bits of the system together to make the integrated HISS. Every time I asked a question I was met with 'I assume', or 'I expect'. . . . So I personally became alarmed by my lack of understanding of the whole!"

The development of modules of the system forced members of the project team to make their tacit knowledge about the hospital explicit, and they became increasingly aware of gaps. The project manager:

> ". . . as we moved through the early part of 1991, where some people were doing what was called product-build—building tables and setting the system up ready to be run—and some people were designing forms, some departmental managers, on the basis of what was being developed in the system, were making assumptions about what their work-load would include, and this takes us

right through to menu design: what would employees have on their menus. Somebody had to do the various functions somewhere and assumptions were being made within the team about who would do what: what nurses would do, what doctors would do, what ward clerks would do; a whole raft of people who all knit together in the real world but whose jobs became focused into the need to know exactly who would do what by the implementation of the system."

Two members of the project team in particular—the nursing officer and the patient administration officer—became increasingly worried, both because they did not have a wide-enough circulation to let people know what they themselves were doing and because of the gaps in their own knowledge. They approached the project manager with the idea of an "integration day", a day on which representatives from across the hospital would be in the same room together, so that assumptions about each other's functions and work could be checked out. As a vehicle for this, they proposed to try to build a case history that would take staff through as many branches of care as possible and use it as a focus for discussion.

To get hospital-wide attendance at such an event, support had to be obtained at senior level. The hospital's general manager was approached, and he adopted the idea with enthusiasm. It was he who issued the invitations to the "integration day" and who ensured that key people attended.

A feature of the situation was that none of the systems had been implemented at that stage. All departments had internal co-ordinators involved in the detailed development or build of their own part of the system. But the managers and other staff attending the integration day would at most have some familiarity with these internal departmental systems being developed:

"If you take radiology as an example, a radiology co-ordinator was building the system for radiology and would have involved all the department in the radiology departmental things, their internal bits, but would be making assumptions about how the interface between radiology and the rest of the hospital worked. Now, while this was working on a word-of-mouth or bits-of-paper basis, in other words in the old way, those assumptions could be fairly woolly. Once we were implementing a full-scale integrated information system, it was necessary to know much more clearly just what those boundaries were, how they would work, who precisely would do what, be responsible for what."

The method

Two scenarios were written, one for the day in a ward and one for the patient, who came to be known as "Poor Old Henry" because so many dire things happened to him. The scenario was written by the diabetes consultant, so the patient was a diabetic.

In the event, integration days using scenarios of this kind to test some aspect of integration were used three times in the course of the next two years. Each time the trigger was a large topic that was going to have a wide impact, so that it was necessary to get together in the same room everybody who would be affected. However, the ward scenario was only used on the first integration day; it was not judged to be relevant for the other two.

The meetings were attended by internal hospital staff. Both senior and junior levels were represented—"those who thought they knew what went on, and those who actually knew what really happened". A decision had been taken not to invite people who were not employed by the hospital, such as social workers. This was linked to the issue of system boundaries, of who should or should not have direct access to the information system.

The work, however, was not primarily systems-oriented. It was intended to focus on people, procedures, and the integration of the hospital. This also meant getting people to understand that they could not simply write a procedure for their part of the work; they had to think in terms of the whole hospital—"Henry allowed the ripples from the pond to be followed."

The structure of the event was the same each time. One member of the project team would "walk" the audience "through" the story step by step, until a question was reached or a discussion broke out.

A member of the project board then acted as facilitator for the discussion. An important feature of the design was to let discussion go on until there was consensus and clarity about what a problem or an issue actually was, but not to let it move further on into problem-solving itself—that was too big and too complex a task to be handled within the space of the day. A few issues could be resolved on the spot; just having the relevant people together to share their knowledge and experience was, in some cases, enough. If a major issue that emerged was not concerned with HISS, in some instances a sub-set of people was convened afterwards to work on it.

The project manager and the training officer acted as scribes, recording the discussion and in particular the issues that emerged. It was felt necessary to have two people doing this, in case one of them missed something (the first integration day yielded one hundred such issues or questions).

After the event, the project manager circulated an "issues list" to all those who had attended. Working on the issues was then prioritized, key issues about parts of the HISS that were being implemented next being looked at first. However, there was a chicken-and-egg element in this: afterwards it was felt that, if some issues that were not immediately identified as urgent had been dealt with, some others would not have arisen at all. The circle was not closed in a formal way, but pencil notes on the various issues lists show that many questions were answered, sometimes very simply, or resolved. Some others, however, remained problematic.

Once the main part of the system had gone live, a regular "Issues Meeting" was institutionalized to continue working on issues that had not been resolved and new ones that came up. Not all issues were resolved.

The first integration day

The first integration day was held to check assumptions in the building of the information system, as described earlier. The people who had instigated it were quite anxious. They knew what they wanted from the event, but they were unsure what the participants would gain. The event took a whole day, with a "walk-through" of the ward in the morning and of the story of Poor Old Henry in the afternoon.

The ward scenario was chronological, dividing the day into phases. A medical ward is a very busy place: some categories of staff come on duty (nurses, junior doctors, a ward clerk; one agency nurse did not turn up) and hand over to each other when their shift ends. Other categories of staff come for specific purposes (physiotherapist, phlebotomist, pharmacist, chaplain, cardiac technician, porter). There are routine events (meals, bed-making, drug rounds) and non-routine events (a patient deteriorates unexpectedly, and doctors and relatives have to be informed); there is a water leak in the bathroom; an oxygen pipe cannot be found. Staff have to have breaks, stores arrive, domestic cleaning takes place. A new patient is admitted, tests have to be ordered. Two patients are ready for discharge but their test results have to be obtained first; transport has to be organized. Records and care plans have to be updated. A consultant does his ward round, and this results in decisions that need to be implemented. And so on, and so on.

"What became apparent were things like the number of times the same pieces of information were requested for different needs—the bed state from the bed bureau, someone from A&E. checking whether the beds available were male or female beds, the senior nurse phoning round trying to find out [bed] availability in terms of needing to move patients around the hospital. . . ."

Another thing the ward scenario highlighted was the number of times people in the meeting said, "The nurses will do that, it will only take them a minute." This was a function of the size of the group; they were all together, they could see the number of times the nursing staff were expected to do things. They even calculated the number of minutes that these various small tasks required and found that this added up to a whole morning of a nurse's time. So there was learning about the knock-on implications of one's actions.

The first story of Henry was as follows:

Henry Smith is an 82-year-old man who lives alone. He has felt unwell for some time, but despite advice from his son (who visits him weekly) he did not seek advice from his GP until he developed a severe pain in his right foot. The following is an abbreviated history of subsequent events:

Henry attends his GP surgery; he is referred to the pathology department at the hospital for tests; when diabetes is confirmed, he is referred to the Diabetic Day Care Centre, then to a consultant's clinic. Admission to hospital is arranged, tests are taken, an antibiotic regime started. Once in hospital, after difficulty in finding a bed, he sees a dietician, a chiropodist, and a surgeon. An arteriogram is arranged and he needs to be put on an insulin drip while he has this test.

After the arteriogram, Henry is told he will need surgery. He is transferred to a surgical ward and to the care of a surgeon. Blood is taken for cross-matching, as he will probably need a blood transfusion. Two days later his foot is amputated; he has a bad reaction to one of the drugs and lands in intensive care for observation. Once back in the ward he has physiotherapy but also has a "funny turn" and is sent to the cardiac ultrasound department for an echocardiogram (which is normal). Before being discharged, arrangements are made for him to attend the Limb Fitting Centre, for an occupational therapist to do a home visit, for a social worker to see him and for a visit to the Eye Clinic.

All being well, Henry is discharged home. He is told that the local district nurse will visit him regularly to look at his wound. He is also given appointments in the follow-up clinic in six weeks' time and asked to return to the hospital one week before his appointment for a blood test. The hospital has arranged transport for all these visits.

Once Henry is recovering at home, back at the hospital much work is going on to document Henry's stay. His case notes are sent to the medical secretaries, where one of the doctors dictates a discharge summary, and once this has been typed his notes are sent to the medical coders before finally being returned to file.

The second integration day

The method was used a second time when the pathology information-system module was about to be implemented. Ordering pathology tests and getting the results was crucial for all other departments, and it was essential to get the pathology system right, or as right as possible:

> "It was really focusing on all the aspects of management that were associated with placing orders: phlebotomy, specimen collection, getting results, urgent results, cumulative reports, a whole raft of things that the organization was interested in in terms of order management for pathology, because it affected everybody. Prior to that we had order management for radiology which was not so pressurized, in the sense that fewer people use it, and when they do use it they generally are not at the same level of intensity. Pathology is the thing that produces the urgent results and reports, the urgent results that somebody has to do something about."

This time, the ward was not thought to be the relevant entity, and the integration day focused only on the experiences of Poor Old Henry. A new scenario, continuing his story, was written. The following is a summary:

> After his last adventures, Henry had successfully gone home and lived a fairly independent life. He still visits the hospital on a regular basis for review of his diabetes in the outpatient department, where he has regular blood tests. However, for some time now Henry has not been well and is losing his independence. His GP decides to undertake some tests to identify the problem.
>
> He sends Henry for an X-ray, ECG, a physiotherapy assessment, and blood tests and also arranges for him to attend [ward] 2A as a "ward attender" for a glucose-tolerance test.
>
> Henry continues to decline and wakes up one morning with a slight left-sided weakness and appears a little confused. The home help becomes very anxious and phones immediately for an ambulance to take Henry to hospital. Several problems are diagnosed, and he is admitted and spends six days in hospital. During this time, investigations are carried out and treatment is started involving several departments of the hospital. In his confused state he attempts to climb out of bed and falls, incurring a fractured femur. This involves another operation, an additional consultant, transfers from one ward to another and back again. Discharging him involves ordering a wheelchair and getting the social work department involved, since he is now going to move into sheltered accommodation.
>
> Five weeks after Henry's discharge, his elderly sister-in-law writes a letter of complaint to "the Matron". She is very unhappy that Henry had the fall and feels she was given little real explanation. She has not given any details on Henry other than his name. She has no telephone.

The scenario took up six pages and the integration day nearly a whole day. This time, sixty-five issues were identified. An example concerned people who were not on the system, such as community midwives and dentists, needing to order tests. The group identified ways of enabling orders to be put in and the implications for coding/statistical analysis of these decisions.

The method raised people's awareness of the complexity of the organization and highlighted how little many people knew about what was done, especially in the area of non-clinical support staff.

The third integration day

The third integration day was organized to help the hospital work on the implications of the framework of provider/purchaser contracting that was being newly implemented in the National Health Service at that time. It was held towards the end of the 1992/93 round of contracting and was particularly aimed at service managers, many of whom had been recently appointed. This time, it was the Unit general manager (the hospital had in the meantime merged with another one to form a single Provider Unit) who asked for it to be organized, not the HISS team. There were over forty people in the room, both very senior and very junior people. Consultants, coders, heads of departments, service managers, the director of finance—all these were involved in the process of making contracts. People who attended found it valuable and instructive, but they wished it had happened earlier so that the learning could have informed the contracting process that year.

Once again only the story of Henry was used, his adventures having many implications for the hospital's contracts. The script used on the last occasion was used again but modified slightly, to open up more implications for contracting. For example, Henry now had a son visiting him who was registered with a distant GP fund-holder and who was also ill. In discussion with the service managers, some issues that had not been part of the story emerged, and these were simply added to the script.

The meeting revealed many problems of definition, such as what is a separate activity—"If I see someone in Outpatients and then do a coronary angiogram, are we then an agent of the [GP] practice, or is it our activity?" Or: "There will only be one consultant against the account, but it can involve up to four others 'assisting'. So where do drug costs get allocated?"

Although the amount of complexity and transfers from one consultant to another in Henry's case was unrealistic, the uncertainty about whose care he was under at any one point generated some questions in the audience about whether he was being clinically cared for. As each consultant episode was being coded separately, "Are the clinicians happy for coders to be diagnosing patients?" Moreover, the patient had a heart condition, which, in the interest generated by the subsequent technical problems, got forgotten.

One issue that surfaced at this meeting had rather wide implications: patients with certain conditions go to any hospital near which they find themselves for routine repeat treatment, such as anticoagulant injections. It was thought to be much cheaper and simpler just to give the treatment than to get the extra-contractual referral agreed by the district of residence first.[1] In the course of the meeting this seemed to become policy, in the hope that local residents away from home would get equivalent benefits where they found themselves, a matter of swings and roundabouts. But the implication was that places where people go on holiday, for instance, would be at a disadvantage because they had more visitors than residents going away; also, there could be quite substantial classes of work for which nobody billed or got paid.

"It's not so much that it was more bother [to obtain an ECR], it was much more fundamental than that. The patient turned up on your doorstep asking to see the haematologist because he had this condition and he needed to have an injection. If he had come from Hartlepool we would not have a contract with Hartlepool, full stop. So in the terms of the rules it had to be an ECR. Now for an ECR you have to ring up the Health Authority involved, tell them that you have one of their patients, what you want to do, get approval for it to be an ECR for them to pay, and the cost of the treatment might only be £3.50. Now you could actually spend £3.50 in administrative fees and telephone calls and paperwork and postage. In the meantime you have got the patient there, so what do you do? Do you keep the patient in the hospital hanging round for several hours while you get the paperwork for the ECR? The District Health Authority person in Hartlepool was not available, he will ring you back tomorrow. . . . . It was the nonsense of the situation which meant you treated the patient and you didn't get the contract sorted out."

Discussion

Initially, the purpose of using Henry and the ward scenario had been to help the people building modules of the information system test their assumptions about other parts of the hospital and get a view of the whole. In addition, there was a purpose about merging the HISS project manager's knowledge of the information system with the team members' knowledge of the workings of the hospital.

However, making use of Henry turned out to have a number of other functions. It gave people across the hospital a better understanding of the problems of others, ranging from the clinical coders' difficulties in reading doctors' handwriting and the problem of what to do if a patient is unable to give his address, to major problems of clinical care and finance. It helped with the induction of new members of management. It highlighted the limitations within which people worked, as they became aware of the consequences for others of their own bright ideas. It helped to get responsibilities identified and ownership for problems taken up.

Example 2:
"I am a Trebor Mint" —
the consultant as product as transitional object

In the late 1970s the Trebor Group, a well-known company in the United Kingdom manufacturing sweets and confectionery, was planning to build a new factory. It was a family firm, with a history of solid growth, and employed some three thousand people. In 1977 it was decided that one of its four factories, in London, could not be adequately refurbished within the existing building and site and should be replaced by an entirely new factory elsewhere. They wanted to take this opportunity to move away from traditional concepts of factory life, and I was engaged to work with them on questions of work satisfaction and the design of the new jobs (Klein & Eason, 1991, chap. 7). This example of a transitional intervention concerns one episode from that work.

A project group at Board level had been formed and when I first met this group, in June 1977, a site had been acquired outside London and planning permission for the new factory obtained. At this meeting, the group was beginning to discuss the choice of architects and the general shape of the building. It was clear that the prospect of an entirely new factory was acting as a focus for a powerful vein of idealism in the company. Not only did they want the jobs in the new factory to be satisfying, they wanted the architecture to be innovative and human in scale, and to make a distinct contribution to the built environment.

Two concepts for the new factory were being debated: on the one hand, the concept of a large hangar-like structure within which there would be freedom and flexibility to arrange and rearrange things; on the other, the concept of a "village street", with small production units, as well as social facilities. Within a few minutes of joining the group, I was confronted with the question, "What do you think—large hangar or village street?"

I had, of course, no basis for an opinion and realized that we were in a dilemma. The concept I intended to work with was that of a production process as a sociotechnical system—that is, one where the human and technical aspects are interdependent and need to be considered simultaneously, with the human aspects and needs playing a strong role. To translate this concept into practical reality, one needs to understand the manufacturing process and its technology in some detail. So within ten minutes of joining one of their meetings for the first time, I encountered a major methodological difficulty in design—that of phasing. The company felt that they could not even begin to talk to architects until they had some idea of the basic shape of the building they wanted; one could not sensibly discuss the shape of the building without some idea of the production layout; and I could not contribute to discussion about the layout from the job-design point of view without some sociotechnical analysis of the production process, which needed time. At that stage, I had not even seen the manufacturing process.

At a second meeting, I worked with the project group to list job-design criteria, discussing priorities among them and relating them to production criteria. I had the opportunity to spend a day in the old factory looking at the production process, but when I attended the third meeting of the project group, I was still far from really understanding the details of the production system I had learned that the first of the products to be manufactured on the new site, a mint, consisted almost entirely of crushed sugar with some additives, which was then compressed into a tablet and packaged.

Instinctively, I went back to basics. I was groping for a more detailed understanding and said: "Look, I still haven't understood the process properly—suppose I'm a piece of sugar. I've just been delivered. What happens to me?" Somebody said, "Well, the first thing that happens to you is that you get blown along a tube. But there is a physical limit to how far you can be blown." I said, "OK, what happens next?" And somebody said, "Next you get crushed into a powder."

In this way, I talked my way through the process in very great detail, role-playing the product. For example, I heard myself saying, "All right, so now I'm a granule—what happens next?"

"Next we drop mint oil on your head."

"Might you miss?"

"Yes, we might."

"How would that be discovered?"

And so on. I checked back a number of times to ask whether to them this was just a game or whether it was useful, but they assured me that they were finding it very useful. The product was a fairly simple one, which they had been making for a long time, and their ways of thinking about it had become rather set. Now, these ways of thinking began to unfreeze, and they began to discover alternatives and to say to each other, "It doesn't have to be like that, it could be like this, if such-and-such conditions are met."

In particular, some things that had been customarily thought of in sequence could, it was found, be done in parallel. This meant that the logic of the production process was not necessarily a straight line, and this, in turn, meant that one could think in terms of a short, squat building. That was the eventual shape of the "product house" that emerged out of this process.

I realized afterwards that my own strategy had instinctively been about leaving options open. Once the factory was staffed and experience of the work system beginning to accumulate, there was more chance of reviewing and revising it in a short, squat building than in one where the logic of the layout led to long, straight lines.

During these design activities and partly through the work that had been done on design criteria, it had emerged that there was a very strong value—not to say ideology—in the company, concerning autonomous work groups and team working. This emphasis was strong and, in my view, somewhat romantic, in that group working was expected to solve a wide and diffuse range of problems. I found myself putting emphasis on unaccustomed ergonomic considerations and other "mundane" aspects of work to try to maintain some balance.

Because of the original experience, the idea of imaginatively playing with alternative ways of doing things became somewhat institutionalized in the company's design activities. The next phase of my involvement was with the management team that the company had been recruiting to develop, and later run, the new factory. A residential seminar with them was organized, and the team arrived with a rough model for the proposed product house. They had invested £200 in Lego bricks and had worked very hard over a weekend to produce a first tentative layout. This they presented, with the question, "What do you think of it?" In a way that was similar to the earlier experience, it seemed unreliable to translate the arrangement of the layout by a sheer act of imagination into the work experiences that might be going on around it.

I said, "I'm not very good at reading drawings. I can't really think my way into this. What is actually happening down there? Suppose it's seven-thirty in the morning, what is going on?" One of them said, "All right, I'll be a press operator." Another said, "We don't know if we're going to have press operators." Gradually, they took on roles according to the tasks that needed to be done, and then someone said, "OK, it's seven-thirty in the morning, the bell's gone and the doors are open . . ." He was interrupted—"What do you mean, bell? Are we going to have bells?" And there followed a long discussion on clocking-in. Their optimism and enthusiasm about the consequences of autonomy was unbounded, and it was I who found myself playing devil's advocate—"suppose a work group has a member who is persistently late? What will they do? How will they demonstrate it if there is no clock to give them the information?" The outcome of this discussion was that there should be space on a wall to install a time-clock if it turned out that the work groups themselves wanted one.

By midday the team had, in this way, worked their way through the start-up and the first hour or so of production. In the process, a number of things in the layout were changed, and it was interesting to see how difficult it was to undo even as ephemeral a decision as the arrangement of a few Lego bricks, given the hard work that had gone into their original arrangement.

Example 3:
Refuelling at London Airport—
a structured, experimental approach

In contrast to the last example, there was very little spontaneity in the design of the final one. And yet it had the same function of allowing people to test out alternative strategies in a safe environment, before becoming committed to one of them. There can be scope for transitional dynamics in places where psychodynamically oriented observers may not look for them; they may well be present even in a highly structured experimental context.

The story concerns the redesign of Esso Petroleum Company's aircraft refuelling function at London Airport (Shackel & Klein, 1976). At the time this work was done, Esso handled about 40% of the refuelling at London's Heathrow Airport. The situation was that, after landing, aircraft parked at any one of about a hundred stands on the long-haul and short-haul "aprons" of the airport. The turn-around time for most aircraft was about one hour, but one airline was already trying to reduce this to half an hour. In this time not only did passengers and fuel have to be loaded, but caterers, maintenance engineers, cleaners, and so on all needed to park near and work on the plane. The job of the controller in the fuelling station was to make sure that fuelling trucks reached the aircraft on time, and the worst thing that could happen for him was that he should be responsible for delaying an aircraft.

For information about aircraft movements, the controller had on his desk the arrival and departure schedules of the airlines who were Esso customers; minute-to-minute information about the actual approach and arrival of the aircraft was received by two tickertape machines from the air traffic control centre; information about the specific fuelling needs of particular aircraft was supplied by electrowriter and by telephone links with the airlines; and information about the availability of drivers and trucks came from duty rosters and truck logs.

This job of controller had been becoming increasingly difficult. The rate of traffic through the airport was increasing by about 15% per year; traffic problems on the ground were increasing in proportion, and one could "lose" a truck in ground traffic for up to forty minutes; and the company was very cost-conscious and kept to a minimum the controller's resources of trucks and drivers.

Job-design criteria concerning skill and autonomy were not a problem. In interviews with the controllers, it became clear that the importance of the job was clear to all and liked by all. They were very much identified with the success of the operation and had many ideas about its improvement. But all of them, in one way or another, complained of "stress", "fatigue", and inability to unwind. Inevitably some informal ways of coping were being found: "When I know I'm going to get a delay, I phone my pal who's maintenance engineer for the airline. He'll pretend there's something the matter with the engine and start pulling it to bits."

Thus, the first part of the project had been an interview study. The next phase, carried out by an external team of ergonomists, was the preparation of detailed analysis papers on all aspects of the system that were important to the controllers or affected their task in some way. The papers included analyses of the tickertape, the documentation in the control-room, the communications with airlines, the movement of people in the control-room and other rooms, the role of the "bolster man" (a back-up support role), the shift-rotation scheme, the resources of men, the resources of trucks, and the implications for Esso of future changes at the airport. These formed a formal information base, checked and agreed by Esso staff, from which the proposed redesign was to be developed and critically evaluated.

From the information and analyses, detailed recommendations were made about the design and layout of the building, control-room, store of truck logs, and structure of the controller's desk, together with recommendations for noise control, heating and ventilation, lighting, and other storage facilities. A magnetic stateboard was designed to give the controller a schematic representation of the state of his re-sources (i.e., drivers and trucks) by means of coloured tags, attached to other tags representing aircraft when they were sent out on a refuelling mission and dismantled once the mission was complete.

A second set of recommendations then detailed the layout of the work area, desk superstructure, aircraft schedules, stateboard and all tags, driver shift board, driver tag store, and colour schemes. Both the redesign of the various rooms and the desk, and the proposed new method of working, were discussed in detail with all the controllers and supervisors, and their suggestions and criticisms were taken into account in the final recommendations.

Once these discussions were complete, a simulated control-room, incorporating the new features, was built in a laboratory, and simu-lation experiments were designed. To obtain an accurate picture of the system, detailed running programmes for the simulation experi-ments were written by three postgraduate students from information supplied by management, supervisors, and controllers. In effect, the programmes were word-for-word theatrical texts for continuous three-hour plays, in which the "actors" were enthusiastic to play their parts. Company personnel were also directly involved in running the experi-ments, since this was the most realistic way of simulating some of the roles in the system. Students took the part of truck drivers.

Each experimental session lasted three hours, and the controller was able to walk into the replica of his office, sit down in the chair, and take over the job as he would in the real situation. The realism of the situation was indicated by the fact that the controllers needed very little explanation of what to do, other than initial briefing with the new equipment. They found that they were able to react in very much the same way as in the real situation.

In this way, the controllers and supervisors came and worked in the simulated control-room, testing and comparing in different sessions four different methods of working, under three different load condi-tions (the current load, the load predicted for the following year's peak period, and the anticipated load for five years ahead). Repeated questionnaires and interviews tested opinions at different stages of the experiments. The intention was that the people who would be operating the system could contribute their experience to its design, would be able to try a number of alternatives before deciding on a solution, and could have some idea of how long that solution would remain viable. In particular, they would be able to try out in safe conditions some of the designers' ideas that were unfamiliar to them and that at first they did not like. The idea of the magnetic stateboard had caused some anxiety, because it did not provide the same permanent record as pieces of paper, since the tags representing each mission were put back into store once the mission was over. However, during the experiments the controllers discovered that they could feel safe with this method.

The solution arrived at in this way was installed and was found to be still in use and well liked both four years and seven years later (one indication of reduced stress for the controllers was that, where they had previously stood and hovered over the desk to do the job, especially during peak load times, they were now sitting to do the job and standing up at intervals to stretch).

Simulation and the testing of alternatives are not, of course, new concepts in design; it is unusual, however, to find such explicit and realistic attention paid to the human aspects of the situation. It is quite possible, for example, to simulate some of the "softer" aspects of social system functioning, such as the effect on a group that has interdependent roles when one member stays away or is slower than the others. In the case of the Esso refuelling controllers, it was found during the experiments that, as they gained increasing control over their own situation, having enough spare capacity through the simplification and streamlining of the work to be able to plan ahead instead of panic-reacting to events as they happened, there were consequences for industrial relations: before, rest-pauses and meal breaks for the drivers had tended to be either very short or very long; now they were instinctively being scheduled in a much more equitable way.

Discussion

Three rather disparate cases have been brought together here because they show how the same ends can be achieved in ways that appear to be quite different.

All three cases, it turned out, had the necessary transitional characteristics of exploring and testing-out in a safe environment, with outcomes not known in advance. In all three there was an element of acting, of theatre. The element of play involved in the use of scenarios in the hospital, especially that concerning Poor Old Henry, was a key feature in the move towards more integrated working. It undoubtedly helped that the meetings were handled in a light-hearted way and contained a good deal of wit and humour. It is a relief to be able to laugh about a patient's misfortunes, since he is only a fiction—"People became very fond of Henry." Humour also featured in the situation of a grown-up woman role-playing a confectionery product, though not so much in the somewhat formal situation of a simulation experiment. In the safety of the laboratory this, too, however, was relatively light-hearted compared with the real hazards of the actual job.

At the same time, it needs to be said that none of the strategies involved in these cases had been planned on this theoretical basis.

Note

1. Where non-emergency treatment was required for a patient with whose GP or "district of residence" the hospital had no contract, agreement needed to be obtained—usually by telephone—that the treatment would be paid for. This was called an extra-contractual referral.

RELATING SCIENTIFIC
AND PROFESSIONAL DEVELOPMENT

The final two papers are more autobiographical than the rest. They lay open the personal journey to becoming a reflective practitioner—in particular, the various efforts to combine and synthesize the two frameworks: the use of knowledge and the dynamics of action.

CHAPTER 15

On the use of psychoanalytic concepts in organizational social science: two sides of a coin

This was a talk given to the International Society for the Psychoanalytic Study of Organizations. The members of this are psychoanalysts—or, at any rate, people in a psychodynamic framework—who work with organizations. I am not a member and in this paper presented a rather personal account of how a non-psychoanalyst comes to learn to use some psychodynamic concepts in working with organizations. Conversely, it suggests what psychoanalysts who want to work with organizations need to take on board from the broader social sciences. It was later published in the journal *Concepts and Transformation* (Klein, 2001). Some of the illustrations have been shortened because they also appear elsewhere in this collection.

The story of "Poor Old Henry" is therefore not repeated in detail, as it appears in the previous chapter. However, it has a particular interest for this area of relating organizational and psychodynamic approaches: from a contingency perspective, the design requirements of an integrated information system forced the members of the hospital to think institutionally, which their previous technologies—paper, the telephone, departmental computer systems—had not demanded of them. Once they were thinking institutionally, they recognized that there were problems and were able to devise a way to proceed that met important psychodynamic criteria.

I joined the Tavistock Institute in 1971, as a social scientist with experience in organizational research and in its application and use. I had been engaged for five years as in-house social sciences adviser in Esso Petroleum Company. I had had some personal analysis and was convinced that people working in consulting roles needed this for the protection of their clients, so that they had somewhere to work on their own problems and would not do so in the course of their work with clients. I had read a good deal of the early Tavistock literature, where more explicit use is made of psychoanalytic approaches.

The excitement of the original Tavistock breakthroughs, which brought psychoanalytic understanding to bear on non-clinical situations, still remains. I trust my guts enough to recognize that this excitement means "there's something there". It is what has kept me interested and intrigued over the years. But excitement is not enough: it is a necessary but not sufficient condition. It should be the trigger that leads to more rigorous investigation, and this has not often happened. Describing the process by which someone discovers and learns to use a set of ideas should at least help to take these ideas out of the realm of mystique and unchallengeable *ex cathedra* pronouncements.

Two sets of ideas had, in fact, been seductive about "the Tavi" over the years (attracting people to it irrespective of what was actually happening there). Both of them are ambiguous, which has been part of the attraction. One is sociotechnical theory: for some people, this has come to be identified with autonomous group working; for some, with participative work design. Many have learned about it as a series of steps in analysing work situations; very few see it as an aid to designing them. For me, this ambiguity has never been a basic problem. It is perhaps the term itself that has proved most useful. The idea of work systems being "sociotechnical" has served as a guide to looking at the interdependencies between their technical and social aspects, in both analysis and design activities. It put what I had been doing already into a conceptual framework, is basic to many different kinds of situation, and has proved useful in many different ways.

The second set of ideas was the use of psychoanalytic concepts in non-clinical situations, and here I was and remain on much less certain ground. The general idea has by now caught on and has indeed become something of a fashion. There is a literature about the "psychoanalysis of organizations", and there is an International Society for the Psychoanalytic Study of Organizations. Clients of these activities may sometimes be attracted by the possibility of gaining personal insights without the difficulty or expense of having an analysis, and therefore they may not worry too much about whether what they are learning has to do with their organizations as well as themselves; consultants have a responsibility not to exploit this need or fudge the distinction.

It is probably tautological to say that the "psychoanalytic study of organizations" brings together two frames of reference: psychoanalysis and the study of organizations. And yet it very much needs to be said, because a good deal of the material that appears under this heading appears to assume that there is only one framework. I want to differentiate between the two, explore some of the links between them, and at the same time also note in what ways they differ. The discussion will need to remain grounded in empirical work, not only because I think it is important to do so, but also because I am not capable of doing anything else.

Some relevant concepts and their use

So what are some of the psychodynamic concepts that I have found useful in working with organizations, and how may they be used? Internalizing a concept and turning it into use is hard work and takes time. In the case of psychoanalytic concepts, I reckon that I can cope with about one per year. The situation is essentially the same with research results in the social sciences. You cannot take a finding developed in situation A and slap it onto situation B. If you internalize the principle of the finding—for instance, that control systems have predictable behavioural consequences—what comes out in situation B, and may be immensely useful, may superficially look quite different from what happened in situation A. Above all, it is unlikely to involve the use of formulae. The problem about using formulaic solutions is that they have not gone through the long and often difficult process of internalizing and turning into use, the outcome of which is generally not predictable.

Splitting

The first psychoanalytic concept that preoccupied me in this conscious and explicit way in the mid-1980s was splitting. "Splitting" is a process of psychic economy whereby we simplify a complex situation for ourselves by attributing all its "x" characteristics to one of a pair, and all its "y" characteristics to the other: the goodies are all-good and wear white hats, and the baddies are all-bad and wear black hats. A stunning—and, with hindsight, stunningly obvious—revelation to which this concept leads is that it explains the sociotechnical problem; by this I mean the unsolved problem of getting sociotechnical work institutionalized.

Clearly, all work systems have technical, human, and social aspects, and these are interdependent. It has simply been easier, more psychically economic, to perceive them in separate configurations. Not only do technologists have difficulty in including the social element in their professional thinking, social scientists have difficulty in including the technical element in theirs: very few social scientists have been willing actually to engage with technology and its design and development instead of generalizing or philosophizing about it from a separate—or split—position.

For, secondly and perhaps even more importantly, the splitting has become deeply institutionalized. It pervades the education system, research, the funding of research, career structures, professional institutions, the literature. Engineers read what engineers have written, social scientists read what social scientists have written. When a social scientist publishes a paper in an engineering journal, as I have occasionally done, it reaches neither database.[1]

The understanding arrived at via the concept of splitting helped to explain why sociotechnical work has been so consistently frustrating. The ideas have, after all, been around for a very long time (they were contained in the work of Karl Marx long before they were conceptualized in this particular way in the coal-mining studies of the Tavistock Institute). My aim, indeed the aim of most approaches described as sociotechnical, had all along been to get the consideration of human and organizational factors integrated with the work of technology development and implementation. After many years of at best partial and ephemeral success, where every change in project-team or steering-group membership virtually meant starting again from scratch, the notion of institutionalized splitting provided a better understanding of why this was so. "Projects" in which social scientists made a contribution to engineering developments, of which there has by now been a large number, were simply too weak a mechanism to counteract the institutionalized splitting. It began to seem more important to tackle the roots of the splitting and search for strategies of integration than to place all the emphasis on collaborative design and development projects, even though these had always been a source of interest and learning. There was a need to look for ways of institutionalizing integrated working—that is, to provide for integration through budgets, through education and training, through management review procedures, and, where appropriate, through standards.

Transference

Gaining some understanding of transference took a long time. My own analysis, I have to say, did not teach me much about it. I knew that it was about transferring feelings developed in relation to one object onto another, in particular onto the analyst; however, I had not seen the relevance or usefulness of this in relation to working with organizations. Then, one day, I was talking through a report on a project with Harold Bridger. It was a difficult project, in which I felt as if I were being batted like a ball between very tough and intransigent management and trade union parties. Harold said: "Read this through again and ask yourself, what are they doing to you that they can't do to each other?" What is apparently meant here is that, in transferring positive or negative feelings onto the analyst, the patient unconsciously makes the analyst play the role of figures to whom those feelings apply (Sándor Ferenczi, cited in Laplanche & Pontalis, 1973). I hadn't realized that. [2]

The use of the self

It is with the concept of the use of the self that the difference between a research frame of reference and a consulting frame of reference emerges starkly. In the research world, the material being worked with is "data", and the aim is to remove the influence of the person of the researcher from it as much as possible. The knowledge is all "out there", and any residual influence of what is "in here" is experienced as threatening to the validity of the knowledge. In consultancy, and especially the kind of consultancy that is informed by psychodynamic understanding, practitioners may make deliberate use of themselves and their own responses. They use themselves like a measuring instrument, asking themselves questions such as: "If this is making me feel angry/anxious/sad/affectionate/muddled, what does that tell me about what is happening out there?"

A social scientist who moves from research into consulting begins to blur and soften this sharp divide. For instance, he or she has to negotiate what is to happen in the assignment; findings have to be fed back into the client system and responses to them dealt with, instead of merely being published to the outside world. There is likely to be some transference to deal with, some need to confront client reactions, some need to respond in ways that are not wholly determined by the data. However, he or she is unlikely to go as far as using him/herself as the principal research tool. That will seem too unreliable a way, too prone to bias and selective perception. Perhaps the greatest value of this limited use of the self is in generating hypotheses for discussion or for testing.

Countertransference

Whereas transference is about feelings and responses of the client towards the consultant, countertransference is about the consultant's reaction to clients. A piece of understanding about the relevance of this to working with organizations came suddenly in the middle of a conference in 1993. After a technical paper on countertransference, someone was making a discussion contribution about organization development, on the lines of "What about our values in all this, our commitment to changing and democratizing organizations?"

I need to explain that, ever since I first heard about OD, I have been very uncomfortable about it. I took the Esso post in 1965 because a feeling was spreading in industry at that time, after a very fruitful period of industrial sociological and psychological research, that the social sciences had something valuable to contribute. The types of contribution were potentially many and varied, and it was to explore this that I joined the company. I had never heard of OD. I thought the task of a social scientist in an organization was to use whatever concepts and methods he or she had available to try to understand what was happening and to work with the organization on whatever issues were encountered. It is a fundamentally different frame of reference from starting out with a clear view of how they ought to behave and trying to change them in that direction. When I later discovered the existence of OD, I thought it very strange for some consultant or group of consultants to call themselves "change agents" when, first, every single member of an organization contributes to its development and/ or change and, second, change is not necessarily what is most needed at any particular time. If change is needed, there has to be a good deal of diagnosis and collaborative work before one can be confident about what kind of change and in what direction.

This uneasy relationship with much of what goes on under the heading of OD has continued ever since, and perhaps reached its peak when I heard an OD practitioner talk about his "hit-list for paradigm change". And then the lightning struck: this normative aspect of OD must be something to do with countertransference, with the consultant transferring his or her own wishes, needs, and feelings onto the client. How else can one explain this urge, this drive, this missionary zeal to change other people and their organizations? Even elegant statements about single-loop and double-loop learning are frequently simply statements about turning bad guys into good guys. And everyone has come across instances of "democratic management" or "participative job design" being introduced in ways that are themselves highly authoritarian and in contradiction to the values being espoused. How else can this be explained except as an urgent effort to make the client do what one cannot do oneself, to effect "out there" what cannot be managed "in here"?

It is good to understand the reason for my unease at last. I don't get it about everything that happens under the heading of OD—but somehow one can smell the difference.

Transitional dynamics

In the case of transitional dynamics, practice preceded theory. When I learned about the use made of Winnicott's ideas about transitional objects and their relevance in everyday life (Winnicott, 1971), I felt a bit like Molière's Bourgeois Gentilhomme, who discovered that he had been talking prose all his life. Many, if not most, social science practitioners are talking this kind of prose already.

A few years ago, Ken Eason and I made a collection of case studies in applied social science (Klein & Eason, 1991). What most of the professionals in these cases were doing, whatever discipline they came from, was devising or helping to devise transitional systems of one kind or another. These might be simulations, pilot exercises, work shops, learning events, negotiating procedures. They were, in any case, situations that could be used for playing, for testing out possible alternative futures, and testing oneself out in relation to such futures. The value of the concept itself in this case lies in checking out whether the method that is being developed has the requisite characteristics that will, in fact, enable it to facilitate transition.

Clients, too, devise transitional systems (see chapter 14 and the story of Poor Old Henry). Question: Is there value in solemnly announcing to the client that Henry is a transitional object?

This brings me to consider the other side of the coin: what the study of organizations has to offer to psychoanalytically oriented consultants.

The other side of the coin

So far, I have considered how a social scientist working with organizations can take on board and use whatever psychoanalytic understanding he or she can arrive at. I hope that the process will continue and that there will be other concepts that one may gradually take on board and internalize. Now I would like both to turn the equation around and say something about what psychoanalytically oriented consultants, who may be used to working with individual patients, need to do to take on board aspects of organization study, and to try to examine where the parallels stop.

The role of evidence

First, the study of organizations is just that: study. This implies a value about taking evidence seriously. Intuitions are valuable, but they need to be checked out. The most fruitful intuitions are those that help to make sense of data that is or can be made accessible to the organization. It may be a new and different kind of sense, and the consultant's frame of reference that produces this new kind of sense is the contribution that he or she brings. It may be the result of rearranging data in an unexpected way. But wild interpretations, which cannot be related to evidence and whose function is merely to startle, seem to me inappropriate and an exploitation of transference.

Individuals and collectives

Second, there is a need to look carefully at the differences between individuals and collectives. I would like to explore this in terms of three examples or situations:

1. Individuals learn, and we know something about the mechanisms by which they do it. Collectives as such do not learn, however seductive the metaphor is. It is just too anthropomorphic. Organizations appear to be learning as entities if individuals within them stay, and in that case we can say something about how such learning may be helped or hindered. But when individuals leave,

the learning of those individuals is lost to the organization. If the learning is institutionalized in some procedure or rule, the value to the organization may be preserved, but new individuals will have less opportunity to learn. It is a continuing dilemma and represents one of the big differences between the social and the natural sciences: in the natural sciences, learning becomes institutionalized in accepted knowledge, which is passed on, and in artefacts. In the social sciences, there are no artefacts and, partly because of this, bodies of "knowledge" are vulnerable to the desire of every new generation to explore and invent. Or, as the late Sir Charles Goodeve so neatly put it, "The natural sciences have developed by people standing on each other's shoulders. In the social sciences they stand on each other's faces."

2. The second example concerns transference—how it is generated and how it is used. The transference that develops during an individual analysis can be used as data because the analyst is not supplying any other kind of data about himself. Therefore, feelings and attitudes that the patient develops must arise from within the patient. This was the model with which Elliott Jaques entered the Glacier Metal Company (Jaques, 1951). It implies social distance of the kind that is maintained in a personal analysis. When I entered Esso, it was with the conviction that the necessary social distance cannot be maintained in a full-time job for eight hours a day. That was one reason why there needed to be found some other, more "ordinary" way of relating to the clients. A second reason for seeking a more ordinary mode of operation was that the use of social science could not otherwise become widespread.

There is, therefore, a strict limit to what you can do with transference phenomena. Mainly, if you spot anything of that kind, you can use it to inform your own learning and behaviour. It may also, as in the example given earlier, generate some hypotheses about the organization's culture.

However, what I did not realize at that time, and still find hard to come to terms with, is the problems associated with maintaining a position of non-mystification, in cultures that get a frisson from mystique and find a prima donna performance more exciting than institutionalized good practice.

The issue is one of professional authority. I am not above envying the impact made by people who announce with confidence, "this is how it is". All I am able to say is, "this is how I have arrived at thinking it is like this". I don't apologize for this, but dynamically it carries less authority and is less likely to go down in history. But to me it seems more real, and in the end reality is what matters and it is one's own face that one has to confront in the mirror.

There is a subset of this issue around the problem of language. As professionals we may fall into the lose/lose situation of being accused either of talking jargon or of "only" talking common sense. Hugh Murray and I once ran a course on sociotechnical design for the Board of a company. In my introductory talk I spoke of the need for design strategies that leave options open, and all round the table heads nodded in agreement. Later, Hugh gave a talk that included reference to "minimum critical specification". In the coffee-break, people complained about the use of jargon and being blinded with science. But they remembered "minimum critical specification", while "leaving options open" was simply too easy to agree with and forget.

3.   The third example where care is needed in distinguishing between an individual and a collective is in the interpretation of phenomena. Let us take as an instance the well-known interpretation of social systems as a defence against anxiety. For an individual, defences against anxiety are motivated but unconscious mechanisms. Is that what they are when we appear to observe them in social institutions? There is an alternative way of looking at it. Ever since the sociologist Robert Merton differentiated between manifest and latent functions, social scientists have found this a most useful distinction to make (Merton, 1957). For once, a sociological concept was as immediately and directly useful to practitioners as it was to theorists. It is easy to explain to clients the latent as well as the manifest functions of some institutional arrangement; but that does not necessarily imply purpose.

If some social arrangements have the effect of limiting anxiety for the members of an institution, does that mean that they have been put in place as an unconscious defence—that is, in some unconscious, purposive way? Or is the limiting of anxiety their latent function—that is, have they survived because by chance they turned out to have valuable functions apart from the manifest ones for which they were set up? In that case, we would need to take a Darwinian rather than a Freudian view—the survival of the most useful. It seems to me that the only way to decide which view to take in any particular situation is to look in detail at its history and circumstances, and not to generalize. In discussing this with Marie Jahoda, the example that came to her mind was that a latent function of the British monarchy is to increase Kodak sales. I suppose one might track some unconscious purposive chain, but it would be difficult.

The relevance of context

Third, there is the relevance of context. I understand that some psychoanalysts now pay more attention than used to be the case to contextual factors in the patient's life. Whatever the technical issues involved in that, when it comes to working with organizations, contextual aspects cannot be omitted. At the very least, the model one has in one's head when working with an individual or a group in an organization needs to include something of the other individuals and departments, the products, the technologies, the markets, the geography, the legal framework, the history. More likely, the work itself needs to encompass these aspects. Otherwise, you are not working with the organization, but with an individual or group that happen to be in an organization. We are here back to the distinction between an individual and a collective. However, collective is too broad a term at this point; one needs to distinguish here between a small group and an organization. An organization simply does not have an inner life that is unconnected with tasks and circumstances.

Conclusions

As I indicated at the beginning, this chapter has been somewhat personal, and, congruent with what I have said about professional authority, this is unavoidable. Ideas and concepts do not come out of thin air; they come from the interplay of field experience and data on the one hand and, on the other, the minds of the people working with those data and the institutional arrangements around that. It therefore becomes necessary to give some context to the history of ideas and concepts—that is, how they arose. This also gives the reader or listener greater freedom to accept or reject.

The question arises whether these attempts to differentiate are worthwhile, and whether the differences matter anyway. But if we are to take further the use of psychoanalytic approaches and the part they can play in organizational design, development, and consultancy, then yes, it does matter to be precise. This field will not make any real progress until we acknowledge that it contains two frames of reference, not one.

Note

1. This analysis is elaborated in a paper on the collaboration between social scientists and engineers (Klein, 1989a).
2. The story of how I was later able to make use of this learning as part of project activity is given here in chapter 5.

CHAPTER 16

Inside and outside—
a struggle for integration

In 1989, Harold Bridger reached the age of 80. I edited a collection of papers to celebrate his birthday (Klein, 1989b) and contributed one paper to it. It describes the continuing effort to integrate external and internal factors in arriving at where one stands. The paper below is an edited version.

In an autobiographical introduction to his book *The Informed Heart*, Bruno Bettelheim (1970) describes the dilemma he experienced as a young man after the First World War, trying to decide where to focus his energies: was it more important to work towards the reform of society, or to change individuals? It was his personal version of the old nature–nurture controversy:

> In order to create the good society, was it of first importance to change society radically enough for all persons to achieve full self realization? In this case psychoanalysis could be discarded, with the possible exception of a few deranged persons. Or was this the wrong approach to the problem and could only persons who had achieved full personal liberation and integration by being psycho-analysed create such a "good" society? In the latter case the correct thing was to forget for the time being any social or economic revolution and to concentrate instead on pushing psychoanalysis;

the hope was that, once the vast majority of men had profited from its inner liberation, they would almost automatically create the good society for themselves and all others. [p. 16]

The dilemma persisted:

So again I found myself asking whether it was the good society that would automatically, or with some effort, produce the good men who would then perpetuate it. . . . If, on the other hand, only the good men could create the good society, then the problem was how to change existing man so that he would become the good man who would then, in his image, create and perpetuate the good society. Of all the known ways of influencing people, psychoanalysis seemed to hold out most promise for a radical change for the better among existing men. . . . [p. 18]

Marx or Freud, then? Structure or dynamics? From outside or from inside? For Bettelheim, "In the end it was psychoanalysis that I turned to more hopefully than political reform."

I know now, with more confidence than I have about anything, that in this dilemma of structure or dynamics, the sociological or the psychological, it is essential to attend to both. What is more, you have to attend to them simultaneously. It is no good thinking that you can postpone the one while you deal with the other, because the dealing-with is unending, so the postponing becomes unending. Also, working on the one produces a frame of mind that is not conducive to working on the other.

So the small problem that remains is *how* to work on them both simultaneously! That is the issue I shall attempt to explore in this chapter, and I shall do it via the influences that have shaped my own understanding. For much of the time, Harold Bridger has been, as he continues to be, one of them.

Starting from outside: industrial sociology

In the social science scene of the 1950s and 1960s, both perspectives were represented, but they were separate. The approach that looks first at structural influences was represented by the industrial sociologists—Joan Woodward, Tom Burns and George Stalker, Tom Lupton. Structure, I probably need to explain, I take to mean that which, though it may be possible to change in the long run, in the short run shapes the environment within which one has to function. For organizations, that means ownership, size, technology, the nature of product and labour markets, the legal framework, the control systems. There are different degrees to which these various structural factors are embedded.

Woodward (1965), looking at economic performance and organization in a grounded way—that is, without a preconceived formal theory—had found some relationships between technology, organization, and behaviour. She always hated being accused of determinism—influencing and determining are not the same thing. Nevertheless, to give the simplest examples, it is clear that, when many decisions are built into the design of a plant, as in process production, people's prestige does not come from being hectically busy, but from being calm and in control; when things are running well, there is less to do than when something has gone wrong. They have time to deal with problems, so problems are more likely to be dealt with. On the other hand, in batch production, where many decisions have to be made in the course of a day, the lives of supervisors and managers are more hectic and there is less time to work through the problems that arise, so more problems remain unresolved. Also, people select themselves in or out, since those who worry and explore the implications of every decision are less likely to cope well in such situations.

In a similar framework of looking at situations in a grounded way but exploring the effects of structure, Burns and Stalker (1961) focused on the influence exerted on the politics, organization, and culture of firms by different characteristics of their product markets, especially the rate at which markets were changing. Lupton (1961) too found that behaviour on the shop-floor was different according to whether a firm was in a stable market or work was seasonal.

My own early fieldwork was in engineering batch production and was in the same frame of reference. The research project we were engaged on was supposed to be looking at the human implications of work study, the assumptions behind it being that, if people's irrational "resistance" was better understood, their motivation might be better harnessed and productivity increased. There were two case studies, one in a packaging company where work study was being newly introduced (Dalziel & Klein, 1960) and one in an engineering company where it had been running for a long time (Klein, 1964). It turned out that, in the short run, work study was experienced as a tight means of exercising control over people, and they disliked and resisted it. In the long run, given time and familiarity, people found ways of regaining and reasserting controls of their own: "fiddling", in the engineering work study situation, had the function of giving scope for the use of initiative and creativity, which the work itself did not permit. The man who explained that he always worked hard on Thursdays, hid the pieces in his locker overnight, and fed them in on Fridays so as not to be too tired for the weekend was, after all, being entirely rational. Fiddles were subtle and complex and involved high intelligence and great understanding of the system and its members; they provided interest, a sense of achievement, and relief from tedium.

The project was carried out from within the then Department of Scientific and Industrial Research, which was administering the Conditional Aid programme, the first major government programme funding industrial social research. Social science and its peculiarities was new to the administrators of government research funds, and it had been thought useful to locate one of the projects in the funding department itself, in order to learn about social science's special characteristics. It was thus a marvellous vantage point from which to learn about what was going on in the whole programme, and it was here that I learned about the work of the Tavistock Institute and read many of its reports and papers. Oh, the agonies of the civil servants dealing with grant applications from people who justified their high salaries on the grounds of having to pay for psychoanalysis!

Towards the end of the project, other members of the team had moved on and I was working on it alone. I was "spotted" by Joan Woodward, who started giving me some professional help, and the project was finished under her supervision at Imperial College, where she was pioneering the link between industrial sociology and the teaching of engineers. I then worked with her for some years, doing research on the behavioural consequences of management control systems.

So here is a contextual influence: Joan was carving out a place for industrial sociology in an environment consisting of scientists and technologists where, whether in reality or imagination, social science was put on the defensive in relation to scientific models and methods. Her work was, indeed, in the model of finding patterns among data which enable you to make constructs, which in turn enable you to make predictions.

I have never had any difficulty with that—that is, with the "scientific" aspects of social science. I find that industrial sociology has considerable predictive value. Tell me how your control system is designed, and I can tell you where the stresses are likely to be. If maintenance is costed in with production, relationships will be different than if the two functions are in separate cost centres. For diagnostic, or consulting, or design activity, it is useful if people can be helped to see how the difficulties they experience may have been designed into a situation and may not all be traceable to their personalities or be solved in terms of personal relationships and dynamics. It is the interplay between structural and human and social factors that yields rich potential for development. If it is normal for production management to have difficulties in relation to marketing management, because of predictable conflict in the way their functions are set up, they don't need to experience the conflict in such a painful way, and residual personal issues can be worked on in the security of "it's not all our fault".

Starting from inside: "the Tavi"

Work coming out of the Tavistock Institute seemed to contain three threads:

1. group dynamics;
2. concepts about work systems as sociotechnical systems;
3. the methodological examination of consultancy roles.

Weirdest, and furthest from where I stood, was the group stuff

In 1956 I heard a lecture by someone who had been to the National Training Laboratories in the United States and had been swept off his feet by something called "group dynamics," whatever that was. It had been the most wonderful experience of his life, he said, which could not possibly be put into words. I decided that I wanted to find out what this was about: if there was anything there worthwhile and real, I felt, it must be possible to find words for it. So when Tavistock announced its own first Group Relations Conference, at Leicester in 1957, I went. I arrived 95% sceptical and came away 90% sceptical.

It was a two-week event, and during the weekend in the middle they showed the film *Twelve Angry Men*, which is about a jury trying to arrive at a verdict. Afterwards, Harold Bridger gave a commentary in terms of the dynamics going on within the group of jurors. The trouble was, he got some of the facts wrong. He would say, "You remember when A got up and went to the window . . ."—only it hadn't been A, it had been someone else.

I felt a sense of outrage and protested, followed by others. If one could not trust these people to get a few simple facts right, how could one trust them about this mysterious, intangible stuff? (Interpretations about "pairing" when three of us had been prevented from attending one of the sessions because someone's car broke down had not helped.) Later, the staff wrote a book and sent a draft of it around to the participants. The "mid-term rebellion" had very fanciful interpretations attached to it.

I wrote to explain why and how the rebellion had actually come about, and they had the integrity to change the draft. I didn't meet Harold again for some years, but it is to this episode that the roots of mutual respect may be traced. When I later learned from him and worked with him, it was this integrity in relation to reality that formed the bridge between a scientific and a dynamic framework. I have never seen him make a dogmatic interpretation just because a theory says that something should be there, or hide behind mystique, or drop unexplained hints about "unconscious forces" in order to put the other at a disadvantage. Rather, he starts from where the other is and works with what is there, using whatever concepts and associations he has to build from there and make linkages between what is and what may become. Such an encounter always leaves one expanded.

As for group relations, I went on trying. Every few years I would muster the courage to have another go, hoping that this time, perhaps, I might find out what a group is. I learned much, but the central core continued to evade me. A group as a setting, a vehicle for exploring many things, certainly. But a group as an entity in its own right or even, heaven forbid, as an "organism"—I simply could not see it. When I began to work with Harold as a consultant in his Working Conferences, he observed that I was working with the dynamics of the content of a group's work, while he was working with the dynamics of the group. (Once, when he had made an intervention that "the group is splitting the task", I said that I knew what he meant, having seen the same events, but did not know whether, with such a comment, he was giving the group a scientific observation or a piece of poetry. That sparked off a two-hour discussion, all the way from Stratford to Hammersmith, the exhilaration of which I still remember.)

Well, this division of labour between the dynamics of the content and the dynamics of the group was quite satisfactory as long as I was working with colleagues who had a greater sense of "the group as such" than I. Then one day recently I found myself working with someone who was looking to me to provide the understanding of "the group"! There is nothing like responsibility to speed up the learning process. It was all right. For the first time, I worked with things that I had relied on others to work with. I found myself able to say "The group is . . ." and not have my fingers metaphorically crossed behind my back. It had only taken thirty-two years.

What of the inside–outside aspects of group relations training? I think there are several:

- One concerns the preoccupation that powerful and to some extent therapeutic experiences generate. I was once on a Social Science Working Party set up by the Trades Union Congress. The research secretary of a large union asked me to come and talk to him about group dynamics—some of his members worked in an organization where managers were undergoing group relations training, and the shop stewards were asking what this was about. I spent a day with him, doing my best to explain. Towards the end, he asked whether this was a form of training that might be useful for shop stewards. I thought that it could be very useful—for instance, when engaged in negotiations—to have some understanding of dynamics and group processes. He seemed to agree but then added: "Of course, we couldn't go to the Tavistock Institute for it." I asked why not, and he left his office and returned with a colleague whom he had apparently collared at random. "What do you think of the Tavistock Institute?" he asked the colleague. The answer came instantly: "A very subversive organization. They only believe in personal conflict, they don't believe in structural conflict."

   Of course it is not true, but there is truth in it. A person has only so much attention and energy. The involvement generated by a good learning experience, especially if it also has a therapeutic component about oneself and one's relationships, may well lead either to the rationalization that other considerations are not impor-tant, or to splitting. An inter-group exercise is too weak to make the point about structural influences. This is why structural explana-tions of difficulties (see above) may well be accepted intellectually, while the protagonists nevertheless continue to seek solutions in terms of work concerned with personality and relationships.

- A second inside–outside aspect concerns numbers. This kind of development experience is staff-intensive and therefore costly. It is only available to a few people, and they are usually at management level. It is said that the only real class distinction these days is between those who have work and those who do not, but I think there is another: it is between those whose development is deemed to end at the age of around 20, and those who have development opportunities throughout life.

- A third inside–outside issue concerns the manner of learning. The value attached to learning from experience, like anything else, should not deteriorate into mere dogmatism. There is no harm in telling people about relevant research findings "out there" when a group has experienced something to which the findings may be related. On the contrary, to compare one's experience with that of others and explore similarities and differences extends the experience. Above all, it provides an experience of linking the outside and the inside and demonstrates that you are not forced to choose between allegiance to one camp or the other. Of course, one has only a small fraction of research findings so well internalized that they surface at the right moment.

Nearest to where I stood already was the sociotechnical work

There was nothing new in pointing to the interdependence between the technical and social aspects of a work system. Karl Marx had done it more than a hundred years before. His chapter on machinery and modern industry is full of examples. For the sheer pleasure of tracing the detective-story chain of cause-and-effect from structure to behaviour and back again, I enjoy citing them. For example:

> In the English letter-press printing trade, for example, there existed formerly a system, corresponding to that in manufactures and handicrafts, of advancing the apprentices from easy to more and more difficult work. They went through a course of teaching till they were finished printers. To be able to read and write was for every one of them a requirement of their trade. All this was changed by the printing machine. It employs two sorts of labourers, one grown up, tenters, and the other, boys mostly from 11 to 17 years of age, whose sole business is either to spread the sheets of paper under the machine, or to take from it the printed sheets. . . . A great part of them cannot read, and they are, as a rule, utter savages and very extraordinary creatures. To qualify them for the work they have to do, they require no intellectual training; there is little room in it for skill, and less for judgement; their wages, though rather high for boys, do not increase proportionately as they grow up, and the majority of them cannot look for advance-

ment to the better paid and more responsible post of machine minder, because while each machine has but one minder, it has at least two, and often four boys attached to it. As soon as they get too old for such child's work, that is about 17 at the latest, they are discharged from the printing establishments. They become recruits of crime. Several attempts to procure them employment elsewhere, were rendered of no avail by their ignorance and brutality. . . . [1867, p. 484]

However, although this is sociotechnical analysis, Marx did not draw sociotechnical conclusions—that is, he did not conclude that social aspects should therefore feature in technology design. He only made one mistake, really: he attributed the problems he saw to ownership and did not take seriously, as an independent contributing factor, the simple need to reduce complexity and the resulting models of man in the minds of engineering designers—in other words, the splitting that has taken place between the human and the technical aspects of work design, and the way this splitting is institutionalized.

What the Tavistock Institute did was, first, to give a name to this interdependence—"sociotechnical" (a term now much misused)—and take it down from the macro-societal level, where you can't do much about it, to the work system level, where you can. Second, since most of those early researchers did have a clinical background, they made it scientifically respectable for feelings, relationships, and experiences to be a valid part of the data when work is being considered. What they did not do was follow through with this thinking into the training of engineers and system designers where it is most needed. Consultancy projects may be more exciting, but no amount of project work can counteract the assumptions about work roles that are built into capital appropriations, technology design, or the software engineering before the consultants turn up, or where there aren't any. In the long run, it is sociotechnical thinking that has to be institutionalized, or there will never be critical mass. Also, the autonomous work group as the answer to everything is a bit of a lazy way out; it means you don't have to keep up with technical developments.

For instance, people cannot behave autonomously if they are technically constrained. Machine-pacing is still with us and brings with it the need to pay attention to buffer zones or stock (the material between one operation and the next that gives people leeway to work at their own pace). As part of one of the projects in the German government's programme to "Humanize Life at Work", a big attitude survey was done in one company. From a range of questions in an enormous questionnaire, the researchers compiled a "job satisfaction index". At the same time, they described the jobs being done in very great detail, "objectively" in the sense that the categories were completed by an observer, not the operator. Then they crunched their data through the computer, relating everything to everything (another contextual influence: the kind of research that gets done depends on the money spent). And they came up with a very interesting finding. When they plotted "job satisfaction", as measured by their index, against the amount of buffer stock available to an operator (measured in terms of time, from 1 minute's worth to, in the case of that company, 180 minutes' worth), there was a straight positive correlation: the bigger the buffer, the greater the satisfaction. The connection was not investigated and is most unlikely to have been causal in a direct sense.

There was more: in their attitude survey, whenever a complaint was expressed, there had been a follow-up question "Can you do anything about that?" Insofar as people felt that nothing could be done about problems, the researchers compiled a "helplessness index". And when the size of buffer was plotted against helplessness, they found a straight negative correlation. In other words, the greater the buffer zone, the fewer complaints people had in the first place, and the less helpless they felt about those things that did give cause for complaint. In that instance, it may simply have been that there is then time to complain or otherwise to tackle a problem and work it through. Freedom from pacing provides the shop-floor version of transitional space: it needs to be technically designed in and then handled dynamically— outside and inside.

In the design of new systems, it is prototypes that facilitate transition. Models, Lego bricks, sophisticated computer simulations may all have this function, *provided that* the roles and experiences that are likely to be involved have a place in the way that the prototyping is done, that there are genuine choices available, and that commitment is to the exploration rather than to the first design.

I have found that the best way to make this point with engineers is to tell them Harold Bridger's story about the little dog: consider the situation of a young man walking in the park who sees a young woman he would like to chat up. It is quite difficult to do directly, even nowadays. If, on the other hand, the young woman is taking a dog for a walk, it is not difficult to talk to the dog or say something about it, and it is not difficult for her to respond in terms of the dog. The dog provides the opportunity to find out what mileage there may be in going any further, and to withdraw with dignity if there isn't any. It functions as a transitional system.

And then there was the question of how

A passionate sense that the social sciences had to be useful and usable drew me first to the work of Elliott Jaques (1951) and the methodological exploration of action research and consultancy. But even while I could see that there was much to be learned here from psychoanalysis—and Joan Woodward, too, thought that people doing consultancy should undergo analysis in order to ensure that their own needs were kept out of the situation—the Glacier Metal Company seemed at the same time too special a case. When I answered Esso Petroleum's advertisement for an in-house social sciences adviser, it was to find out how this might be done in more ordinary circumstances—where the social scientist was not experienced as an analyst and there was not such personal enthusiasm on the part of the managing director (Klein, 1976).

It was about two-thirds of the way through the time with Esso that I began to use Harold Bridger as a consultant. He taught, clarified, gave support, and eventually, when the Esso experiment ended in 1970, suggested that I should join the Tavistock Institute. Through all the research and consulting since then, the struggle to integrate some psychodynamic understanding appropriately into organizational work has been a constant thread and fascination: dynamics *and* structure, inside *and* outside, the individual *and* society. The utilization of social science implies vision, understanding, infrastructure, and institutions. All of them.

* * *

My dear Harold: we both know that intellectual and professional positions don't just come from "out there". That is why, in this piece, I have described where I stand in terms of how I got there, at least at one level. That makes it seem less authoritative than it might be—people want to be told this is how it is, not this is what I am learning. But, as I've said before, in the end it is my face in the mirror that I have to answer to. So now you are 80. To my own great astonishment I am 60. The struggle continues.

REFERENCES

Amado, G., & Ambrose, A. (Eds.) (2001). *The Transitional Approach to Change*. London: Karnac.

Bennis, W. G. (1966). Theory and method in applying behavioural science to planned organizational change. In: J. R. Lawrence (Ed.), *Operational Research and the Social Sciences*. London: Tavistock Publications.

Bettelheim, B. (1970). *The Informed Heart*. London: Paladin.

Blake, R. R., & Mouton, J. S. (1964). *The Managerial Grid*. Houston, TX: Gulf Publishing.

Bowra, M. (1971). *Periclean Athens*. New York: Dial Press.

Bridger, H. (1990). Courses and working conferences as transitional learning institutions. In: E. Trist & H. Murray (Eds.), *The Social Engagement of Social Science: A Tavistock Anthology. Vol. 1: The Socio-Psychological Perspective*. Philadelphia, PA: University of Pennsylvania Press.

Brown, J. A. C. (1954). *The Social Psychology of Industry: Human Relations in the Factory*. London: Penguin.

Burns, T., & Stalker, G. (1961). *The Management of Innovation*. London: Tavistock Publications.

Cabinet Office (1993). *Realising Our Potential: A Strategy for Science, Engineering and Technology*. Cmnd 2250. London: HMSO.

Cherns, A. (1968). The use of the social sciences. *Human Relations, 21*: 313–325.

Cherns, A. (1979). *Using the Social Sciences*. London/Boston/Henley: Routledge & Kegan Paul.

Coch, L., & French, J. R. P. (1948). Overcoming resistance to change. *Human Relations, 1.*

Comfort, A. (1967). *The Anxiety Makers: Some Curious Preoccupations of the Medical Profession*. London: Thomas Nelson & Sons.

Dalziel, S., & Klein, L. (1960). *The Human Implications of Work Study: The Case of Pakitt Ltd*. DSIR, Warren Spring Laboratory.

Department of Education and Science (1965). *Report of the Committee on Social Studies* (Lord Heyworth, chairman). Cmnd 2660. London: HMSO.

Department of Scientific and Industrial Research/Medical Research Council (1958). *Final Report of the Joint Committee on Human Relations in Industry 1954–57, and Report of the Joint Committee on Individual Efficiency in Industry 1953–57*. London: HMSO.

Department of Scientific and Industrial Research/Ministry of Technology (1957–67). *Problems of Progress in Industry Series, Nos. 1–16*. London: HMSO.

Havelock, R. G. (1969). *Planning for Innovation: A Comparative Study of the Literature on the Dissemination and Utilization of Scientific Knowledge*. Ann Arbor, MI: CRUSK.

Jaques, E. (1951). *The Changing Culture of a Factory*. London: Tavistock Publications.

Klein, L. (1964). *Multiproducts Limited: A Case Study in the Social Effects of Rationalised Production*. London: HMS0.

Klein, L. (1965). Rationality in management control. *British Journal of Management Studies, 3* (1).

Klein, L. (1969). Social science: Customers beware. *New Society, 14* (377): 978–980.

Klein, L. (1976). *A Social Scientist in Industry*. London: Gower Press.

Klein, L. (1980). *The Role of the Anaesthetist: An Exploratory Study*. London: Association of Anaesthetists of Great Britain and Ireland.

Klein, L. (1989a). On the collaboration between social scientists and engineers. In: H. H. Rosenbrock (Ed.), *Designing Human-centred Technology: A Cross-disciplinary Project in Computer-aided Manufacturing*. London: Springer-Verlag. [Also in: *The Meaning of Work*. London: Karnac, forthcoming.]

Klein, L. (Ed.) (1989b). *Working with Organisations: Papers to Celebrate the 80th Birthday of Harold Bridger*. London: Tavistock Institute of Human Relations.

Klein, L. (2001). On the use of psychoanalytic concepts in organisational social science. *Concepts and Transformation: International Journal of Action Research, 6* (1).

Klein, L. (forthcoming). *The Meaning of Work.* London: Karnac.

Klein, L., & Eason, K. (1991). *Putting Social Science to Work: The Ground between Theory and Use Explored through Case Studies in Organisations.* Cambridge: Cambridge University Press.

Laplanche, J., & Pontalis, J.-B. (1973). *The Language of Psychoanalysis.* London: Karnac, 1988.

Lawrence, P. R., & Lorsch, J. W. (1967). *Organizations and Environment: Managing Differentiation and Integration.* Boston, MA: Graduate School of Business Administration, Harvard University.

Lazarsfeld, P. F., Sewall, W. N., & Wilenesky, H. L. (Eds.) (1968). Introduction. In: *The Uses of Sociology.* London: Weidenfeld & Nicholson.

Lewin, K. (1942). *The Relative Effectiveness of a Lecture Method and a Method of Group Decision for Changing Food Habits.* Mimeo, Commission on Food Habits, National Research Council, Washington, D.C.

Lewin, K. (1943). *Forces behind Food Habits and Methods of Change. National Research Council Bulletin, No. 108*: 35–65.

Likert, R. (1961). *New Patterns of Management.* New York/London: McGraw-Hill.

Likert, R. (1967). *The Human Organization: Its Management and Value.* New York: McGraw-Hill.

Lupton, T. (1961). *On the Shop Floor.* Oxford: Oxford University Press.

Manchester Centre for Healthcare Management et al. (2001). *Research Evaluation of NHS EPR/ICWS Pilot Sites.* Available online: www. disco. port.ac.uk/ictri/projects/EPR_pilot_eval.htm.

Marx, K. (1867). *Capital.* London: Lawrence & Wishart, 1958.

McGregor, D. (1960). *The Human Side of Enterprise.* New York: McGraw-Hill.

Menninger, K. (1958). *Theory of Psychoanalytic Technique* (pp. 15–42). London: Imago.

Merton, R. K. (1957). *Social Theory and Social Structure* (revised and enlarged edition). New York: Free Press.

Ministry of Technology (1960). *Training Made Easier: A Review of Four Recent Studies. Problems of Progress in Industry, No. 6.* London: HMSO.

National Institute of Industrial Psychology (1951). *The Foreman.* London: Staples Press.

National Institute of Industrial Psychology (1952). *Joint Consultation.* London: Staples Press.

Paterson, T. T. (1955). *Morale in War and Work: An Experiment in the Management of Men*. London: Max Parrish.

Perrow, C. (1986). *Complex Organizations: A Critical Essay* (3rd edition). New York: Random House.

Phillipson, H. (1989). The creative use of chance events. In: L. Klein (Ed.), *Working with Organisations: Papers to Celebrate the 80th Birthday of Harold Bridger*. London: Tavistock Institute of Human Relations.

Pugh, D. S., Mansfield, R., & Warner, M. (1975). *Research in Organizational Behaviour*. London: Heinemann.

Roethlisberger, F. J., & Dickson, W. J. (1939). *Management and the Worker*. Cambridge, MA: Harvard University Press.

Rosenbrock, H. H. (1979). "The Redirection of Technology." IFAC Symposium on Criteria for Selecting Appropriate Technologies under Different Cultural, Technical and Social Conditions, 21–23 May, Bari, Italy.

Rosenbrock, H. H. (1983). Developing a technology which provides satisfactory work. *IFAC Newsletter*, 5 (October).

Rothschild, Lord (1982). *An Enquiry into the Social Science Research Council*. Cmnd 8554. London: HMSO.

Scott, W. H. (1952). *Industrial Leadership and Joint Consultation*. Liverpool: University Press.

Shackel, B., & Klein, L. (1976). ESSO London Airport refuelling control centre redesign—an ergonomics case study. *Applied Ergonomics, 7* (1): 37–45.

Shimmin, S., & Wallis, D. (1994). *Fifty Years of Occupational Psychology in Britain*. Leicester: British Psychological Society.

Shove, E. (1997). *Researchers, Users and Window Frames*. Lancaster: Centre for the Study of Environmental Change, Lancaster University.

Smith, A. (1776). *An Enquiry into the Nature and Causes of the Wealth of Nations*. London: Methuen, 1904.

Stansfield, R. G. (1981). Operational research and sociology. *Science and Public Policy, 8* (4).

Trist, E. L., Higgin, G. W., Murray, H., & Pollock, A. B. (1963). *Organizational Choice: Capabilities of Groups at the Coalface under Changing Technologies*. London: Tavistock Publications.

Whyte, W. H. (1956). *The Organization Man*. New York: Doubleday.

Williams, R. (1980). Social research and sociology: Problems in the funding of knowledge. In: D. C. Anderson (Ed.), *The Ignorance of Social Intervention*. London: Croom Helm.

Winnicott, D. W. (1971). *Playing and Reality*. London: Tavistock Publications.

Woodward, J. (1965). *Industrial Organisation: Theory and Practice*. Oxford: Oxford University Press.

Woodward, J. (Ed.) (1970). *Industrial Organisation: Behaviour and Control*. Oxford: Oxford University Press.

INDEX